AF267427

The World is Always Never Ending

A Modern Antidote for the Worried
Well-Informed and Terminally Online

Karina Vunnam

Creative Nudge Press

The World is ~~Always~~ Never Ending: A Modern Antidote for the Worried Well-Informed and Terminally Online

Written by Karina Vunnam

Copyright © 2026 by Karina Vunnam

All rights reserved.

Published by Creative Nudge Press, LLC

First Edition, 2026

For permission requests

contact@creativenudge.net

TheResilienceCompass.com

Library of Congress Cataloging-in-Publication Data

Vunnam, Karina

The World is ~~Always~~ Never Ending: A Modern Antidote for the Worried Well-Informed and Terminally Online / Karina Vunnam

978-1-966193-08-1 (paperback)

978-1-966193-09-8 (hardback)

1. Social psychology

2. Collective behavior

3. Social movements—History

4. Mass media—Social aspects

5. Anxiety—Social aspects

Printed in the United States of America

10 9 8 7 6 5 4 3 2 1

Contents

Introduction

SPINS & ROUNDABOUTS

There are books written to change the world. This isn't one of them. Those books arrive with manifestos and battle cries, demanding action and promising revolution. They add to the noise, the urgency, the weight on your shoulders.

This book offers something else: permission to exhale.

In a time that feels perpetually on fire, where each headline warns of another crisis, where tribal lines are drawn ever deeper, these pages don't ask you to fight harder or worry more. They invite you to look up at the stars, to remember how vast time is, how small we are, and how this moment, with all its noise and fury, is just one flickering point in humanity's long journey.

Because sometimes the most revolutionary act isn't changing the world, but changing how you see it.

I began writing this book during my own period of despair, when I found myself increasingly alarmed by ideological movements that seemed to threaten everything I valued. Each day brought new reasons for outrage, new evidence that society was crumbling. I felt that familiar clutch of anxiety with every notification, that sense that we were living in end times.

Then one night, I looked up at the stars.

It was something I had done countless times as a child, lying on my back in the grass, feeling simultaneously tiny and infinite. The perspective was immediate and humbling, just as it had been when I was young. Those pinpricks of ancient light stirred that familiar mixture of awe, fear, and wonder, a feeling at once terrifying and exhilarating.

Those same stars had witnessed countless civilizations rise and fall, had shone over periods of both terrible darkness and brilliant enlightenment. They had seen humans at their worst and at their best, and through it all, we persisted, adapted, and often improved. When was the last time you looked up and allowed yourself to feel that vastness?

The stars, in their silent patience, have observed our human drama with a perspective we can barely comprehend. They watched as early humans gathered in caves, painting stories on walls to make sense of their world. They've witnessed our greatest triumphs: the building of cities, the development of writing, the discoveries that have expanded our understanding of the universe they inhabit. They've also seen our darkest moments: wars that consumed continents, plagues that decimated populations, conflicts born from our inability to recognize our shared humanity. Yet through all these cycles of creation and destruction, advancement and retreat, the stars have seen humanity's remarkable resilience, our capacity to rebuild, to learn, to gradually find better ways of living together.

What became clear to me beneath that star-filled sky was a pattern that stretches across human history, a movement like a pendulum, swinging between periods of progressive change and conservative reaction. Each swing, to those living through it, feels monumental, often apocalyptic. The Salem witch trials, the Red Scare, the moral panics of the 1980s: each represented moments when society, gripped by fear, pulled back from change and sought refuge in the familiar.

Yet with each complete arc, this pendulum doesn't return precisely to its starting point. Instead, it traces a gradual upward path. We revisit similar societal fears and reactions, but rarely do we completely undo the progress of previous generations. The witch hunts of Salem won't return in their original form. The homophobia of the AIDS crisis won't lead to the internment camps some once advocated. Each cycle teaches us something, and slowly, sometimes painfully slowly, we move forward.

This isn't to say that progress is inevitable or that we can passively wait for improvement. The upward trajectory of history has always required human intervention: courage, compassion, and the willingness to engage with difference rather than retreat from it.

This book isn't arguing that your concerns aren't valid. Today's challenges are real and significant. The polarization, the environmental threats, the economic uncertainties: none of these should be dismissed or minimized.

Nor is this book promising that everything will magically work out if we just wait long enough. History teaches us that positive change has always required human intervention: people coming together, communicating, and taking action despite their differences.

What this book offers instead is context. It's a quiet space where you might find historical companions who felt as you do now, who faced their own versions of apocalypse, who struggled with belonging and meaning in times of upheaval. Their stories aren't told here to convince you that your problems are insignificant, but to assure you that you're not alone in feeling overwhelmed by your era.

You'll find no political agenda between these pages, no attempt to pull you toward one tribe or another. Instead, you'll find an invitation to practice holding opposing truths without immediately reacting, what I call entering "No Man's Land." This contemplative space allows us to acknowledge complexity without demanding immediate resolution. In a world of increasing polarization, this skill might be our most powerful tool for maintaining both sanity and compassion.

From their celestial vantage point, the stars have observed how humans throughout time have struggled with complexity and contradiction. They've watched as societies oscillate between periods of rigid certainty and chaotic disruption, between eras when one truth overshadows all others and times when all truths seem equally valid. The stars, perhaps, recognize something we often forget: that the most enduring human wisdom has emerged not from the extremes, but from that middle territory where seemingly opposing truths can be held in creative tension. They've witnessed how civilizations that survive longest are those that find this balance, that create space for both tradition and innovation, for both individual expression and collective cohesion. This "No

Man's Land" between polarities isn't a place of compromise or indecision, but a fertile ground where deeper understanding can take root.

The path of human history isn't a perfect upward line, but neither is it an endless circle. It's a spiral, revisiting themes while gradually ascending. Understanding this pattern doesn't eliminate our responsibility to engage with today's challenges, but it might help us approach them with greater wisdom and less despair.

Consider this book a resource rather than a prescription. Turn to it when the news cycle leaves you breathless, when social media makes you feel like a stranger in your own country, when you need a reminder that humans have weathered storms before. Use it as you would a quiet garden bench where you can sit and gain perspective without abandoning your commitments to making the world better.

In the pages that follow, we'll explore historical cycles that echo our present moment, examine the universal human need for belonging, and practice the art of perspective. We'll look at what science tells us about navigating uncertainty and finding peace without disengaging from the world around us.

This isn't a book that promises answers, but one that creates space for better questions. It doesn't offer escape, but perspective, a widening of the lens that might help you carry your concerns with greater ease.

In a world that constantly demands you take a side, stake a claim, and fight for your position, these pages invite you to something radical: contemplation. Not as a replacement for action, but as its necessary companion.

Welcome to a journey through time, meaning, and our shared human experience. There's an ancient saying, often attributed to Chinese wisdom: "May you live in interesting times." It's meant as a curse, as interesting times are rarely peaceful ones. We certainly live in interesting times now. But perhaps there's a blessing we can pair with this curse: "May you find the perspective to navigate them."

May this book bring you not just knowledge, but also moments of peace in turbulent times, and the perspective to face our interesting times with wisdom, courage, and even wonder.

No Man's Land: An Invitation to Contemplation

Before we journey together through history's spiraling patterns, I invite you to pause and recognize the territory we're about to enter, a contemplative space that exists neither in certainty's fortress nor doubt's wilderness, but in the fertile ground between them. This space, which we'll call "No Man's Land," appears throughout this book as both destination and practice.

What is this middle territory? Imagine standing at twilight, when the world is neither fully illuminated nor completely dark. Objects take on a different quality then, their edges softened, their essence somehow more apparent even as their details become less defined. This liminal hour invites a particular kind of seeing, one that perceives not through categorization but through presence, not through judgment but through receptive attention.

Let's try a simple demonstration of this practice together, using tensions we all encounter in our daily lives.

Find a quiet moment. Take a slow, deep breath, allowing your awareness to settle into the present moment. Then consider these two statements:

Change is essential for growth and progress; without it, societies stagnate and individuals wither.

Pause. Notice what arises in you, perhaps agreement, examples from your own life, or a sense of energy and possibility.

Stability and continuity provide necessary foundations; without them, communities fragment and individuals lose their sense of meaning.

Pause again. Notice what emerges, perhaps different examples, concerns about too much change, or a feeling of groundedness.

Rather than immediately deciding which statement is "more true" or trying to reconcile them into a neat compromise, simply allow both to exist simultaneously in your awareness. Notice if there's an urge to choose one over the other, to mentally argue for your preferred position, or to quickly resolve the tension between them.

Instead, rest in the spacious awareness that can hold both truths. This isn't indecision or relativism; it's a more expansive form of understanding that recognizes how these apparently opposing principles actually depend upon and complement each other in the full spectrum of human experience.

The stars themselves exist in this kind of balance, between the tremendous forces of gravity pulling inward and the nuclear reactions pushing outward. It is precisely this tension, this perfect equilibrium between opposing forces, that allows them to shine for billions of years, providing light and life-giving energy. Perhaps there is a cosmic wisdom in this balance, a pattern reflected throughout nature and human experience, that creative tension between opposing forces often produces the most sustainable and generative states.

As you sit with this tension, you might notice something subtle shift within you, not toward resolution, but toward a different quality of attention. This middle territory, where seeming opposites can coexist without battle, contains a particular kind of wisdom that neither pole alone can offer.

This simple practice, holding opposing truths with gentle awareness, becomes increasingly valuable as we explore more charged polarities throughout this book. It cultivates a capacity to engage with complexity without being overwhelmed by it, to hear different perspectives without immediately categorizing them as ally or adversary.

No Man's Land is not about abandoning discernment, but about enriching it, creating space for more nuanced understanding to emerge from the conversation between different aspects of truth. It's a practice as ancient as wisdom traditions and as relevant as today's headlines.

As we journey together through history's cycles, this contemplative middle ground will offer not only perspective on the past but a different way of meeting our present moment, with neither the false certainty that blinds us to complexity nor the resignation that prevents us from acting with conviction when needed.

Cycle 1: When Shadows Had Names

Chapter One

When God Seemed Far Away

"S omething wicked this way comes." The phrase whispered through Salem Village in the bitter winter of 1692 wasn't borrowed from Shakespeare; it was a genuine fear that gripped ordinary people as young girls began to contort in strange fits, speaking in tongues and crying out against invisible tormentors. What began as peculiar behavior in a minister's household soon escalated into a community-wide panic that claimed twenty lives and permanently scarred the American consciousness. The afflicted girls pointed fingers at neighbors who had allegedly signed "the Devil's book," and reasonable men and women believed them. The most powerful men in the colony established special courts, abandoned normal rules of evidence, and sent innocent people to the gallows based largely on testimony about specters only accusers could see.

How could this happen? How could rational people, many well-educated by the standards of their day, accept claims that now seem so obviously fantastical? And perhaps more unsettlingly, what does this historical episode reveal about our own vulnerability to fear-driven thinking?

When we look up at the stars today, we see points of light in scientific terms, distant suns and planets following the predictable laws of physics. But the night sky that watched over Salem in 1692 spoke a different language to those beneath it. For the Puritans, celestial bodies formed part of God's creation, their movements portending divine favor or judgment. This represented a coherent worldview where the natural and supernatural existed in continuous conversation. Understanding this perspective opens the first gateway toward comprehending how reasonable people could believe in witches who brought tangible harm to their communities.

The world of the seventeenth century bore the aftershocks of religious upheaval. The Protestant Reformation, barely a century old, had shattered the religious uniformity of medieval Europe, leaving behind a landscape of competing faiths and contested truths. Both common people and elites experienced this fragmentation of religious certainty as a deep spiritual vulnerability. The scars of recent religious wars remained visible across the continent, both in the physical destruction of towns and villages and in the collective memory of communities torn apart by doctrinal differences.

In England, these tensions played out through decades of tumult. The English Civil War (1642-1651) had recently concluded, leaving a society deeply traumatized by religious conflict. The war pitted Parliamentarians against Royalists, but underneath these political labels lay deeper religious divisions between Puritans and Anglicans, with Catholics caught dangerously in between. The execution of King Charles I in 1649 went beyond removing a monarch; it violated the divine order that many believed underpinned society itself.

For most people of this era, religious uniformity stood as essential to social stability and divine protection, not simply a preference. The concept of religious tolerance as we understand it today was virtually unthinkable to most seventeenth-century minds. Society viewed dissenting religious views not as personal choices or matters of individual conscience, but as dangerous contagions threatening to corrupt the community and invite God's wrath upon all. When your neighbor's heresy might bring divine punishment to your village, their religious choices became everyone's concern.

Such perceptions created a social environment primed for fear and suspicion. The term "atheist" emerged as one of the most damning accusations possible, a label applied not only to those who denied God's existence (extremely rare in this period) but to anyone whose beliefs strayed too far from orthodox

Christianity. To be called an atheist in the seventeenth century marked someone as having rejected the very foundation of moral order.

Faith and social order intertwined fundamentally in seventeenth-century worldviews. Religion offered spiritual guidance while simultaneously providing the essential structure for understanding one's place in society, the workings of the natural world, and the course of human history. Threats to this structure triggered anxiety that manifested in ways that seem extreme to modern sensibilities, including heightened vigilance against perceived enemies of the faith, whether internal or external.

The Puritan settlements of New England embodied these religious concerns in concentrated form. Beyond creating places to live and work, colonists established these communities as spiritual experiments, "cities upon a hill" demonstrating godly living in its purest form. This sense of divine mission generated enormous pressure to maintain religious and moral purity.

By the late seventeenth century, the Massachusetts Bay Colony faced a significant identity crisis. The founding generation was passing away, and with them, many feared, the original spiritual fervor that had driven the colony's establishment. Economic pressures mounted as agricultural land grew scarce for the third generation of settlers. The initial covenant with God, which had promised prosperity in exchange for righteousness, appeared increasingly strained as hardships multiplied.

Puritans viewed Satan's presence as tangible and immediate rather than symbolic. They understood the devil to be actively working in the world, seeking to corrupt God's people and undermine their covenant. Unlike modern conceptions that might view evil as an abstract force or psychological phenomenon, Puritans experienced Satan as a real entity, constantly testing their faith and virtue. This belief formed a central pillar of their theology, shaping how they understood their daily struggles and community challenges.

Sermons, the primary media of the time, constantly reinforced this perspective. Puritan ministers delivered what were known as "jeremiad" sermons, powerful, emotionally charged warnings about moral decline and its consequences. Following a consistent pattern, these orations celebrated the community's founding principles, lamented current failings, and warned of divine punishment if repentance didn't follow. Week after week, ordinary Puritans absorbed this message of imminent spiritual danger, fostering a psychological environment of perpetual vigilance against sin and corruption.

External threats amplified these internal fears. King William's War (1688-1697) brought violence to the New England frontier as English colonists clashed with French and Native American forces. Beyond physical danger, the conflict created a refugee crisis, as displaced frontier families sought safety in more established towns like Salem. These newcomers strained local resources and social bonds already under pressure.

Information in seventeenth-century New England traveled through channels vastly different from our own, yet served similarly powerful functions in shaping public perception and response to perceived threats. Sermons dominated as the primary form of mass communication, equivalent to today's television broadcasts or viral social media. Ministers speaking from their pulpits went beyond advising on spiritual matters; they interpreted current events, defined community boundaries, and established the frameworks through which people understood their world.

The sermon's power stemmed partly from its regular rhythm in community life. Attendance was mandatory, with penalties for those who failed to participate. Lasting between one and two hours, the typical Puritan sermon reached congregants who stood or sat on hard benches in unheated meeting houses. This physical discipline paralleled the mental focus expected of listeners, who were taught to internalize and meditate upon the minister's words throughout the week.

Printed religious materials formed the second major channel of information flow, complementing spoken sermons. Literacy rates in New England reached remarkably high levels for the period, with laws requiring communities to establish schools so children could read the Bible. This fostered a population especially receptive to printed texts, particularly religious works that explained unusual events or warned of spiritual dangers.

Cotton Mather's *Remarkable Providences*, published in 1684, nearly a decade before the Salem trials began, ranked among the most influential printed works. This collection documented supernatural occurrences throughout New England, including alleged instances of witchcraft, demonic possession, and divine intervention. Beyond entertainment, the book established a template for identifying and understanding satanic influence in the community. When strange symptoms later appeared in Salem Village, Mather's framework offered ready-made explanations that guided how authorities responded.

Stories of possession and witchcraft spread through communities via a complex web of oral and written transmission. Women's household visits, market conversations, and church gatherings served as vectors for circulating accounts of unusual happenings. These informal networks often transmitted information faster than official channels and played crucial roles in amplifying concerns about witchcraft. Hearing such accounts directly from trusted neighbors, rather than from distant authorities, gave them particular potency in generating fear and suspicion.

While New England developed its distinct religious culture, England confronted its own perfect storm of religious and political anxiety. By the 1680s, England faced a crisis centered on King James II, whose open Catholicism posed what many saw as an existential threat to the Protestant identity that had defined English national consciousness for over a century. In the English mind, this crisis transcended theological preference, striking at national security and constitutional order itself.

Earlier religious conflicts continued to shape English politics through collective trauma. John Foxe's widely-read *Book of Martyrs* kept alive the memory of "Bloody Mary" Tudor's persecution of Protestants in the 1550s, graphically detailing the torture and execution of Protestant dissenters. More recently, the anti-Catholic Gordon Riots of 1666 had demonstrated the volatile nature of religious tensions in English society. English Protestants largely viewed Catholicism as more than a different Christian denomination; to them, it represented a foreign allegiance to Rome that threatened English sovereignty and freedoms.

These fears erupted dramatically in the Popish Plot scare of 1678-79. Titus Oates, a former Anglican clergyman, claimed to have uncovered a vast Catholic conspiracy to assassinate King Charles II and massacre English Protestants. Despite eventually being proven false, these claims triggered a wave of anti-Catholic hysteria. Between 1678 and 1681, authorities executed at least fifteen Catholics based on fabricated testimony, while imprisoning many more or confiscating their property. The panic demonstrated how quickly unfounded accusations could lead to deadly consequences when they aligned with existing social fears.

The succession crisis known as the Exclusion Crisis (1679-1681) further heightened religious tensions. Parliamentary efforts to prevent the Catholic James, Duke of York, from inheriting the throne from his brother Charles II ultimately failed, but the conflict created lasting political divisions and intensified suspicions about Catholic influence in government. When James II became king in 1685, his policies confirmed Protestant fears, appointing Catholics to high positions, establishing a standing army with Catholic officers, and promoting religious toleration policies perceived as favoring Catholics.

The final catalyst arrived in June 1688 with the birth of James's son. This event created the prospect of a permanent Catholic dynasty rather than a temporary Catholic monarch who would be succeeded by his Protestant daughters Mary and Anne. For many English Protestants, this development signaled an unbearable threat to their religious and political future.

Behind the witch trials and religious panics of the seventeenth century lay psychological mechanisms that continue to operate in human societies today. Modern research in psychology, neuroscience, and group behavior offers insights that help us understand these historical events not as simple superstition but as manifestations of universal human tendencies under specific conditions of stress and uncertainty.

Mass psychogenic illness, once known as "mass hysteria," provides one framework for understanding aspects of the Salem crisis. This phenomenon occurs when symptoms of illness spread through a community without an identifiable physical cause, transmitted instead through social networks and shared beliefs. Contemporary studies of such outbreaks reveal common patterns: they often begin among people of lower social status (frequently young women or children), occur in communities under significant stress, and spread most effectively in environments with strong social connections and shared belief systems, all conditions present in Salem Village in 1692.

The neuroscience of fear illuminates the physiological mechanisms behind such events. When the human brain perceives a threat, the amygdala triggers a cascade of stress hormones that prepare the body for fight-or-flight response. This system evolved to protect us from immediate physical dangers, but it also activates in response to social threats and uncertainties. Prolonged exposure to stress, such as that experienced by colonial communities facing economic hardship, frontier violence, and religious anxiety, can heighten this response system, making people more reactive to perceived threats and less capable of calm, rational assessment.

Salem Village's power dynamics reveal another psychological dimension of the witch trials. The young female accusers, who under normal circumstances occupied positions of limited influence, suddenly gained unprecedented authority as community leaders took their accusations seriously. This inversion of the usual social hierarchy, where children, especially girls, were expected to be silent and obedient, created a feedback loop that may have reinforced accusatory behavior through attention and status rewards previously unavailable to these individuals.

Perhaps most fundamental to understanding events like the Salem trials is the human tendency toward in-group/out-group thinking. Evolutionary psychologists suggest that humans evolved to quickly categorize others as either part of their group (therefore trustworthy) or outside it (potentially threatening). This cognitive shortcut, while adaptive in ancestral environments, can lead to dangerous stereotyping and scapegoating, particularly when communities feel threatened. In Salem, accusations targeted disproportionately those who already existed at the community's margins, people with reputations for conflict, unusual behaviors, or limited social connections.

Economic and social stressors created fertile ground for scapegoating. When communities face hardships with no clear cause or solution, such as crop failures, inexplicable illnesses, or economic decline, assigning blame to identifiable individuals offers psychological relief and an illusion of control. By identifying "witches" as the source of community problems, people transformed diffuse, uncontrollable anxieties into concrete threats that could be eliminated through decisive action.

The convergence of these factors, theological beliefs about Satan's active presence, fear of declining religious fervor, economic pressures, and external threats, created a social powder keg. When unusual events began to occur, particularly involving young women and girls displaying strange behaviors, the community possessed a ready explanatory framework: witchcraft, the devil's most insidious tool for corrupting godly communities.

On those cold winter nights in Salem Village, as accusers named neighbors who had allegedly tormented them, the stars above remained constant in their courses. Yet the people below found themselves caught in a spiral of fear that would recur in different forms across centuries. As we journey further through human history's recurring patterns, this first cycle offers a sobering reminder: when societies experience the collision of genuine external threats, internal anxieties, and explanatory frameworks that invite fear, the resulting interactions can override even the most basic protections for individual rights and reason.

These psychological patterns aren't relics of a superstitious past but enduring aspects of human psychology that manifest in different forms across time. Understanding them doesn't excuse the injustices committed during the witch trials, but it helps us recognize our own vulnerability to similar patterns under conditions of fear and uncertainty, the first step toward developing greater resilience against modern forms of panic and scapegoating.

NO MAN'S LAND: PROTECTION VS. FREEDOM

Communities have a responsibility to protect their members from genuine threats, establishing boundaries that preserve safety and shared values.

Pause. Notice what arises in you.

Every person deserves the freedom to hold different beliefs, explore new ideas, and live according to their conscience without fear of persecution.

Pause. Notice what arises in you.

You do not have to agree with or justify either statement. Simply hold them both in your mind and observe what comes up.

The tension between these two principles, community protection and individual freedom, rests at the heart of our exploration of religious fear. The communities we've examined genuinely believed they were protecting themselves and their most sacred values. Yet in their determination to establish security, they sacrificed the freedom and sometimes the lives of those who stood outside prevailing orthodoxies.

Neither principle alone offers a complete answer. A society without protective boundaries disintegrates into chaos; a society without freedom of conscience becomes tyrannical. The challenge, then and now, lies not in choosing between these values but in finding ways to honor both, to create communities that are both secure and free.

As we move forward in our exploration of historical cycles, this tension will resurface repeatedly in different contexts. The question is not which principle to abandon, but how to hold both with wisdom rather than fear.

Chapter Two

When Neighbors Pointed Fingers

"I am no more a witch than you are a wizard, and if you take my life away, God will give you blood to drink." These defiant words, reportedly spoken by Sarah Good from the gallows in 1692, haunt us still. A homeless pregnant woman deemed troublesome by her neighbors, Good became among the first to die in a panic that consumed Salem Village and echoed similar terrors that had already claimed thousands of lives across the Atlantic. As her final prediction of divine retribution hung in the summer air, witnesses might have paused to consider the path that had led them to this moment, but the machinery of fear, once set in motion, demanded its sacrifices.

The Salem witch trials stand as America's most infamous episode of collective madness, yet they were neither the first nor the largest of such panics. What makes these events so compelling, and so chilling, is not their uniqueness but their familiarity. Their progression from private suspicion to public execution, from marginalized scapegoats to respected victims, from unquestioning certainty to eventual regret, follows patterns that would repeat across continents and centuries. Salem's story offers not just a historical curiosity but a mirror reflecting enduring human vulnerabilities.

The stars that watched over Salem Village that winter of 1691-1692 had witnessed centuries of similar persecutions across Europe. From their celestial vantage point, these recurring human dramas might appear as predictable as astronomical patterns: the rise and fall of fear, the eclipse of reason by terror, the gravitational pull of scapegoating when societies face uncertainty. Examining these events more closely reveals not incomprehensible superstition but recognizable human responses to perceived threats.

Bitter cold settled over Salem Village, seeming to penetrate the very soul of the community as something strange began happening in Reverend Samuel Parris's home. His daughter Betty, age 9, and niece Abigail Williams, age 11, exhibited bewildering symptoms: uncontrollable fits, contorted body positions, complaints of being pinched and pricked by invisible tormentors, and unintelligible speech that some interpreted as hellish languages. Soon these behaviors spread to other girls in their circle, including 12-year-old Ann Putnam Jr. and 17-year-old Elizabeth Hubbard.

Local physician William Griggs, called to examine the afflicted girls, found himself baffled. After exhausting natural explanations, he pronounced a diagnosis that would set tragedy in motion: "The evil hand is upon them." With this medical opinion confirming supernatural causes, attention turned to identifying the source of the demonic affliction. When pressed to name their tormentors, the girls identified three women from the community.

The first three accused, Tituba, Sarah Good, and Sarah Osborne, reveal much about how witch panics functioned and whom they targeted. Tituba, an enslaved indigenous woman from the Caribbean, served in Reverend Parris's household. She occupied multiple outsider categories: racial, cultural, and socioeconomic. Sarah Good wandered between neighbors' homes as a homeless beggar seeking charity, often muttering to herself when turned away. Currently pregnant and with a young child, she embodied a troublesome dependency on the community. Sarah Osborne, an elderly widow, had scandalized the village by failing to attend church regularly and by living with a man before marriage. All three existed at the community's margins, making them perfect repositories for social anxieties.

Targeting society's most vulnerable wasn't coincidental but rather a defining feature of witch accusations throughout history. Those with the least social capital made the safest targets for projection of fear and blame. Their marginal status meant fewer defenders would step forward, and their previous conflicts with neighbors provided ready-made narratives of malice.

The initial hearings before local magistrates John Hathorne and Jonathan Corwin took place in Salem Village's meetinghouse in early March 1692. The proceedings bore little resemblance to modern judicial standards. The accused faced their accusers directly, without legal representation. Questions presumed guilt rather than innocence: "Why do you hurt these children?" rather than "Did you hurt these children?" When the girls collapsed in fits during the hearings, spectators accepted these reactions as proof of the accused's power.

The trajectory of the three initial cases diverged in ways that would prove fateful for the community. Tituba, perhaps recognizing the hopelessness of denial, confessed to practicing witchcraft. Her dramatic testimony included lurid details of signing the devil's book, meeting with other witches, and riding through the air on a pole. Far from saving herself, Tituba's confession validated the entire framework of supernatural conspiracy, making further accusations more credible. Sarah Good and Sarah Osborne maintained their innocence but were nonetheless jailed. Osborne would die in prison before trial, while Good proceeded to conviction and execution.

The accusers, having tasted a new kind of power, soon expanded their allegations. Within weeks, respected community members Martha Corey and Rebecca Nurse found themselves accused, a significant escalation that should have prompted skepticism but instead heightened panic. Suspicion against obvious outsiders transformed into a more pervasive threat, with witches potentially hiding among even the seemingly devout.

By May 1692, what began as strange behaviors among a handful of girls had exploded into a regional crisis. Dozens stood accused, jails in Salem, Boston, and Ipswich overflowed with suspects, and the colonial government established a special Court of Oyer and Terminer ("to hear and determine") to address the emergency. This unprecedented legal intervention signaled how seriously officials took the alleged witch conspiracy, elevating local suspicions into matters of colony-wide concern.

Central to the court's procedure was the controversial acceptance of "spectral evidence," testimony that the accused's supernatural form or "specter" had appeared to victims, even when the accused's physical body was elsewhere. This legal innovation effectively removed traditional alibis, since witnesses could claim to see a person's spectral form committing mischief while the actual person was visibly elsewhere, even at church or asleep in bed. The admission of such evidence ran counter to established legal traditions but aligned with deeply held religious beliefs about the devil's powers.

The court's chief justice, William Stoughton, strongly supported spectral evidence despite reservations expressed by some clergymen. When pressed on the possibility that the devil might impersonate innocent people, Stoughton reportedly declared that if the devil could represent an innocent person, "he would choose to represent such persons as he knew were at the time reputed to be good persons so that when such shall be accused they might be the more readily believed to be witches." This circular logic made it virtually impossible for the accused to establish innocence.

As accusations multiplied, so did confessions, not because of widespread guilt, but through the mechanics of fear and survival. Those who confessed and named accomplices generally received postponed sentences, while those maintaining innocence faced swift execution. This created a perverse incentive structure: lie and live, tell truth and die. By summer, some accused had begun strategically confessing, fueling the perception of an extensive witch network.

The trials themselves became public spectacles that further reinforced collective belief. Held in the Salem Town courthouse, proceedings attracted large crowds who witnessed the accusers' dramatic fits when confronted with the accused. These performances, and we must consider the possibility that some accusers became trapped in roles they couldn't abandon, created powerful theater that demanded a satisfying conclusion: conviction and punishment.

On June 10, 1692, Bridget Bishop became the first accused witch executed by hanging at Gallows Hill. Her death, rather than sating the hunger for retribution, only accelerated the process. Five more executions followed on July 19: Sarah Good, Rebecca Nurse, Susannah Martin, Elizabeth Howe, and Sarah

Wildes. Five more died on August 19, and five on September 22. Men were not exempt; George Burroughs, a former Salem minister, was among those executed, despite reciting the Lord's Prayer perfectly at his hanging (supposedly impossible for a witch). Giles Corey, refusing to enter a plea to prevent his property's forfeiture, was pressed to death under heavy stones over three days, the only such execution in American history.

The geographical scope of accusations expanded alongside their social reach. From the initial focus on Salem Village, accusations spread to Andover, Beverly, Charlestown, and beyond. In Andover alone, more than forty people were accused. No longer confined to society's margins, accusations reached respected church members, wealthy landowners, and even the wife of Governor Phips himself. This extension into the highest circles of society would ultimately help end the trials, but not before immense damage had been done to lives, communities, and the colonial legal system.

Behind the statistics of the Salem witch trials, over 200 accused, 30 convicted, 20 executed, lie individual human stories that reveal the trials' profound personal costs. Each victim faced not only loss of life or liberty but also reputation, property, and the psychological torture of false accusation. Their stories, preserved in trial records and family accounts, put human faces to what might otherwise remain abstract history.

Rebecca Nurse exemplified the trials' escalation beyond society's margins. At 71, she was a respected church member, mother of eight, grandmother to many more, and known for her piety. When first accused, many neighbors signed petitions attesting to her good character. Even the initial jury found her not guilty, until judge Stoughton sent them back to reconsider after objections from the accusers. Her family's desperate petition for clemency after conviction noted her "known and old age" and that she was "hard of hearing and full of infirmities." Governor Phips initially granted a reprieve, then withdrew it under pressure. Her final words before hanging reportedly included, "I am innocent as the child unborn, but surely what sin hath God found in me unrepented of that He should lay such affliction upon me in my old age?"

Giles Corey's brutal death by pressing represents another dimension of the tragedy. At 80 years old, this prosperous farmer refused to enter a plea, knowing that a trial would likely end in conviction, allowing the government to seize his property and leaving his children destitute. Massachusetts law permitted "peine forte et dure," placing heavy stones on a defendant's chest until they entered a plea or died. Over three days in September 1692, stones were piled on Corey's chest as he lay in a field. His only recorded words during this torture: "More weight." By refusing to participate in what he clearly viewed as a corrupt process, Corey maintained legal standing that protected his family's inheritance, a final act of resistance and protection.

Martha Carrier, described by Cotton Mather as "the Queen of Hell," faced testimony from her own children, who had been imprisoned separately and tortured or coerced into accusing her. This family betrayal under duress illustrates how the trials tore apart fundamental social bonds. Thirteen-year-old Thomas Carrier Jr. testified that his mother made him a witch when he was seven, forced him to baptize himself in a brook in the devil's name, and threatened to break his neck if he refused. No record tells us how Martha felt facing her children in court or how those children lived with their forced testimony after her execution.

The psychological state of the accusers remains one of the trials' most debated aspects. The core group of accusers consisted primarily of adolescent girls and young women, with 12-year-old Ann Putnam Jr. among the most prolific accusers. Were they suffering from conversion disorder (historically called hysteria), experiencing the effects of ergot poisoning from contaminated rye, or consciously performing? Perhaps most likely, they became trapped in escalating roles that garnered unprecedented attention and power in a society where young women, especially those of lower status, had little agency.

What began as strange symptoms may have evolved into conscious or unconscious performance as the girls discovered their new influence. Abigail Williams and Betty Parris, the first afflicted, eventually stopped their accusations and left Salem. Both lived into adulthood but vanish from historical records, suggesting possible shame or efforts to escape their pasts. Ann Putnam Jr., however, made a public confession in 1706, claiming she had been "deluded by Satan" into accusing innocent people, including Rebecca Nurse specifically. Whether this represented genuine remorse or social rehabilitation remains unclear.

As accusations multiplied in New England, England was experiencing its own crisis of fear and accusation across the Atlantic, though political rather than supernatural in nature. The Glorious Revolution of 1688-89 saw Protestant William of Orange invade England and displace Catholic King James II in a nearly bloodless coup. While lacking Salem's supernatural elements, this revolution employed similar psychological mechanisms of fear-mongering, scapegoating, and propaganda.

William of Orange's invasion succeeded partly through an unprecedented propaganda campaign that transformed a military takeover into a "deliverance." His "Declaration of Reasons," distributed before his landing, framed his invasion not as a foreign attack but as a rescue mission to protect English "liberties" and the Protestant religion from Catholic tyranny. Copies were smuggled into England and Scotland, circulated through coffeehouses and taverns, and read from sympathetic pulpits. This document portrayed James II not simply as a Catholic, which he openly was, but as a secret papal agent bent on destroying England's constitutional freedoms.

The revolution relied heavily on fear of Catholic conspiracy, building on decades of anti-Catholic sentiment. The Popish Plot panic of 1678-79 had already demonstrated English Protestants' receptiveness to allegations of Catholic schemes, resulting in the execution of at least 15 innocent Catholics based on forged evidence. William's propaganda exploited these fears by emphasizing the birth of James's Catholic heir, painting the prospect of a Catholic dynasty as an existential threat to Protestant England.

Coffeehouses and taverns served as the social media of the era, places where political news and rumors spread through oral transmission and pamphlet sharing. London's estimated 2,000 coffeehouses by 1700 provided spaces for political discussion previously impossible in traditional public settings. Similarly, taverns in New England had facilitated the spread of witchcraft accusations beyond immediate communities. Both crises demonstrate how new communication technologies and spaces, whether coffeehouses or meeting houses, could accelerate fear contagion.

What connects these seemingly different events, a colonial witch panic and a bloodless revolution, is their reliance on similar mechanisms of fear propagation. Both crises succeeded by identifying an enemy within threatening the community's existence, creating a narrative of conspiracy requiring extraordinary defensive measures, establishing legitimacy through official declarations and proceedings, controlling information flow to favor the dominant narrative, and providing explanatory frameworks for complex social and political anxieties.

The panic in Salem, though infamous in American history, pales in comparison to the scale and duration of European witch persecution. While Salem's tragedy claimed 20 lives over less than a year, Europe's witch-hunting era lasted roughly three centuries (1450-1750) and resulted in approximately 40,000-60,000 executions. Understanding this broader context helps place Salem within a transatlantic pattern of fear and persecution, revealing both shared characteristics and important differences.

The European witch hunts began earlier and ended later than many realize. While popular imagination places them firmly in the medieval period, they actually reached their peak during the early modern era, the same period that saw the Scientific Revolution and early Enlightenment. The most intense persecution occurred between 1580 and 1630, particularly in the German states, where some villages lost significant portions of their female population to executions. Salem's outbreak in 1692 actually came near the end of the European witch-hunting era, when many regions had already abandoned such prosecutions.

Scotland presents perhaps the closest European parallel to Salem. Under King James VI (later England's James I), Scotland experienced several intense witch panics. The North Berwick trials of 1590 began when a servant girl confessed under torture to conspiring with others to use witchcraft against the king. The investigation eventually implicated over seventy people and included dramatic public trials where accusers demonstrated their torments before the king himself. James's personal involvement, and his publication of *Daemonologie* (1597), a treatise on witchcraft, gave royal legitimacy to witch-hunting. Scottish prosecutions continued into the early 18th century, with the last execution in 1727.

The legal frameworks for European witch trials differed significantly from Salem's approach. Many European jurisdictions relied on the legal concept of *crimen exceptum* ("exceptional crime") for witchcraft cases, explicitly setting aside normal evidence standards for this "exceptional" threat. Torture, rarely used in English or colonial American legal systems, became standard procedure in many Continental witch trials. The "swimming test" (floating indicated guilt, sinking innocence) and "pricking" to find insensitive spots considered "devil's marks" supplemented judicial torture in gathering "evidence." These methods almost guaranteed confessions and further accusations.

The influential text *Malleus Maleficarum* ("Hammer of Witches"), published in 1487 by German clergymen Heinrich Kramer and Jacob Sprenger, codified methods for identifying, trying, and executing witches. While never officially endorsed by the Catholic Church, this manual spread widely and shaped judicial approaches across denominations. It particularly emphasized women's supposed susceptibility to demonic influence, claiming "women are intellectually like children" and "more superstitious." While both men and women faced accusations, approximately 75-80% of European witch trial victims were female, reflecting these gendered assumptions.

The scale of some European witch hunts dwarfed Salem's outbreak. The Bamberg witch trials (1626-1630) claimed approximately 1,000 lives in that German city-state alone. Würzburg saw 900 executions. Entire communities fell under suspicion, with accusations spreading through family networks and extracted through torture. Unlike Salem, where executions involved hanging, most European witch executions involved burning at the stake, considered necessary to prevent the witch's return and purify the community through fire.

Despite these differences, European and American witch hunts shared key characteristics: they targeted predominantly women, particularly those lacking social protection; they flourished during periods of religious conflict, war, or social instability; they relied on special legal procedures that disadvantaged the accused; they typically began with marginalized individuals before spreading to more respectable community members; and they eventually collapsed when accusations reached powerful figures or when intellectual elites withdrew support.

Beyond the direct persecution of alleged witches, the late 17th century saw broader mechanisms for enforcing religious and intellectual conformity. Blasphemy prosecutions, book censorship, and suppression of scientific ideas formed part of the same impulse that drove witch hunts: the desire to protect communities from dangerous influences, whether demonic or intellectual. These parallel systems of control reveal how deeply fear of unorthodoxy penetrated society.

The case of Thomas Aikenhead stands as a stark example of blasphemy enforcement. This 20-year-old Edinburgh University student was executed for blasphemy in January 1697, just four years after the last Salem execution. Aikenhead's "crime" consisted mainly of questioning Christian doctrines in private conversations with fellow students, including expressing doubts about biblical miracles and suggesting the Old Testament might contain "allegories" rather than literal truth. When these comments became known, Aikenhead faced prosecution under Scotland's strict blasphemy laws.

Despite his youth and written recantation begging forgiveness for his "horrible extravagancies," Aikenhead was sentenced to hang. His execution represented the last judicial killing for blasphemy in Britain and came during a period when such prosecutions were already becoming rare. Like Salem's final executions, Aikenhead's death marked the end of an era rather than its height. The public reaction, surprisingly muted, with some expressing discomfort at the severity of the punishment, suggested changing attitudes toward religious enforcement.

Book censorship operated alongside personal prosecution to control dangerous ideas. The Catholic Church maintained its Index Librorum Prohibitorum (Index of Forbidden Books), which by the late 17th century included works by Galileo, Copernicus, Descartes, and other scientific and philosophical pioneers.

Protestant countries employed their own censorship systems, with England's Licensing Act requiring pre-publication approval for printed materials until its lapse in 1695. Colonial printing presses operated under even tighter control, with Massachusetts limiting printing to Cambridge until 1674 and maintaining close supervision of publications.

Scientific ideas that challenged scripture faced particular scrutiny. Galileo's famous conflict with the Church over heliocentrism (the sun-centered model of the solar system) exemplified this tension. Although his infamous trial occurred earlier (1633), its effects continued to influence scientific communication throughout the century. Many scientists adopted self-censorship, framing discoveries as illuminating God's design rather than challenging biblical authority. Newton himself, whose mathematical work undermined traditional cosmology, remained outwardly devout and carefully positioned his discoveries within religious frameworks.

What powered the spiral of accusation and confession in Salem and beyond? Beyond religious explanations and psychological theories lies a simpler, more universal human tendency: in times of uncertainty and threat, people seek explanation, control, and safety. Identifying witches offered all three: an explanation for misfortunes, control through identification and punishment, and the illusion of safety through removal of perceived threats. As the cycle fed itself, stopping the momentum required challenging deeply held beliefs and admitting the possibility of grave injustice, both profoundly difficult steps for any society.

If we could stand among the stars and look down upon Earth during these centuries of fear, we might see not isolated outbreaks of superstition but a recurring pattern of human communities under stress, reaching for explanatory frameworks that offered control when confronted with uncertainty. The paths from accusation to execution followed similar trajectories whether in Salem Village or German principalities, with initial targeting of marginalized individuals expanding to threaten the social fabric itself. By century's end, this system of enforced orthodoxy showed signs of weakening. The Salem trials' excesses had demonstrated the dangers of unchecked religious fervor. Scientific advances increasingly proved their practical value. The proliferation of print culture made complete censorship impossible. Growing religious diversity within Protestant communities forced greater tolerance of differing interpretations. What had once seemed essential protection against dangerous corruption gradually appeared more like unnecessary restriction.

The concurrent decline of witch trials, blasphemy executions, and strict censorship around the turn of the 18th century suggests a broader shift in Western attitudes toward difference and dissent. Communities began recognizing that diversity of thought might not necessarily threaten social cohesion, and that enforcement mechanisms themselves could cause more harm than the ideas they sought to suppress. This shift didn't happen overnight, but the excesses of cases like Salem and Aikenhead helped accelerate reconsideration of how societies should respond to perceived threats, whether supernatural or intellectual.

NO MAN'S LAND: Security vs. Liberty

Communities require protection from genuine threats, and sometimes must limit certain freedoms to ensure collective safety and stability.

Pause. Notice what arises in you.

Individual liberty, to think differently, question authority, and live according to one's conscience, forms the foundation of human dignity and societal progress.

Pause. Notice what arises in you.

You do not have to agree with or justify either statement. Simply hold them both in your mind and observe what comes up.

The tension between security and liberty has defined human societies across time. The Salem witch trials and their European counterparts arose from genuine concerns about community protection, yet resulted in profound violations of individual freedom and dignity. Neither security without liberty nor liberty without security offers a viable path forward.

The most stable societies find ways to protect themselves from genuine threats while preserving space for individual conscience and expression. The events we've explored reveal what happens when this balance fails, and invite us to consider where similar imbalances might exist in our own time.

This tension isn't something to "solve" once and for all, but rather a dynamic balance to maintain with wisdom rather than fear.

Chapter Three

When the Fever Broke

"I do humbly beg forgiveness of all those that I have given just grounds of sorrow and offense through my imprudence." In the hushed Salem meeting house in 1706, now-grown Ann Putnam Jr. stood before her community as her confession was read aloud. Fourteen years after pointing an accusing finger at innocent neighbors, Putnam acknowledged being "deluded by Satan" into condemning people "that were innocent." Her statement came too late for those executed, but marked a community's painful recognition of its mistakes. The path from certainty to regret, from persecution to atonement, reveals as much about human psychology as the panic itself.

The Salem witch trials prove particularly instructive not just in how they began but in how they ended. Unlike some historical persecutions that continued for decades, Salem's witch hunt collapsed with remarkable speed, less than a year from first accusation to final execution. The mechanisms that halted this deadly machinery of fear reveal how societies can recover from collective madness, offering insights that extend far beyond colonial New England. The story's resolution across both the American colonies and England demonstrates a pattern of awakening that occurs repeatedly throughout history: the movement from fear-driven reaction toward more measured response.

The stars that had witnessed Salem's descent into panic now watched its awakening from the same impassive distance. If those celestial observers could have perceived the subtle shift in human consciousness below, they would have noted how quickly certainty can give way to doubt, and how systems designed to propagate fear can transform into instruments of correction. The night sky that had seemed filled with omens of divine judgment in the winter of accusation now looked down upon a community beginning its long journey toward reconciliation with its own dark chapter.

The Salem witch trials didn't gradually fade away; they collapsed almost as suddenly as they had begun. By September 1692, the crisis had reached its peak with 20 executions completed and dozens more awaiting trial. Yet just one month later, the special Court of Oyer and Terminer had been dissolved, spectral evidence rejected, and the path toward resolution begun. What happened to end a panic that had seemed unstoppable?

Several factors converged to halt the trials' momentum. First came growing skepticism among influential voices. Increase Mather, one of New England's most respected ministers and father of Cotton Mather, published "Cases of Conscience Concerning Evil Spirits" in October 1692, directly challenging the use of spectral evidence. Though affirming belief in witchcraft itself, Mather argued that spectral testimony was inherently unreliable: "It were better that ten suspected witches should escape, than that one innocent person should be condemned." This rhetorical shift, prioritizing protection of the innocent over capturing every guilty party, represented a fundamental change in approach.

Practical concerns reinforced intellectual doubts. As accusations reached into Boston's elite circles and even implicated Lady Mary Phips, wife of the governor, powerful stakeholders recognized the threat to social order. Governor William Phips, who had initially authorized the special court, moved to restrict the proceedings, writing to English authorities that "some were accused of whose innocency I was well assured." On October 12, 1692, Phips prohibited further arrests for witchcraft, and on October 29, he dissolved the Court of Oyer and Terminer entirely.

The establishment of a new Superior Court of Judicature in January 1693 marked the final phase of the trials' collapse. Operating under more traditional legal standards, this court disallowed spectral evidence and required material proof for conviction. The results proved dramatic: of 52 cases tried under these stricter standards, 49 resulted in acquittals. The three convicted received reprieves from Governor Phips. By May 1693, Phips had pardoned and released all remaining accused witches from prison, effectively ending the Salem witch hunt.

This swift reversal raises important questions. If spectral evidence was so clearly problematic that its rejection immediately collapsed almost every case, why had respected legal authorities accepted it initially? The answer lies partly in the momentum of fear itself. Once set in motion, with lives already taken based on certain standards of evidence, acknowledging those standards as flawed required admitting terrible mistakes had been made. Such admission comes at high psychological cost, which helps explain why reversals of persecutions often seem to require a breaking point, in Salem's case, the overreaching of accusations into elite circles.

The collapse also demonstrates how quickly social consensus can shift when influential voices change position. The same community that had enthusiastically supported witch-hunting in spring 1692 accepted its end by winter. This pattern, rapid social contagion followed by equally rapid abandonment, suggests that many participants may have privately harbored doubts even while publicly supporting the proceedings. When authorities signaled a change in direction, these private doubts could safely become public, accelerating the persecution's end.

Most striking is how the legal system that had enabled the persecutions ultimately provided the mechanism for their resolution. By returning to traditional standards of evidence and due process, the courts transformed from instruments of panic to guarantors of justice. This self-correction capability, though it came too late for twenty victims, illustrates how institutional safeguards, when properly applied, can help societies recover from periods of excessive fear.

The Salem witch trials left deep scars on New England society, creating a legacy of guilt, recrimination, and eventually, attempts at atonement. The five years following the trials' end saw a community struggling to process what had happened and reconcile with a shameful episode that had claimed innocent lives.

On January 14, 1697, Massachusetts observed a colony-wide "Day of Repentance" ordered by the General Court. The resolution establishing this day explicitly acknowledged "the late tragedy raised among us by Satan and his instruments through the awful judgment of God," language that still attributed events to supernatural forces but recognized human error. In Salem Village, minister Joseph Green read a statement confessing the community's collective guilt before a congregation that included many former accusers and family members of the executed.

Judge Samuel Sewall made perhaps the most remarkable public acknowledgment of wrongdoing. On this day of fasting, Sewall stood in Boston's South Church while his minister read his confession, acknowledging "the blame and shame of it" and asking "pardon of men," particularly for his role in the death of innocent victims. Sewall would observe a private day of fasting annually thereafter on the anniversary of the first executions, a personal ritual of remembrance and atonement he maintained for the rest of his life.

Most officials involved in the trials, however, never publicly acknowledged wrongdoing. William Stoughton, the chief justice who had most aggressively accepted spectral evidence, refused to admit error and reportedly walked out of a meeting when Governor Phips suggested the court had made mistakes. Stoughton's resistance illustrates the psychological difficulty of admitting participation in injustice, especially for those most deeply invested in the process. The accusers themselves largely disappeared from public record, with Ann Putnam Jr.'s 1706 confession standing as a rare exception.

The legal rehabilitation of the accused proceeded alongside these moral reckonings. In 1697, the Massachusetts legislature passed a bill reversing the attainder (legal penalties) against those who had been convicted but not executed. In 1702, the General Court declared the 1692 trials unlawful, and in 1711, it passed a more comprehensive bill officially exonerating those convicted and providing compensation to their heirs, though the amounts (ranging from £7 to £79) hardly matched the losses suffered. The last official exoneration wouldn't come until 2001, when the Massachusetts legislature finally cleared the name of Elizabeth Johnson Jr., overlooked in previous actions.

The families of victims followed different paths in response to the tragedy. Some, like the Nurses, remained in Salem and worked to restore their family's good name, eventually establishing a separate cemetery where Rebecca's body was properly reinterred after her hasty burial at the execution site. Others left the community entirely, seeking fresh starts where their family names carried no stigma. The Proctors (John Proctor was executed while his wife Elizabeth was spared due to pregnancy) relocated to Lynn, Massachusetts, abandoning the land that had been in their family for generations.

Salem Village itself sought to escape the legacy of the trials through literal renaming, becoming Danvers in 1752. This attempt at reinvention reflects the community's desire to distance itself from events that had become synonymous with injustice and hysteria. Yet the psychological impact lingered in local consciousness far longer than any official records, with family stories of persecution and false accusation passing down through generations.

While New England grappled with the aftermath of witch trials, England was establishing a new political and religious equilibrium following the Glorious Revolution. The settlement that emerged from this period represented a similar movement away from fear-driven policies toward more balanced approaches to difference and dissent.

The English Bill of Rights, enacted in February 1689, established key protections that would prove foundational for later democratic development. It prohibited the monarch from suspending laws, maintaining a standing army during peacetime without Parliamentary consent, or imposing excessive bail and "cruel and unusual punishments." These provisions directly addressed the perceived abuses of James II while establishing stronger institutional safeguards against future monarchical overreach. Like Salem's return to stricter legal standards, these protections represented a society stepping back from fear-based suspension of normal constraints.

Religious settlement proved more complex than political adjustment. The Toleration Act of May 1689 extended legal protection to Protestant dissenters (Presbyterians, Baptists, Congregationalists) but specifically excluded Catholics and those denying the Trinity. This partial toleration reflected pragmatic recognition of Protestant diversity rather than embracing full religious freedom, a limited but significant step from the previous insistence on strict conformity. Catholics remained subject to various legal disabilities, demonstrating how fear of perceived threats diminishes gradually rather than vanishing instantly.

Military resolution of potential counter-revolution threats reinforced the settlement's stability. William III's victories over Jacobite forces (supporters of the deposed James II) in Ireland (1690) and ongoing suppression of Scottish resistance removed immediate threats to the new regime. This security allowed some relaxation of anti-Catholic measures over time, as the feared Catholic restoration became increasingly unlikely. Here too, reduced threat perception enabled more moderate policy, echoing Salem's abandonment of witch-hunting as the perceived conspiracy threat diminished.

Perhaps most transformative was what happened in Salem Village and beyond: the gradual reshaping of collective memory. What began as a community's desperate response to perceived supernatural threat was increasingly reframed as a cautionary tale about human fallibility and institutional failure. By the early 18th century, Salem had already begun to function as a cultural reference point for the dangers of unchecked fear and abandoned due process. Ministers and civic leaders invoked the trials as warnings against future excess, establishing what would become an enduring place in American moral consciousness. This transformation, from immediate trauma to instructive history, represents an essential process in how societies integrate difficult episodes into their cultural memory and identity.

The early 18th century witnessed a broader intellectual shift that would profoundly influence how Western societies approached difference and dissent. The emerging Enlightenment, with its emphasis on reason, evidence, and skepticism toward authority, provided intellectual frameworks that would permanently alter how phenomena like witch panics were understood and addressed.

John Locke's "Letter Concerning Toleration" (1689) offered philosophical arguments for religious pluralism that went beyond political expedience. Written during his exile in Holland and published upon his return to England after the Glorious Revolution, Locke argued that coerced belief wasn't merely unjust but fundamentally contradictory: "Such is the nature of the understanding that it cannot be compelled to the belief of anything by outward force." By distinguishing between civil interests (properly regulated by government) and spiritual salvation (beyond governmental competence), Locke established intellectual foundations for separating church authority from state power, a separation that would eventually limit religion's role in prosecuting dissent.

The gradual relaxation of censorship created space for more open intellectual exchange. England's Licensing Act lapsed in 1695, ending pre-publication censorship of printed materials. While seditious or blasphemous content remained prosecutable after publication, the absence of prior restraint allowed wider circulation of controversial ideas. The proliferation of newspapers, periodicals, and pamphlets created a more diverse information environment where single narratives couldn't dominate as easily as in Salem's isolated community. This expanding "marketplace of ideas" made it more difficult for fear-driven explanations to go unchallenged.

Coffeehouses and salons emerged as important physical spaces for this new discourse. London's coffeehouses grew from dozens in the 1650s to thousands by the early 18th century, providing venues where people from different social backgrounds could gather, read newspapers, and discuss current events. Unlike churches with their hierarchical communication (minister to congregation), coffeehouses facilitated horizontal exchange and debate. Similarly, in France and elsewhere, salon culture created spaces for philosophical discussion outside traditional institutions. These new social forms enabled questioning of traditional explanations for misfortune, disease, and social problems.

Scientific explanations increasingly challenged supernatural interpretations of natural phenomena. The Royal Society (founded 1660) had established protocols for experimental verification that privileged empirical evidence over received authority. Isaac Newton's "Principia Mathematica" (1687) had demonstrated how natural laws could explain celestial movements previously attributed to divine action. By the early 1700s, this scientific approach was extending to weather, disease, and other areas previously explained through supernatural frameworks. While most scientists remained religious, they increasingly sought natural rather than supernatural explanations for observable phenomena.

Public attitudes showed growing fatigue with religious conflict after generations of persecution and counter-persecution. The English writer Jonathan Swift captured this sentiment in 1708, lamenting how religious differences led people to "hate one another for God's sake." This exhaustion with sectarian strife created receptiveness to more tolerant approaches advocated by Enlightenment thinkers. Having witnessed the human costs of religious persecution, from witch trials to international wars, many began questioning whether enforcing orthodoxy justified such suffering.

The transition from the 17th century's religious fears to the 18th century's more measured approaches unfolded not suddenly but through concrete legal and social changes that gradually transformed how Western societies responded to perceived threats, whether supernatural or ideological.

The repeal of witch-hunting statutes marked a crucial legal shift. Britain's Witchcraft Act of 1735 repealed previous laws that had made witchcraft a capital offense, replacing them with penalties for those claiming to possess magical powers, effectively recategorizing witchcraft from demonic conspiracy to fraudulent pretense. Similar legal reforms followed across Europe, with France abolishing witch trials in 1682 and Prussia in 1714. These changes didn't necessarily indicate disbelief in supernatural powers but reflected changing assessments of appropriate legal responses to such beliefs.

Standards of evidence evolved alongside statutory changes. Courts increasingly required material proof rather than spectral evidence or coerced confessions in all types of cases. The legal concept of "corpus delicti," requiring proof that a crime actually occurred before convicting someone of committing it, gained importance. These standards made witchcraft particularly difficult to prosecute, as the crime itself (communion with Satan) left no physical evidence. More broadly, legal systems moved toward principles that would later be expressed as "innocent until proven guilty" and requirements for evidence beyond reasonable doubt.

The execution of religious dissenters similarly declined through institutional rather than purely philosophical changes. Thomas Aikenhead's 1697 execution for blasphemy marked the last such judicial killing in Britain. While blasphemy remained legally prohibited (as it would until the 20th century in many jurisdictions), punishment gradually shifted from execution to imprisonment, fines, or social censure. This de-escalation of consequences reflected both changing views about proportionate punishment and growing recognition that diversity of belief didn't necessarily threaten social cohesion.

Churches' roles in public life underwent subtle but significant transformation. While established churches maintained formal privileges, their practical influence over civil authority diminished. Clergy increasingly focused on moral persuasion rather than coercive enforcement of orthodoxy. This shift wasn't just institutional but reflected changing expectations among congregants themselves, who increasingly distinguished between conforming to community moral standards and persecuting those who differed. Religious leadership adapted to maintain relevance in a changing cultural environment that valued evidence and reason alongside faith tradition.

The emergence of periodicals encouraging rational discourse provided vital infrastructure for this cultural evolution. Publications like The Spectator (founded 1711) popularized reasoned argument and polite disagreement as alternatives to dogmatic assertion. Editor Joseph Addison explicitly aimed to "bring philosophy out of closets and libraries, schools and colleges, to dwell in clubs and assemblies, at tea-tables and coffee-houses," making rational analysis accessible to broader audiences. This democratization of analytical thinking helped displace fear-based reactions to difference with more considered responses.

Conservative religious thought adapted rather than simply disappeared. Cotton Mather himself, so associated with Salem's panic, later championed smallpox inoculation based on empirical evidence of its effectiveness, despite facing religious objections that it interfered with divine providence. This integration of scientific observation with religious perspective exemplifies how many reconciled traditional faith with emerging empirical approaches. Religious conservatism remained vibrant but increasingly engaged with, rather than simply rejected, emerging scientific and philosophical developments.

These legal and social adaptations created what historian Keith Thomas called "the decline of magic," not an overnight revolution but a gradual recalibration of how societies explained misfortune, regulated difference, and managed fear. The pattern shows how institutional changes often precede and facilitate broader cultural shifts, creating space for new understandings to develop and spread. Legal reform doesn't merely reflect changed attitudes but helps create conditions for them to evolve.

The Salem witch trials left an indelible mark on American consciousness, evolving from historical event to powerful cultural symbol that continues to shape understanding of group psychology, legal process, and the dangers of unchecked fear. This transformation of historical experience into meaningful cultural narrative represents the final stage in the cycle we've examined, not just the end of persecution but its integration into societal understanding in ways that might prevent future recurrence.

Salem became America's cautionary tale about the dangers of abandoning due process in the face of fear. Legal scholars and jurists have frequently invoked the trials when arguing against relaxed evidentiary standards or heightened procedural protections for the accused. Supreme Court opinions have cited Salem when upholding rights to confront accusers and requirements for reliable evidence. This legal legacy demonstrates how historical excesses can generate corrective principles that guide future practice, a pattern seen repeatedly as societies learn from their most troubling episodes.

Arthur Miller's 1953 play "The Crucible" powerfully reinterpreted Salem for modern audiences, explicitly connecting colonial witch hunts to contemporary anti-Communist persecutions under McCarthyism. Miller's work exemplifies how historical events gain renewed relevance through analogy to current concerns, becoming flexible metaphors rather than merely fixed past incidents. The term "witch hunt" itself has entered common vocabulary as shorthand for persecutions driven by fear rather than evidence, though often claimed by conflicting sides in contemporary debates, demonstrating the enduring resonance of Salem's legacy across political perspectives.

The psychological insights from historical panics have proven enduringly valuable. Modern understanding of concepts like mass psychogenic illness, confirmation bias, and scapegoating mechanisms owes much to analysis of historical episodes like Salem. When psychologists Robert Rosenthal and Lenore Jacobson coined the term "Pygmalion effect" to describe how expectations influence perception, they drew on witch-hunting history, noting how "the expectation alone is sufficient to cause projection and subsequent 'confirmation' of the expectation." This scientific legacy demonstrates how historical experience informs understanding of persistent human tendencies.

Salem's influence extended beyond America to shape attitudes toward evidence and due process internationally. As colonial legal systems developed worldwide, Salem repeatedly served as cautionary reference for maintaining procedural safeguards even during periods of perceived threat. This legal memory helped establish presumption of innocence and requirements for reliable evidence as fundamental principles rather than dispensable luxuries during crises, principles that would be formally enshrined in documents like the Universal Declaration of Human Rights following 20th-century persecutions that echoed witch-hunting dynamics.

If we return to our stargazing metaphor, we might imagine how differently the night sky appeared to observers at the beginning and end of this historical cycle. The same stars that had seemed to portend divine judgment in 1692 now represented the constancy of natural laws to early 18th-century eyes. This shift in perception, from supernatural to natural, from fear-driven to evidence-based, didn't change the stars themselves but transformed how humans interpreted their meaning. Similarly, the human capacity for both panic and correction remains constant across centuries, with each generation learning anew how to balance legitimate concern with measured response.

Perhaps most importantly, Salem and similar historical episodes help us recognize pattern rather than anomaly in human behavior. What once might have been dismissed as superstitious aberration is now understood as manifestation of recurrent human tendencies, tendencies that persist in modern form. This recognition doesn't make us immune to similar dynamics but increases our collective capacity to identify and potentially interrupt destructive patterns before they reach their most damaging phases.

The enduring lesson of this first historical cycle lies not in cataloging past errors but in recognizing their continued relevance to present challenges. The specific content of fears changes across time, from witches to communists to terrorists to emerging technologies, but the human patterns of response remain strikingly consistent. By understanding these patterns, we develop greater capacity to distinguish between genuine threats requiring response and manufactured fears exploiting psychological vulnerabilities. This discernment represents the most valuable legacy of Salem and similar historical episodes: not just knowledge of what happened, but insight into why it happened and how similar dynamics might manifest in our own time.

NO MAN'S LAND: Conviction vs. Correction

Maintaining conviction in our beliefs provides necessary stability, direction, and meaning in a complex and challenging world.

Pause. Notice what arises in you.

Willingness to recognize error, change course, and admit mistakes enables growth, justice, and the correction of harmful patterns.

Pause. Notice what arises in you.

You do not have to agree with or justify either statement. Simply hold them both in your mind and observe what comes up.

This tension between conviction and correction lies at the heart of both personal development and societal evolution. The Salem judges who maintained absolute certainty in the reality of witchcraft conspiracy could not recognize their errors until devastating harm had occurred. Yet their conviction wasn't entirely misplaced; they were responding to what they genuinely perceived as threats to their community, guided by the best understanding available to them.

The capacity to hold strong beliefs while remaining open to correction represents a vital balance rarely achieved by individuals or societies. Too much conviction without correction leads to rigidity and potential injustice; too much correction without conviction creates instability and lack of coherent purpose.

As we continue exploring historical cycles, this dynamic tension will reappear repeatedly in different forms. The challenge isn't choosing between these values but developing the wisdom to honor both, maintaining conviction where warranted while embracing correction when necessary.

Cycle 2: When Reason Met the Mob

Chapter Four

When Words Became Weapons

The small printing shop on Philadelphia's Market Street buzzed with activity in January 1776. Workers hunched over their presses, fingers stained with ink, as they rushed to meet unprecedented demand. Outside, a line had formed: farmers in rough homespun, merchants in finer garb, and laborers with calloused hands, all waiting to purchase the same slim pamphlet. Just published a few days earlier, Thomas Paine's *Common Sense* was already creating a sensation. The 47-page tract, which attacked the very concept of monarchy as "exceedingly ridiculous" and made a passionate case for American independence, would sell an astonishing 150,000 copies in its first few months, equivalent to one copy for every twenty inhabitants in the colonies.

Across the Atlantic, similar scenes unfolded in Parisian print shops, where workers produced countless political pamphlets and newspapers that challenged traditional authority. In both contexts, words transformed into weapons in a revolution that would reshape not just nations but how humans conceived of governance itself. The explosion of print culture in the 18th century didn't simply report on revolutionary changes; it helped create them.

As we lift our gaze from Salem's witch trials to this new historical cycle, the stars remain fixed in their celestial patterns, but human understanding of them has fundamentally shifted. Where once these heavenly bodies served as divine signs, by the mid-18th century they had become objects of scientific study, their movements governed by Newton's mathematical laws rather than supernatural whims. This transformation in perspective, from mystical to rational, from fearful submission to confident inquiry, reflects the broader intellectual revolution unfolding below. The Age of Reason brought a fresh way of examining not just the heavens but human societies themselves, questioning arrangements once considered divinely ordained and unchangeable.

The 18th century witnessed an unprecedented surge in print communication. What had been a technology largely controlled by and serving authorities, the church, the state, established publishers, now became more accessible, affordable, and resistant to control. This shift represented a media revolution that would dramatically alter how people formed their political opinions and identities.

In America, newspapers multiplied rapidly in the decades before revolution. By 1775, the colonies supported thirty-eight newspapers, an impressive number for a population of just over two million. These papers reprinted political essays, shared reports of British actions from different colonies, and gradually wove isolated grievances into a shared narrative of threat. Benjamin Franklin's "Join, or Die" cartoon, originally created during the Seven Years' War to urge colonial unity against the French, emerged as a powerful symbol of necessary colonial cooperation against British policies.

The committees of correspondence, established first in Boston in 1772 and quickly spreading to other colonies, created what one historian calls "a geography of resistance," a parallel communication structure outside official channels that could rapidly disseminate information and coordinate responses to British actions. This network elevated local issues into continental concerns and helped forge a shared revolutionary consciousness.

In France, a similar explosion in political publishing took place. Between 1789 and 1799, over 1,300 newspapers sprang up in Paris alone. Radical publications like Jean-Paul Marat's "L'Ami du peuple" (The Friend of the People) constantly urged Parisians to root out "traitors," effectively inciting mob action against those deemed enemies of the revolution. The press evolved beyond a forum for debate into an active agent in radicalizing public opinion.

This print revolution paralleled in many ways our modern social media environment, enabling rapid information sharing, emotional contagion across distance, the formation of like-minded communities, and the ability to bypass traditional authorities. Just as Twitter and Facebook proved instrumental in mobilizing movements like the Arab Spring, 18th-century pamphlets and newspapers galvanized populations for revolutionary action.

For traditional authorities, this democratization of information posed an existential threat. Information beyond their control meant power they couldn't maintain. Both British and French authorities attempted to suppress revolutionary publications through various censorship measures, but the technology had evolved faster than their ability to regulate it. The print revolution had altered the information landscape, shifting advantage to those who could best navigate the new media environment, often those advocating for change rather than those defending the status quo.

Behind the revolutionary pamphlets and newspapers lay a set of transformative ideas. The Enlightenment, a broad intellectual movement that championed reason, science, and human capacity, provided the philosophical foundation upon which revolutionary movements would build their case against traditional authority.

John Locke's ideas proved particularly influential. His concept of natural rights, that humans are born free and possess inherent rights to life, liberty, and property, directly challenged the notion that monarchs ruled by divine right. His social contract theory established that legitimate government derives from the consent of the governed and exists to protect their natural rights. When government fails in this essential purpose, Locke argued, citizens not only have the right but the duty to replace it.

These ideas found eager audiences in both America and France. Thomas Jefferson drew heavily on Locke when drafting the Declaration of Independence, particularly the concepts of life, liberty, and the right to overthrow oppressive governments. The document's stirring preamble, "We hold these truths to be self-evident, that all men are created equal," heralded a new era of government by consent.

In France, philosophers like Jean-Jacques Rousseau, Voltaire, and Montesquieu supplied similar intellectual ammunition against the ancien régime. Rousseau's concept of the "general will" placed sovereignty properly in the people themselves, not their rulers. Voltaire's withering critiques of religious intolerance and arbitrary authority eroded the legitimacy of both church and monarchy. Montesquieu's analysis of the separation of powers offered practical models for constraining governmental authority.

These Enlightenment ideas "influenced ordinary readers, politicians, and even heads of state" across the Western world. They challenged more than existing systems; they questioned the very legitimacy of traditional power arrangements. In doing so, they sparked a significant psychological shift, what had once seemed divinely ordained and immutable now appeared as conventional and subject to rational critique.

For those in power, these ideas loomed as dangerous contagions threatening the very foundations of social order. For those seeking change, they offered intellectual justification for revolutionary action. Both reactions highlighted the transformative power of new ways of thinking, ideas that, once introduced, refused to be contained by traditional authority.

The Seven Years' War (1756-1763) created the perfect storm of conditions for revolution. While British forces emerged victorious in this first truly global conflict, their triumph came at tremendous cost. The British national debt nearly doubled during the war, creating an urgent need for new revenue sources. Colonial America, which had benefited from British military protection against French encroachment, appeared a logical place to recover costs.

From London's perspective, colonial taxation represented not tyranny but fiscal necessity and imperial responsibility. Parliament's passage of the Sugar Act (1764), Stamp Act (1765), and Townshend Acts (1767) sought to address war debt while asserting parliamentary authority over increasingly independent-minded colonies.

Yet through the colonial lens, shaped by distance, developing identity, and Enlightenment ideals, these same policies appeared as dangerous innovations threatening cherished liberties. Colonial resistance sprang not primarily from economic burden, the taxes were relatively modest, but from the principle of taxation without direct representation in Parliament and fears about the precedent being established.

"No taxation without representation" emerged as a powerful rallying cry, condensing complex constitutional arguments into a simple, memorable phrase. The Stamp Act, which required a royal stamp on all printed materials and legal documents, ignited particular outrage because it directly affected colonial printers, the very people who controlled communication channels. Boston printer Benjamin Edes transformed his newspaper, the Boston Gazette, into a powerful voice of resistance, publishing inflammatory articles that portrayed British policies as part of a deliberate conspiracy against liberty.

Colonial assemblies, accustomed to significant self-governance in local affairs, increasingly clashed with royal governors attempting to implement parliamentary directives. This conflict raised fundamental questions about the proper relationship between center and periphery within the British Empire, questions that would ultimately find resolution only through separation.

The Boston Tea Party of December 1773 marked a pivotal moment when resistance escalated from political protest to direct action. When American colonists dumped 342 chests of British tea into Boston Harbor, they symbolically rejected British commercial control and parliamentary authority. The British response, closing Boston Harbor and imposing direct rule on Massachusetts through the Coercive Acts (which colonists called the "Intolerable Acts"), only confirmed colonial fears about British intentions.

Through each escalation, the revolutionary communication network spread news, shaped interpretation, and mobilized resistance. What might have remained isolated local grievances became, through the power of print and correspondence networks, a shared narrative of threat that transcended colonial boundaries and created the psychological foundation for united action.

While American colonists chafed under British taxation, France faced a more comprehensive crisis that threatened its entire social structure. The ancien régime, a system defined by rigid social hierarchy, aristocratic privilege, and absolute monarchy, confronted simultaneous challenges of financial collapse, ideological challenge, and social unrest.

France's social structure consisted of three estates: the First Estate (clergy), the Second Estate (nobility), and the Third Estate (everyone else, from wealthy urban merchants to impoverished peasants). Despite comprising less than 2% of the population, the First and Second Estates owned approximately 35% of the land and enjoyed exemption from most taxation. Meanwhile, the tax burden fell almost entirely on the Third Estate, an arrangement considered "one of the causes of the French Revolution."

This unjust taxation system might have endured longer had France not faced acute financial crisis by the 1780s. Decades of royal extravagance and costly wars, including substantial support for the American Revolution, had nearly bankrupted the kingdom. When poor harvests in 1788 and 1789 caused bread prices to soar, widespread hunger and mounting anger swept through a populace that viewed the court as indifferent to common suffering.

Louis XVI, well-intentioned but indecisive, proved incapable of implementing necessary reforms. When his finance ministers suggested taxing the privileged classes, they encountered fierce resistance from aristocrats determined to preserve their traditional exemptions. The king's attempts to impose new taxes on the nobility were blocked by the Parlement of Paris, ironically using Enlightenment language about rights and consent to protect aristocratic privilege.

As the crisis deepened, the influence of Enlightenment ideas among the educated classes fostered growing skepticism about the legitimacy of absolute monarchy and hereditary privilege. The American example had demonstrated that revolution against monarchical authority could succeed; it "set the stage for an effective uprising" in France. The combination of material suffering, intellectual critique, and practical example created increasingly favorable conditions for fundamental change.

By 1789, with the royal treasury virtually empty, Louis XVI was forced to call the Estates-General, a representative assembly of all three estates that hadn't met since 1614. This desperate measure, intended to address the financial crisis, instead provided the mechanism through which revolutionary forces would begin to dismantle the ancien régime itself.

As both the American colonies and France approached their revolutionary moments, a distinctive psychological climate took hold, a mixture of fear, hope, anticipation, and determination that transcended simple political disagreement. This revolutionary mood reflected fundamental uncertainty about the future combined with growing certainty that the present system could not continue unchanged.

In America, colonists' hope for rightful treatment within the British Empire gradually yielded to fears of a deliberate conspiracy against their liberties. Every new British policy seemed to confirm these suspicions. A Massachusetts minister captured this mood in 1774, writing that Britain intended "to get the children's necks under a yoke that neither we nor our fathers could bear." This fear of tyranny mobilized resistance while providing psychological justification for increasingly radical action.

British authorities and loyalists harbored their own fears, of disorder, of the collapse of legitimate authority, of what might replace established institutions if revolution succeeded. General Thomas Gage, dispatched to Massachusetts in 1774 to restore order, found himself in a society already transformed by years of revolutionary communication. "The flames of sedition," he reported back to London, "have spread universally throughout the country beyond conception."

In France, decades of social inequality bred similar revolutionary anticipation. The Third Estate increasingly questioned not just specific policies but the legitimacy of a system that placed enormous burdens on the majority while granting privileges to a tiny minority. The American Revolution had demonstrated that alternative political arrangements were possible. Revolutionary pamphlets circulated widely, preparing minds for radical change even before formal revolutionary structures emerged.

France's elites harbored their own anxieties. Some forward-thinking aristocrats recognized the need for reform but feared losing control of the process. Others stubbornly defended traditional privileges, believing that any concession would lead to complete collapse of the social order. The King and his court, isolated at Versailles and deeply disconnected from daily realities, failed to fully comprehend the revolutionary mood until it was too late to address it through moderate reforms.

What makes this period so instructive is how differently these shared fears manifested in different contexts. In America, revolutionary leaders maintained a crucial balance between mobilizing fear and controlling it, channeling anxiety into organized political action rather than chaotic outburst. In France, by contrast, revolutionary fear would eventually spiral beyond control, leading to the Terror and its thousands of executions.

As both societies approached their revolutionary thresholds, hope and fear became powerful catalysts for action. The revolutionary mood combined anticipation of a better future with anxiety about what would be lost in transition. This psychological climate, once established, developed its own momentum, carrying societies toward transformations that even revolutionary leaders could not fully control or predict.

If we could observe these events from the cosmic perspective of the stars, we might notice how the cycle of fear from our previous chapter repeats, but with a crucial difference. Where Salem's panic arose from perceived supernatural threats to the community's spiritual cohesion, revolutionary fears centered on tyranny and disorder, secular concerns about governance and liberty. Yet the underlying pattern remains recognizable: once again, societies face uncertainty about their future, perceive threats to their essential values, and mobilize defensive reactions that sometimes exceed rational boundaries. The spiral of history turns, not repeating exactly but echoing familiar human patterns in new contexts.

No Man's Land: Order vs. Liberty

Social order is necessary for human flourishing and must sometimes be protected through authority and tradition.

Pause. Notice what arises in you.

Personal liberty is fundamental to human dignity and justifies resistance to oppressive authority.

Pause. Notice what arises in you.

You do not have to agree with or justify either statement. Simply hold them both in your mind and observe what comes up.

This tension between order and liberty defined the revolutionary era. Those defending traditional authority genuinely feared that dismantling established hierarchies would lead to chaos, violence, and societal collapse. These weren't merely self-interested fears; history provided ample examples of social breakdown following rapid change.

Revolutionaries, meanwhile, feared continued oppression if traditional authority remained unchallenged. They saw personal liberty not as a luxury but as essential to human dignity and fulfillment. The question wasn't whether to choose order or liberty, but how to create systems that could deliver both, protecting rights while maintaining sufficient stability for society to function.

The revolutionary periods we've examined reveal that both fears, of excessive control and excessive freedom, contain legitimate insights about human needs. Social stability provides the foundation for human flourishing, yet without personal liberty, that stability becomes a prison rather than a support structure.

Later, we'll see how post-revolutionary societies attempted to resolve this tension through constitutional systems that divided and balanced power. But first, we must understand how revolutionary movements transformed from intellectual critiques to active rebellions, and how the fear that mobilized revolution sometimes spiraled beyond the control of revolutionary leaders themselves.

Chapter Five

When Kings Lost Their Heads

T he morning of January 21, 1793 dawned cold and foggy in Paris. Louis XVI, once sovereign ruler of France by divine right, woke early in his cell at the Temple prison. After receiving communion, he was escorted through hushed streets to the Place de la Révolution, where a freshly constructed guillotine awaited. As he mounted the scaffold, the king attempted one final address to his people, a people who, less than four years earlier, had been his subjects. "I die innocent of all the crimes laid to my charge," he began, only to be drowned out by a roll of drums ordered by the authorities. Minutes later, the blade fell, separating the king's head from his body. A witness recorded that when the executioner held the severed head aloft, "the youthful face had not yet lost its pink color."

The crowd, estimated at 100,000, greeted the king's death with a thunderous cry: "Vive la République!" Some rushed forward to dip handkerchiefs in the royal blood as souvenirs or talismans of the revolution. The execution of a king, once unthinkable, had become not just possible but celebrated. A symbolic line had been crossed that would shock Europe and mark a point of no return for the French Revolution.

This moment represents the culmination of revolutionary forces that had been building on both sides of the Atlantic. The anxieties that revolution both responded to and created would reshape the modern world, establishing patterns of fear, hope, and reaction that continue to resonate in our own time. How did the revolutionary impulse, born of Enlightenment ideals and legitimate grievances, sometimes spiral into terror? And what does this tell us about the delicate balance between necessary change and social stability?

The stars that had witnessed the Salem witch trials now looked down upon a world transformed by Enlightenment thought. The same celestial bodies that Puritans had interpreted as divine omens had become, for revolutionary thinkers, evidence of natural laws and mathematical precision. This shift in perspective, from superstition to science, from divine predetermined order to human agency, illuminated not just the heavens but the earth below. If the movements of planets followed natural laws rather than supernatural whims, perhaps human societies too should be governed by reason rather than tradition, by natural rights rather than inherited privileges. This revolutionary idea would ignite not just philosophical debates but actual revolutions that would reshape the political landscape of the Atlantic world.

The transformation from theoretical rebellion to actual revolution came suddenly in the American colonies. On April 19, 1775, British troops marched from Boston toward Concord to seize a colonial arms cache. At Lexington Green, they encountered a small band of militia, ordinary farmers and townsmen who had trained to defend their communities. Someone fired, historians still debate which side, and the battle erupted. By day's end, 49 Americans and 73 British soldiers lay dead, and the rhetorical conflict had become a shooting war.

The psychological impact of this transition cannot be overstated. Colonists who had spent years engaging in political resistance now faced the reality of armed conflict against what was then the world's premier military power. The prospect terrified even those committed to the cause. John Adams later recalled the mixture of "hope and fear, of joy and sorrow, of apprehension and energy" that the outbreak of hostilities created among Americans. For every colonist who greeted the news with revolutionary enthusiasm, others experienced deep anxiety about the uncertain path ahead.

This anxiety manifested in practical concerns about military readiness. The hastily formed Continental Army under George Washington faced severe shortages of weapons, ammunition, trained officers, and basic supplies. Washington himself wrote despairingly of the "want of arms, ammunition, and proper accoutrements" among his troops. The prospect of facing Britain's professional army and navy with such limited resources created a constant undercurrent of fear, even among the most dedicated patriots.

Beyond military concerns lay deeper existential questions: What would happen if the revolution failed? For the signers of the Declaration of Independence, who had publicly committed an act of treason against the Crown, the consequences were clear. As Benjamin Franklin reportedly remarked, "We must all hang together, or assuredly we shall all hang separately." For ordinary colonists, failure might mean property confiscation, imprisonment, or being targeted by loyalist neighbors seeking revenge. These were not abstract fears but practical calculations that influenced decisions about whether to support the revolutionary cause.

Even success brought uncertainties about the unknown future. The Declaration of Independence, adopted July 4, 1776, represented a radical break with political tradition. By rejecting monarchy for republican government, the revolutionaries ventured into largely uncharted territory. Few successful republics existed in the world, and those that did were small city-states, not sprawling territories like the united colonies. John Adams expressed these concerns in a letter to his wife Abigail: "The Second Day of July 1776, will be the most memorable Epocha, in the History of America... I am apt to believe that it will be celebrated, by succeeding Generations... But I must submit all my Hopes and Fears, to an overruling Providence, in which, unfashionable as the Faith may be, I firmly Believe."

These anxieties, military, personal, and philosophical, created a climate of tension that would persist throughout the revolutionary period. Yet American revolutionary leaders proved remarkably adept at channeling these fears productively, using them to motivate action while preventing the kind of terror and extremism that would later emerge in the French context. The contrast between these two revolutionary paths reveals much about the relationship between fear and social transformation.

The American Revolution was fought not just with muskets and cannons but with words and images. Revolutionary leaders recognized that maintaining public support required a sophisticated propaganda campaign that could unite disparate colonies, demonize the enemy, and justify radical action. This battle for hearts and minds reveals both the power of revolutionary communication and its potential to amplify fears in service of political mobilization.

Visual propaganda played a crucial role in this effort. Benjamin Franklin's "Join, or Die" illustration, showing a snake cut into segments representing the colonies, became an iconic symbol of the need for colonial unity. Originally created during the Seven Years' War to urge cooperation against the French, the image was repurposed for the revolutionary cause, proving "so effective it rallied the colonies and influenced politics throughout two wars." The segmented snake communicated a powerful message: remain divided and perish, unite and survive. Such imagery tapped directly into existential anxieties while offering a clear call to action.

Paul Revere's engraving of the Boston Massacre represented another masterpiece of revolutionary propaganda. Though the actual event in 1770 was more complex and ambiguous than the image suggests, Revere's depiction showed British soldiers firing in formation upon helpless civilians, with blood dramatically pooling in the foreground. The engraving circulated widely, becoming one of the most effective pieces of visual propaganda of the era. By simplifying a complex event into a clear narrative of British brutality, the image transformed a street fight into a symbolic atrocity that demanded resistance.

The committees of correspondence, established first in Boston in 1772, created a revolutionary communication infrastructure that could rapidly disseminate news, coordinate responses to British actions, and maintain revolutionary fervor across vast distances. These committees served as a parallel government in waiting, establishing patterns of leadership and cooperation that would survive the transition to independence. As one historian notes, "Through both their form and content, the committees' communications created what might be called a 'geography of resistance,' a network that allowed local grievances to become collective concerns."

The language of revolution underwent careful cultivation. King George III transformed in revolutionary discourse from a respected sovereign to "the Royal Brute of Great Britain," a "tyrant," and even "the bloody Nero of the British Crown." Such rhetoric wasn't just colorful exaggeration; it served the crucial psychological function of making resistance and eventual separation morally justified in the minds of colonists who had long identified as loyal British subjects. By portraying the king as monstrous, revolutionary propagandists helped colonists overcome their deeply ingrained reverence for monarchy.

The Declaration of Independence itself represents the culmination of revolutionary persuasion. Though ostensibly addressed to "a candid world" seeking international sympathy, its primary audience was the American public, many of whom still harbored doubts about the revolutionary project. The document's rhetorical power came from its combination of universal philosophical principles with a specific list of grievances against the king. By emphasizing that independence came only after "a long train of abuses," the Declaration portrayed revolution not as radical choice but as reluctant necessity, the last resort of a people pushed beyond endurance.

France's revolutionary moment arrived on July 14, 1789, when the simmering tensions in Paris boiled over into direct action. That morning, a crowd of Parisians, primarily working-class laborers, craftsmen, and small merchants, gathered outside the Bastille, a medieval fortress that had been converted into a state prison. Though it held only seven prisoners at the time (none for political offenses), the Bastille had become a powerful symbol of royal authority and arbitrary power. The crowd's immediate goal was to secure the gunpowder stored there, but the moment carried far deeper significance.

Nicolas Ruault, a bookseller who witnessed the events, recorded: "Immense crowds gathered on all sides; people raced through the streets shouting 'To arms! To arms! They are slaughtering the people in the Saint-Antoine district!'" This sense of emergency, whether based on fact or rumor, created the conditions for collective action. After hours of tense negotiation with the fortress governor, the marquis de Launay, the crowd's patience evaporated. They stormed the outer courtyard and, after a chaotic battle that claimed the lives of 98 attackers, overwhelmed the garrison.

What followed revealed how quickly revolutionary action could transcend conventional moral boundaries. De Launay, who had surrendered with the promise of safe conduct, was instead dragged to the Hôtel de Ville (city hall), beaten, and beheaded by the crowd. His severed head, along with that of Jacques de Flesselles, the city's chief merchant who was accused of deceiving the people about arms supplies, was mounted on a pike and paraded through the streets. A witness reported that the crowd displayed "a kind of savage joy" during these processions. The symbolic re-ordering of society through violence had begun.

News of the Bastille's fall spread rapidly throughout France, triggering powerful psychological responses. For those sympathetic to revolutionary ideals, it demonstrated that "liberty" was something the people could seize by force. A Paris newspaper reported that "Serene and blessed liberty, for the first time, has at last been introduced into this abode of horrors." The taking of a royal fortress by ordinary citizens represented a radical inversion of the traditional power hierarchy, a concrete embodiment of revolutionary possibility.

In rural France, news of the Bastille's fall contributed to a wave of peasant revolts known collectively as the "Great Fear." Rumors spread that aristocrats had hired brigands to attack villages and destroy crops, leading peasants in many regions to form militias and arm themselves. These armed groups often turned against local manor houses, where they burned feudal documents recording peasant obligations and sometimes the buildings themselves. The Great Fear represented a massive, spontaneous uprising across much of rural France that fundamentally altered power relations in the countryside.

The psychological impact of seeing royal authority defeated created a dramatic shift in how ordinary people perceived political possibility. As historian Timothy Tackett observes, "Events like the storming of the Bastille, which no one could have imagined beforehand, suggested that anything was now possible." This expansion of perceived possibility contributed to an atmosphere where traditional restraints and authorities held less sway, creating conditions for both liberation and excess.

King Louis XVI, upon being informed of the Bastille's fall, reportedly asked, "Is it a revolt?" His advisor, the duc de La Rochefoucauld-Liancourt, famously replied, "No, Sire, it is a revolution." This exchange captures the transformative nature of the event, not merely a temporary disturbance but the beginning of a fundamental restructuring of French society and government. The anxiety this created among elites would drive much of the subsequent counter-revolutionary response, both within France and across Europe.

The early phase of the French Revolution carried an extraordinary sense of moral and political possibility. In the heady days of 1789, it seemed that France might transform itself peacefully into a more just and rational society based on Enlightenment principles. This period of revolutionary idealism produced lasting achievements while containing seeds of the extremism that would follow.

The Declaration of the Rights of Man and Citizen, adopted by the National Assembly on August 26, 1789, embodied the revolution's highest aspirations. Its opening proclamation that "Men are born and remain free and equal in rights" represented a radical challenge to the hierarchical foundations of the ancien régime. The document outlined natural rights to "liberty, property, security, and resistance to oppression" and established the principle that "law is the expression of the general will" in which all citizens have the right to participate. Published in newspapers and posted in public spaces throughout France, the Declaration provided a philosophical framework for revolutionary changes.

Just weeks earlier, on August 4-5, 1789, the National Assembly had enacted the "abolition of feudal privileges," a sweeping reform that eliminated many traditional obligations peasants owed to lords, the Church's right to collect tithes, exclusive hunting rights for nobility, the purchase and sale of judicial positions, and numerous other aristocratic privileges. This dramatic legislative session, which began with individual nobles voluntarily renouncing their privileges and escalated to comprehensive reform, represented revolutionary idealism in action. As one participant described it, "We were swept along by an enthusiasm which led us to ever more radical measures."

Revolutionary festivals and public celebrations sought to forge a new civic culture based on revolutionary values. The Festival of Federation, held on the first anniversary of the Bastille's fall (July 14, 1790), drew hundreds of thousands to Paris, where representatives from all 83 departments gathered at the Champ de Mars for a grand ceremony of national unity. With the king in attendance, participants swore loyalty to "the nation, the law, and the king," a formulation that placed royal authority within a constitutional framework rather than above it. Such festivals attempted to channel revolutionary energy into constructive civic ritual rather than destructive violence.

For nearly two years, revolutionaries attempted to transform France into a constitutional monarchy that would preserve the stability of royal governance while guaranteeing citizens' rights and representative government. The Constitution of 1791 established a limited monarchy with a legislative assembly elected through a property-based franchise. This moderate approach reflected the desire of many early revolutionaries to reform France without completely dismantling its traditional institutions, to achieve revolutionary goals through evolutionary means.

The execution of Louis XVI in January 1793 marked the revolution's decisive turn toward extremism. The king's death shocked Europe and signaled that traditional boundaries would no longer constrain revolutionary action. Austrian Chancellor Kaunitz called it "a deed which the wildest savages would scarce commit," while Edmund Burke declared it "the most important event that has happened in our world in our day, perhaps in our century." For many observers, the act confirmed their deepest fears about where revolutionary impulses might lead.

Maximilien Robespierre emerged as the dominant figure of the Terror that followed. Once a provincial lawyer who opposed the death penalty, Robespierre transformed into the embodiment of revolutionary purity and uncompromising virtue. His philosophy justified extreme measures: "Terror is nothing other than justice, prompt, severe, inflexible; it is therefore an emanation of virtue." This fusion of terror with virtue created a moral framework that could justify almost any action in service of revolutionary goals. By identifying opposition to revolutionary measures with treason against the nation itself, Robespierre and his allies made moderation increasingly dangerous.

The institutional apparatus of terror took shape with frightening efficiency. The Committee of Public Safety, established in April 1793 and eventually dominated by Robespierre, wielded near-dictatorial power. The Law of Suspects, passed in September 1793, allowed for the arrest of anyone suspected of counter-revolutionary sympathies, a category defined so broadly that it could include almost anyone. Revolutionary Tribunals dispensed hasty justice with minimal procedural protections. As one committee member explained, "The proof necessary to condemn the enemies of the people is any kind of evidence, either material or moral, either verbal or written, which can naturally gain the assent of any just and reasonable mind."

The statistics of the Terror tell a grim story: approximately 17,000 people were officially executed by guillotine between September 1793 and July 1794, while as many as 10,000 more died in prison or without trial. Victims included not only aristocrats and clergy but also peasants, laborers, and eventually revolutionary leaders themselves as factions turned against each other. Lavoisier, the father of modern chemistry, was executed with the cold observation that "the Republic has no need of scientists." The Girondin faction, once revolutionary allies of the Jacobins, found themselves condemned as enemies of the people. The revolution was indeed devouring its children.

Due process protections were systematically dismantled in the name of revolutionary efficiency. The Law of 22 Prairial (June 10, 1794) eliminated defendants' right to counsel, limited trials to determining whether the accused was an "enemy of the people," and provided only two possible verdicts: acquittal or death. As one observer noted, "The guillotine has become the supreme law of the Republic, whose emblem should be neither a tree of liberty nor a bonnet rouge but solely a guillotine."

The psychological transformation of revolutionaries from idealists to executioners reveals how extreme circumstances can normalize behavior once considered unthinkable. Many who participated in the Terror had earlier advocated for humane legal reforms. How did they come to accept and implement methods so contrary to their initial values? The psychology involves several elements: the dehumanization of opponents as "enemies of the people," the rationalization that extreme measures were temporary necessities, and the constant fear that showing mercy might be interpreted as counter-revolutionary sympathy.

What began as legitimate defense against very real threats, foreign invasion, internal rebellion, economic crisis, spiraled into a cycle where fear generated repression, which created more fear. The Committee of Public Safety's justification that "terror is the order of the day" transformed a tactic into a governing principle. By July 1794, the Terror had become so extreme that even revolutionary hardliners began to fear for their own safety. On 9 Thermidor (July 27, 1794), the Convention turned against Robespierre, voting for his arrest. The next day, he and his closest allies faced the same fate they had imposed on so many others: death by guillotine. The most extreme phase of the Revolution had consumed its most fervent advocate.

The revolutionary periods in both America and France revealed powerful psychological forces that operate when traditional authority weakens and collective action replaces individual decision-making. Understanding these dynamics helps explain how reasonable people can participate in extreme actions that they might never consider as individuals.

Mass psychology during revolutionary moments creates distinctive patterns of behavior. As individuals join crowds, they often experience what psychologists call "deindividuation," a reduced sense of personal identity and responsibility that facilitates actions that would normally be constrained by individual conscience or fear of consequences. One contemporary observer of Parisian crowds noted that "gathered together, they become intoxicated by the emotion they feel in common; they become exalted, carried away, and their dominant passions are intensified by sharing."

This emotional contagion, the rapid spread of feelings through groups, operates through what modern neuroscientists identify as "mirror neurons," which allow humans to unconsciously match their emotional states to those around them. In revolutionary Paris, the rapid transmission of anger, fear, or euphoria created volatile situations where rationality could quickly yield to collective passion. During events like the September Massacres of 1792, when prison inmates were summarily executed by mobs fearing counter-revolutionary conspiracies, participants later reported being swept up in a "collective madness" they struggled to explain when questioned individually.

The role of revolutionary leaders in channeling mob emotions reveals the complex interplay between spontaneous crowd action and directed political purpose. Leaders like Robespierre rarely participated directly in street violence, but they provided the rhetorical frameworks that justified it and created institutional channels to direct it toward political ends. As historian Simon Schama observes, "The revolutionary government did not create popular violence, but it did harness it, canonize it, and transform it from a brutal necessity to a patriotic virtue."

Contemporary accounts of crowd behavior from both revolutions highlight the striking transformation of ordinary people in collective settings. Gouverneur Morris, American minister to France during the Terror, wrote of witnessing a crowd in Paris: "Such a mingled mass of enthusiasm, rage, drunkenness, and savagery I could never have imagined, the women particularly outdoing the men in every form of ferocity." In the American context, reports of crowd actions like tarring and feathering loyalists similarly emphasized the temporary suspension of normal social constraints.

Crucially, the two revolutions developed different mechanisms for managing these psychological forces. American revolutionary leaders generally channeled popular energy into more structured forms of resistance, committees of correspondence, militia organizations, formal political bodies, that provided institutional constraints on mob action. When crowd violence did occur, as in attacks on loyalists' property, revolutionary leaders often tried to restore order while redirecting popular energy toward legitimate targets.

The French Revolution, by contrast, increasingly institutionalized revolutionary violence through entities like the Committee of Public Safety and Revolutionary Tribunals. As Edmund Burke observed, when revolutionary violence becomes "an instrument of government... it will be the sanguinary means of its conservation." This difference helps explain why the American Revolution produced relatively few domestic casualties while the French Revolution descended into the Terror.

If we could position ourselves among the stars looking down on these revolutionary societies, we might observe the same pattern we witnessed in Salem's witch trials now playing out on a grander scale: the spiral from legitimate concern to excessive fear, from defensive response to offensive persecution. Yet we would also notice crucial differences in how these revolutionary societies managed their fears. The American revolutionaries created institutional channels that could direct revolutionary energy toward constructive nation-building; the French revolution's more radical phase dismantled traditional restraints faster than new ones could be established. Both sought to reach the stars of human potential, but through paths that revealed different understandings of how quickly human nature and institutions can safely change.

The legacy of these revolutionary movements includes not just their political achievements but the psychological insights they provide about human behavior under conditions of radical social transformation. The line between liberation and excess, between necessary change and destructive chaos, often depends not on the justice of the cause but on the institutional and psychological mechanisms available to manage the powerful energies that revolution unleashes.

NO MAN'S LAND: RAPID CHANGE VS. GRADUAL EVOLUTION

Societies sometimes require rapid, fundamental change to address deep injustices and prevent worse outcomes.

Pause. Notice what arises in you.

Gradual, incremental change allows for adaptation and prevents destructive disruption of social systems.

Pause. Notice what arises in you.

You do not have to agree with or justify either statement. Simply hold them both in your mind and observe what comes up.

The revolutionary periods we've explored embody this tension between rapid transformation and gradual evolution. Both approaches seek improvement, but through profoundly different paths and rhythms.

The advocate for rapid change points to moments when incremental reform proves inadequate to address fundamental injustices. The French peasantry had endured centuries of exploitation with minimal improvement; American colonists had petitioned for redress of grievances for years before declaring independence. Some situations, this perspective suggests, require breaking rather than bending, a clean rupture with the past to create space for something genuinely new. As Thomas Jefferson wrote, "The tree of liberty must be refreshed from time to time with the blood of patriots and tyrants."

The advocate for gradual change observes how revolutionary enthusiasm can outpace human adaptation, creating destructive backlash and unintended consequences. Edmund Burke, witnessing the French Revolution's excesses, argued that societies are complex organisms that cannot be suddenly reconstructed according to abstract principles. "The nature of man is intricate," he wrote, "the objects of society are of the greatest possible complexity; and therefore no simple disposition or direction of power can be suitable to man's nature, or to the quality of his affairs."

Both perspectives contain wisdom. The revolutionary moments that have most sustainably improved human welfare typically balanced transformative vision with practical constraints, recognizing both the need for fundamental change and the value of institutional continuity. The American revolutionaries created a new government while preserving many aspects of English common law and local governance. The more extreme phases of the French Revolution, by contrast, attempted to remake society entirely, down to the calendar and forms of address, creating disorientation that contributed to its excesses.

Perhaps the most valuable insight comes not from choosing between these approaches but from understanding when each might be appropriate, and how they might complement rather than oppose each other. Some institutions may require gradual reform while others demand immediate transformation; some aspects of society benefit from revolutionary energy while others need evolutionary patience.

Chapter Six

When Order Found Its Voice

On a chilly autumn morning in 1796, President George Washington published his Farewell Address in the American Daily Advertiser. After two terms as the first leader of the new republic, Washington made an unprecedented decision: he would voluntarily relinquish power. In a world accustomed to rulers who clung to authority until death or overthrow, this peaceful, intentional transfer of leadership embodied something revolutionary in itself. "The acceptance of, and continuance hitherto in, the office to which your suffrages have twice called me," Washington wrote, "have been a uniform sacrifice of inclination to the opinion of duty and to a deference for what appeared to be your desire." The system that had emerged from revolution would endure beyond its founding leader through institutional strength rather than personal authority.

Across the Atlantic, a dramatically different scene unfolded as European monarchs and ministers gathered in Vienna in 1814-1815 to restore order after the revolutionary era. In opulent palaces adorned with crystal chandeliers, diplomats like Metternich, Talleyrand, and Castlereagh redrew the map of Europe, balancing power among nations while reinstating "legitimate" rulers toppled by revolutionary forces. Yet even in this bastion of conservative restoration, the world had irrevocably changed. The ideas unleashed by the American and French Revolutions, about rights, sovereignty, and governance, could be suppressed but not eliminated.

These contrasting scenes illustrate the fundamental question facing post-revolutionary societies: how to establish stability while preserving, abandoning, or transforming the principles that sparked revolution in the first place. The answers would shape the modern world.

The stars that had witnessed the revolutionary terror now looked down upon societies struggling to find balance. The same celestial bodies that had illuminated the guillotine's blade and Washington's crossing of the Delaware now witnessed humanity's attempts to forge stable frameworks from revolutionary principles. From this celestial vantage point, one might observe the spiral of history continuing its turn, not returning to its starting point, but advancing to a new position that incorporated elements of both the old order and revolutionary transformation.

The American Revolution secured independence but left a crucial challenge: constructing a functioning government from revolutionary principles. The initial attempt at national organization, the Articles of Confederation (ratified in 1781), proved severely inadequate for the fledgling republic. The Articles established a loose association of sovereign states with a weak central government that lacked taxation and enforcement powers. Problems quickly mounted: the national government couldn't pay its Revolutionary War debts; states engaged in destructive economic competition with one another; and the nation appeared increasingly vulnerable to foreign powers.

In 1786, the weakness of the system was dramatically exposed during Shays' Rebellion, when debt-ridden Massachusetts farmers led by Revolutionary War veteran Daniel Shays forcibly prevented courts from foreclosing on farms. The uprising revealed the inability of both state and national governments to maintain domestic order. George Washington lamented in a letter: "There are combustibles in every State, which a spark might set fire to... I am mortified beyond expression that... the powers of government... are insufficient to check the tumult."

These mounting crises convinced American leaders that a stronger constitutional framework was needed. The Constitutional Convention, convened in Philadelphia in May 1787, brought together delegates from twelve states (Rhode Island abstained) to address the nation's governance problems. Over four months of intense debate, these men, educated in Enlightenment principles yet deeply practical in their concerns, crafted a document that reflected both revolutionary ideals and the need for stable authority.

The Constitution they produced embodied a fear-driven balance: fear of both tyranny and anarchy. The memory of British oppression remained vivid, but so did the chaos of Shays' Rebellion and the ineffectiveness of the Articles of Confederation. The solution emerged in a carefully structured system of divided powers. Horizontally, the new government separated authority between executive, legislative, and judicial branches, with each able to check the others. Vertically, power was divided between federal and state governments. As James Madison explained in Federalist No. 51, "Ambition must be made to counteract ambition... If men were angels, no government would be necessary."

Still, many Americans worried that the new Constitution provided insufficient protection for individual liberties. The absence of explicit rights guarantees fueled significant opposition to ratification. Addressing this concern, the first Congress proposed twelve amendments in 1789 (ten of which were quickly ratified as the Bill of Rights), specifically protecting freedoms of speech, religion, press, and assembly, along with procedural rights for the accused and limits on federal power. These amendments directly addressed the fear of government overreach that had motivated the revolution itself.

The American system's practical success hinged not only on its constitutional structure but on the precedents established during Washington's presidency (1789-1797). By consulting cabinet members, respecting congressional authority, and avoiding foreign entanglements, Washington established patterns of governance that balanced effective leadership with constitutional constraints. Most significantly, his voluntary retirement after two terms set a powerful example of peaceful power transition that distinguished the American republic from the monarchies and dictatorships of Europe. When John Adams succeeded Washington in 1797 despite their political differences, the fragile republic demonstrated that it could transfer power between rival factions without violence or collapse, an achievement that would elude revolutionary France.

This stabilization represented neither a complete fulfillment nor a betrayal of revolutionary principles, but their translation into practical governance. The new system maintained the revolutionary commitment to popular sovereignty, as expressed in the Constitution's opening words: "We the People of the United States..." Yet it tempered direct democracy with representative mechanisms and institutional checks, reflecting both Enlightenment ideals and practical concerns about mass democracy's potential instability.

The resulting government proved remarkably durable, yet also contained profound tensions and contradictions. Most glaringly, the nation founded on the principle that "all men are created equal" preserved and protected slavery through constitutional compromises like the Three-Fifths Clause and Fugitive Slave provision. Women, Native Americans, and property-less white men likewise remained excluded from full political participation. These limitations represented not merely hypocritical failures but fundamental tensions between universal principles and particular interests that would shape American development for generations.

While Americans constructed their republic through constitutional negotiation and peaceful transitions, France's path from revolution to stability proved far more turbulent. The fall of Robespierre in July 1794 (9 Thermidor, Year II, in the revolutionary calendar) marked a crucial turning point. Exhausted by the Terror's excesses and fearful of becoming its next victims, members of the National Convention turned against Robespierre and his closest allies. Within twenty-four hours, the architect of revolutionary virtue found himself facing the guillotine he had so frequently employed against others. A witness reported that when the blade fell on Robespierre, "a deafening chorus of cheers and applause rose from the crowd and continued for several minutes."

The Thermidorian Reaction that followed represented less an ideological shift than a pragmatic retreat from extremism. The new leadership maintained republican government but dismantled the apparatus of terror: the Revolutionary Tribunal was restructured, the Law of Suspects repealed, and thousands of political prisoners released. The Jacobin Club, once the engine of radical political mobilization, was closed, and many former terrorists faced retaliation from citizens who had lived in fear during the preceding year.

In 1795, the Convention adopted the Constitution of Year III, establishing what became known as the Directory government. This system featured a bicameral legislature and a five-member executive Directory, with various mechanisms designed to prevent the concentration of power that had enabled the Terror. Property requirements for voting were reinstated, reflecting the revolution's shift from democratic radicalism toward protection of bourgeois interests. Yet the Directory proved chronically unstable, facing threats from both royalist counterrevolution and continued jacobin radicalism, while also managing ongoing war with other European powers. The government repeatedly resorted to military intervention to maintain power, ironically undermining the constitutional system it was meant to uphold.

This cycle of instability created the conditions for Napoleon Bonaparte's rise. A brilliant young general who had gained fame through military victories in Italy and Egypt, Napoleon possessed the military credibility, administrative skill, and political ambition to seize the moment of crisis. On November 9, 1799 (18 Brumaire, Year VIII), with support from key political figures including director Emmanuel Joseph Sieyès, Napoleon executed a coup d'état against the Directory. Initially establishing a three-man Consulate, Napoleon quickly consolidated power, becoming First Consul and effectively ruling alone. In 1804, he crowned himself Emperor of the French, symbolically ending the republican experiment even while claiming to preserve its principles.

Napoleon's regime represented a complex compromise between revolutionary principles and authoritarian governance. He maintained key revolutionary gains like legal equality, religious tolerance, and meritocratic advancement while abandoning democratic governance and republican virtue. Napoleon himself articulated this balance: "I closed the gulf of anarchy and brought order out of chaos. I rewarded merit regardless of birth, station or wealth, wherever I found it." Yet he also declared, "I found the crown of France lying in the gutter, and I picked it up with my sword," revealing how military force had replaced popular sovereignty as the regime's foundation.

The Napoleonic Code of 1804 exemplified this balanced approach to revolutionary principles. This comprehensive legal system preserved essential revolutionary achievements like equality before the law, protection of property rights, and religious freedom. It abolished feudal privileges and established uniform national law. Yet it also restricted freedoms, particularly for women, who lost many rights they had gained during the republic and were legally subordinated to male authority in marriage and civic life. The code would become Napoleon's most enduring legacy, influencing legal systems across Europe and beyond.

Napoleon's domestic success stemmed partly from his ability to offer the French people what one historian calls "glory instead of liberty." His military campaigns, which initially extended revolutionary principles across Europe but increasingly served French imperial ambitions, generated national pride and economic opportunities while distracting from the loss of political rights. Yet this militaristic foundation proved ultimately unsustainable. Following his disastrous Russian campaign in 1812 and subsequent defeats, Napoleon was forced to abdicate in 1814, briefly returned during the "Hundred Days" in 1815, and was permanently exiled after his defeat at Waterloo.

France's post-Napoleonic settlement reflected the revolution's mixed legacy. The restoration of the Bourbon monarchy under Louis XVIII represented a conservative victory, yet came with concessions unimaginable before 1789. The Constitutional Charter of 1814 preserved many Napoleonic institutions, including the legal code, and established a limited constitutional monarchy with some representative elements. When reactionary Charles X attempted to restore absolute monarchy, the July Revolution of 1830 replaced him with the more moderate Louis-Philippe, demonstrating how revolutionary principles, though moderated, continued to shape French politics. The pendulum between revolutionary change and conservative order would continue to swing throughout the nineteenth century, but France would never fully return to pre-revolutionary absolutism.

While France and America navigated their distinct paths from revolution to stability, the broader European response to revolutionary ideas took shape through the Congress of Vienna (1814-1815). This unprecedented diplomatic gathering brought together representatives from across Europe to reconstruct the continental order after twenty-five years of revolutionary and Napoleonic upheaval. The Congress represented the coordinated conservative reaction to revolutionary principles, an attempt to restore stability while containing the ideas that had threatened traditional authority.

The Congress was dominated by five major powers: Austria (represented by Prince Klemens von Metternich), Russia (Tsar Alexander I), Prussia (Prince Karl August von Hardenberg), Great Britain (Viscount Castlereagh), and, remarkably, defeated France (represented by the skilled diplomat Charles-Maurice de Talleyrand). Lesser powers also participated, but key decisions emerged from negotiations among the major states. The Congress faced a monumental task: redrawing the map of Europe, reestablishing legitimate authority, and creating mechanisms to prevent future revolutionary contagion.

Three guiding principles shaped the Vienna settlement: balance of power, legitimacy, and conservatism. Balance of power aimed to prevent any single state from dominating Europe, as France had under Napoleon. This required carefully distributing territory to ensure that major powers could check each other's ambitions. The principle of legitimacy, particularly championed by Metternich, called for restoring "rightful" rulers who had been deposed during the revolutionary period, especially the Bourbon dynasties in France, Spain, and Naples. Underpinning these specific objectives was a broader conservative ideology that sought to roll back revolutionary reforms and reinforce traditional authority.

The territorial rearrangements established at Vienna fundamentally reshaped Europe. France was contained within roughly its 1792 borders, preventing future expansion. A ring of strengthened buffer states surrounded France: the Kingdom of the Netherlands (combining the former Dutch Republic and Belgian territories), a reinforced Piedmont-Sardinia, and Prussian territories in the Rhineland. Germany was reorganized from hundreds of states into the German Confederation, a loose association of 39 states under Austrian presidency. Poland was again partitioned, with Russia gaining a "Congress Kingdom" under the tsar's rule. Austria emerged as the dominant power in Italy, directly annexing Lombardy and Venetia while establishing Habsburg relatives as rulers in other Italian states.

Beyond these territorial adjustments, the Congress established a framework for maintaining the conservative order: the Concert of Europe. This system, formalized through the Quadruple Alliance (later expanded to include France as the Quintuple Alliance), created mechanisms for Great Power cooperation to preserve peace and suppress revolutionary movements. Through regular diplomatic consultations and coordinated interventions, the Concert aimed to prevent the spread of revolutionary ideas and maintain the status quo established at Vienna.

This conservative restoration soon faced challenges from liberal and nationalist movements that had absorbed revolutionary principles. The conservative powers responded with coordinated suppression. Following minor revolutionary stirrings among German university students in 1819, Metternich persuaded German states to adopt the Carlsbad Decrees, imposing strict censorship, outlawing nationalist student organizations, and establishing mechanisms to investigate suspected revolutionaries.

The principle of intervention against revolution was codified at the Congress of Troppau in 1820. In response to liberal revolutions in Spain and Naples, the Holy Alliance powers (Austria, Prussia, and Russia) declared that states which had undergone revolutionary change threatened the European order and should be forcibly restored to legitimate rule. This principle was quickly applied: Austrian forces crushed the Neapolitan revolution in 1821, while French troops intervened in Spain in 1823 to restore absolute monarchy. These actions highlighted the divergence within the Concert, as Britain refused to endorse the principle of intervention, viewing it as an unacceptable infringement on state sovereignty.

The conservative powers' most brutal suppression targeted the Polish November Uprising of 1830-1831. When Polish patriots revolted against Russian rule, demanding restoration of their constitution and national rights, Tsar Nicholas I responded with overwhelming military force. After the fall of Warsaw, Russia abolished Poland's constitution and autonomy, effectively incorporating Congress Poland into the Russian Empire. Thousands were executed or exiled to Siberia in harsh reprisals that demonstrated the limits of European sympathy for nationalist aspirations.

Despite these successful interventions, the conservative order established at Vienna rested on increasingly unstable foundations. The Concert of Europe maintained peace among Great Powers for an unprecedented period, preventing general European war for nearly forty years. Yet it could not eliminate the revolutionary principles of liberty, equality, and national self-determination that continued to spread through education, literature, and clandestine political networks. The system managed to delay, rather than resolve, the fundamental conflicts brewing within European society, conflicts that would erupt with continent-wide force in the Revolutions of 1848.

Both the American republic and post-revolutionary Europe revealed significant gaps between revolutionary ideals and post-revolutionary realities, not merely failures of implementation but fundamental tensions between universal principles and particular interests, between transformative visions and practical constraints.

The American Revolution declared that "all men are created equal" and possessed "unalienable rights," yet the nation it established initially extended these rights primarily to white, property-owning men. The Constitution provided explicit protection for slavery through provisions like the Three-Fifths Clause (counting enslaved persons as three-fifths of a person for representation and taxation) and the Fugitive Slave Clause (requiring the return of escaped slaves). When the new federal government counted the population in its first census of 1790, it recorded nearly 700,000 enslaved people, about 18% of the total population, living in a nation founded on liberty.

This contradiction between universal language and particularist implementation reflected not just hypocrisy but genuine tension within the revolutionary settlement. Many Founders, including Thomas Jefferson, recognized the moral incoherence of claiming liberty while practicing enslavement. Jefferson wrote that when considering slavery, "I tremble for my country when I reflect that God is just," yet he continued to own over 600 people during his lifetime. This tension between revolutionary principles and entrenched interests would eventually lead to the Civil War, in which the nation "conceived in liberty" would finally begin to fulfill its founding promise.

Women similarly experienced the gap between revolutionary rhetoric and post-revolutionary reality. During the revolution, women had contributed significantly to the patriot cause through political organizing, boycotts, and domestic production. Abigail Adams famously implored her husband John to "remember the ladies" when forming the new government, warning that women "will not hold ourselves bound by any laws in which we have no voice or representation." Yet the post-revolutionary settlement largely confined women to a "republican motherhood" role: educating future citizens while lacking full citizenship themselves. Women would not gain the right to vote nationally until 1920, nearly 150 years after the Declaration of Independence proclaimed universal equality.

Native Americans experienced an even starker betrayal of revolutionary ideals. Despite some tribes' support for the patriot cause, the new nation's commitment to westward expansion directly threatened indigenous lands and sovereignty. As the revolutionary generation transitioned from revolution to governance, their rhetoric shifted from universal rights to particular interests. Thomas Jefferson, who had eloquently defended natural rights, would later as president oversee the Louisiana Purchase and promote policies removing Native peoples from their ancestral territories to make way for white settlement.

The French Revolution's trajectory revealed even more dramatic tensions between revolutionary ideals and their implementation. The Declaration of the Rights of Man and Citizen had proclaimed that "men are born and remain free and equal in rights," yet this principle underwent severe restriction in practice. Revolutionary leaders initially extended political rights to property-owning men, briefly expanded them during the radical phase, then restricted them again under the Directory and Napoleon. Women, who had played crucial roles in revolutionary journées (days of mass action) like the Women's March on Versailles and formed political clubs during the republic, saw their rights severely curtailed under the Napoleonic Code.

From these contradictions emerged conservatism as a coherent political philosophy, itself a paradoxical legacy of the revolutionary era. Edmund Burke, who had supported the American Revolution as a defense of traditional English liberties, viewed the French Revolution as a dangerous experiment in abstract reason that ignored the accumulated wisdom of tradition. In his *Reflections on the Revolution in France* (1790), Burke argued: "The effect of liberty to individuals is that they may do what they please; we ought to see what it will please them to do, before we risk congratulations." Burke's conservatism emphasized historical continuity, social order, and skepticism toward radical change, principles that would shape European political thought throughout the nineteenth century.

Joseph de Maistre developed an even more reactionary response, arguing that the revolution represented divine punishment for human pride in challenging God's ordained order. Where Burke advocated measured evolution guided by tradition, de Maistre championed absolute monarchy and church authority, stating bluntly that "every nation gets the government it deserves." The emergence of these sophisticated conservative thinkers demonstrated how the revolutionary era had permanently altered political discourse, forcing traditional authority to justify itself through reasoned argument rather than mere tradition. Even counter-revolution adopted revolutionary methods of persuasion.

The divergent paths of post-revolutionary societies offered profound lessons about the relationship between revolutionary change and sustainable governance, lessons that continue to resonate in modern political development.

The most fundamental lesson concerned the dangers of revolutionary excess and the backlash it inevitably provokes. The French Revolution's descent into the Terror demonstrated how revolutionary idealism could transform into its opposite. As revolutionary leaders from Danton to Robespierre fell victim to the very system they had created, they illustrated the revolution's tendency to "devour its own children." This self-destructive spiral resulted partly from escalating fear: fear of counter-revolution led to extreme measures, which generated new fears, which demanded even more extreme responses. The American Revolution largely avoided this cycle by maintaining stronger institutional constraints and clearer legal protections even during the crisis of establishing independence.

The American experience highlighted the importance of institutions in anchoring revolutionary changes. The Constitution transformed abstract principles like popular sovereignty and separation of powers into concrete mechanisms and procedures that could withstand political conflict and leadership transitions. These institutional frameworks proved remarkably durable: despite intense partisan conflict beginning in the 1790s, American political opponents continued to operate within constitutional boundaries rather than resorting to extra-legal violence. When institutions maintain legitimacy, they become the arena for political contest rather than its casualty.

The contrasting outcomes of the American and French Revolutions stemmed partly from their different relationships to existing social structures. The American Revolution, though politically radical in rejecting monarchy, remained socially conservative in many respects. It preserved existing property relations (except for loyalist confiscations), maintained local governance patterns, and left significant power in the hands of traditional social elites. The French Revolution, by contrast, radically reorganized French society, abolishing feudal privileges, redrawing provincial boundaries, attacking the Church, and executing much of the aristocracy. These comprehensive social changes prevented the emergence of stable institutions that could channel and constrain revolutionary energy.

Looking toward the night sky from these post-revolutionary societies, observers might notice a certain order emerging from the apparent chaos. Just as celestial bodies follow patterns that ancient astronomers could only partially discern, the tumultuous political transformations of the revolutionary era gradually revealed underlying patterns that would shape modern governance. The pendulum swings between revolutionary change and conservative reaction, between universal principles and particular contexts, between liberty and order, all formed part of a spiral that carried human societies not back to their starting points, but forward toward new syntheses of tradition and transformation.

The revolutions of the late eighteenth century, despite conservative attempts to contain their influence, permanently altered the landscape of global politics. Their enduring legacy transcends specific institutional arrangements to encompass fundamental changes in political discourse, popular expectations, and the relationship between the governed and governing.

Most immediately, these revolutions transformed political vocabulary, introducing concepts that remain central to modern political thought. Terms like "citizens" rather than "subjects," "rights" rather than "privileges," "republic" rather than "realm," and "constitution" rather than "tradition" reflect profound shifts in how humans conceive of political relationships. The very concept of "left" versus "right" emerged from the French Revolution, where delegates supporting revolutionary change sat to the president's left in the National Assembly, while those favoring tradition sat to his right. This spatial metaphor continues to organize political discourse around the tension between change and continuity, progress and tradition, itself a legacy of the revolutionary era.

The notion of the nation as a community of citizens rather than the patrimony of a monarch represents another transformative legacy. The French Revolution's language of the "nation" and "the people" transformed political identity from vertical allegiance to a sovereign toward horizontal solidarity among citizens. This concept, captured in the revolutionary address "citizen" that replaced hierarchical titles, fundamentally altered political psychology. Even after the restoration of monarchy, Europeans increasingly understood themselves as members of nations with distinct cultural identities and collective interests. This nationalist legacy would reshape Europe throughout the nineteenth century, ultimately redrawing the continent's borders along national lines rather than dynastic claims.

Revolutionary constitutionalism spread far beyond its origins, becoming the dominant framework for legitimate governance. While pre-revolutionary states derived authority from tradition, divine right, or conquest, post-revolutionary political systems increasingly claimed legitimacy through written constitutions that limited government power and guaranteed rights. Even conservative regimes found themselves adopting constitutional forms, though often with significant limitations. When Louis XVIII returned to France after Napoleon's defeat, he issued the Constitutional Charter of 1814, not as a concession granted by the sovereign people, but as a gift bestowed by royal authority. This conservative adaptation of revolutionary forms demonstrated how thoroughly constitutionalism had transformed political expectations.

Perhaps most profoundly, the revolutions initiated ongoing interrogation of the gap between universal principles and particular applications, a tension that continues to drive political development. Revolutionary societies proclaimed universal rights while restricting their application based on race, gender, property, and religion. Each limitation generated movements demanding consistency between universal rhetoric and practical implementation: abolitionists citing the Declaration of Independence, suffragists invoking revolutionary principles of representation, workers applying equality to economic conditions. This dynamic process of expanding revolutionary principles beyond their initial boundaries represents one of the era's most significant legacies.

The revolutionary legacy thus continues to unfold through an ongoing conversation about human governance. The American and French Revolutions did not simply replace one system with another; they initiated a new manner of thinking about politics as an intentional human project rather than a natural or divine inheritance. This conceptual transformation, more than any specific institutional arrangement, represents their most profound contribution to human civilization, one that continues to inspire both hope and caution as societies navigate the perennial tensions between liberty and order, universalism and particularism, tradition and progress.

NO MAN'S LAND: Universal vs. Particular

Universal principles and rights apply equally to all humans regardless of culture, nationality, or historical context.

Pause. Notice what arises in you.

Particular traditions, cultures, and historical contexts shape different legitimate ways of organizing society.

Pause. Notice what arises in you.

You do not have to agree with or justify either statement. Simply hold them both in your mind and observe what comes up.

This tension between universal principles and particular contexts defined the revolutionary era and its aftermath. The American Declaration proclaimed "self-evident" truths about universal human equality and rights, while the French Declaration of Rights similarly asserted that its principles applied "at all times, in all places." These universal claims inspired dramatic change yet often met resistance when applied to specific cultural, economic, and social arrangements.

Edmund Burke, the foundational conservative thinker, articulated the case for particularity: "Circumstances give, in reality, to every political principle, its distinguishing color and discriminating effect. The circumstances are what render every civil and political scheme beneficial or noxious to mankind." For Burke, abstract principles neglected the wisdom embedded in traditions that had evolved over generations to address a society's particular needs and values.

Yet universalists countered that appeals to tradition and circumstance often masked simple privilege and prejudice. Thomas Paine responded to Burke: "He pities the plumage, but forgets the dying bird." Without universal principles of justice, particular arrangements often protected the powerful at the expense of the vulnerable.

Both perspectives contain wisdom. Universal principles provide critical standards for evaluating social arrangements beyond mere tradition or authority. They remind us that humans share fundamental needs and capacities regardless of circumstance. Yet particular contexts shape how principles can be meaningfully implemented in specific times and places. They remind us that human flourishing occurs within concrete communities with their own histories and challenges.

The societies that have most successfully navigated this tension recognize both dimensions, grounding governance in universal principles while adapting implementation to particular circumstances, maintaining aspirational standards while acknowledging the gradual nature of social transformation. This balanced approach represents not a compromise between opposing positions but a deeper understanding that embraces both universal human dignity and the rich diversity of human communities.

Cycle 3: When Progress Felt Like Loss

Chapter Seven

When Machines Stole Dreams

The full moon illuminated the Yorkshire countryside on that April night in 1812, casting long shadows as a group of men moved silently toward Rawfolds Mill. Their faces blackened with soot, they carried hammers, axes, and crude firearms. Leading them was a tall figure who called himself "General Ludd," though this was no military campaign in the conventional sense. These men, skilled weavers and croppers whose livelihoods had been threatened by the mechanized looms inside, had come to destroy the machines they believed were destroying them.

The mill owner, William Cartwright, had anticipated such an attack. He had fortified his factory and stationed armed guards inside. As the Luddites approached, they shouted their demands: dismantle the power looms or watch the mill burn. When their ultimatum was refused, they smashed windows and tried to force entry. Gunfire erupted from inside. Two Luddites fell mortally wounded; the rest scattered into the darkness. The machines remained intact, but the fear and rage that drove men to risk everything to destroy them continued to smolder across industrial England.

This violent confrontation reflected a society grappling with transformative change. Just as the mechanical looms threatened centuries-old traditions of textile craftsmanship, the political and social landscape of Europe was being reshaped in the aftermath of the revolutionary era. Fear, whether of machines, revolutionary ideas, or social disorder, drove reactions that would define the early nineteenth century. From the halls of the Congress of Vienna to the factories of northern England, the quest for stability and order would collide with the inexorable forces of change.

The stars that had witnessed the revolutionary tumult and Napoleon's rise and fall now looked down upon a Europe seeking to restore order from chaos. These same celestial bodies that had illuminated battlefields from Austerlitz to Waterloo now watched as the continent attempted to rebuild from decades of upheaval. The spiral of history continued its turn, not returning to its starting point but advancing to a position that incorporated both fear of revolutionary excess and anxiety about technological transformation. This next cycle would reveal how societies respond when faced with not just political but industrial revolution, when the very fabric of daily life is rewoven by forces that seem beyond individual control.

The Battle of Waterloo marked the end of an era. On June 18, 1815, Napoleon Bonaparte's final gamble collapsed in the muddy Belgian country-side. After twenty-five years of revolutionary upheaval and imperial expansion, France's military power was definitively broken. "Nothing except a battle lost can be half so melancholy as a battle won," wrote the Duke of Wellington, looking out over a field strewn with 40,000 dead and wounded soldiers. The human cost of revolutionary chaos and constant warfare had exhausted Europe, creating a desperate longing for stability.

This exhaustion created fertile ground for conservative restoration. The generation that had witnessed the execution of Louis XVI, the Terror, and the seemingly endless Napoleonic campaigns craved normality. "They cannot be expected to weep at the passing of ideas that nearly destroyed them," noted one historian of the period. Ordinary citizens who had endured food shortages, conscription, and economic disruption welcomed the promise of peace, even at the cost of revolutionary ideals.

In France, the restoration of the Bourbon monarchy under Louis XVIII represented this desire for stabilization through familiar institutions. Returning from exile, the portly brother of the executed king attempted to strike a balance between the old regime and revolutionary changes. "I have lived near the throne all my life," Louis declared upon his return, "and I know that revolutions are not ended by unlimited concessions." His Constitutional Charter preserved some revolutionary gains, including legal equality, administrative reforms, and limited parliamentary government, while restoring monarchical authority and aristocratic privilege.

Across Europe, the Napoleonic era had left a complex legacy. French revolutionary armies had swept away ancient feudal structures, introduced modern legal codes, and dismantled old barriers to commerce. They had also awakened national consciousness in many regions, particularly in the German and Italian states. Napoleon himself embodied contradiction: a revolutionary general who crowned himself emperor, spreading liberal ideals through authoritarian means. His defeat created both opportunity and challenge: how to restore stability without simply turning back the clock to a pre-revolutionary world that could never truly be recovered.

The Congress of Vienna, convened in September 1814, represented the most ambitious attempt to establish a post-revolutionary settlement. Representatives from every European power gathered in the Austrian capital to redraw boundaries, restore monarchies, and create mechanisms to prevent future revolutionary upheaval. The Congress brought together an extraordinary assembly of talent: Austria's Prince Klemens von Metternich, the calculating architect of the conservative order; Britain's Viscount Castlereagh, the pragmatic defender of balance-of-power politics; Russia's Tsar Alexander I, who combined mystical religiosity with imperial ambition; and the wily French diplomat Talleyrand, who skillfully inserted defeated France back into the European concert.

These statesmen approached their task with both determination and anxiety. "The revolutionary spirit still wanders like a ghost through these conferences," wrote a German observer. Despite the military victory over Napoleon, they understood that the ideas of liberty, equality, and national self-determination could not be defeated on the battlefield. Their response was to create a comprehensive system of containment: a "tranquilizer" as one historian described it, designed to prevent revolutionary contagion through coordinated conservative governance.

The territorial settlement they established aimed to prevent future French expansion while strengthening the conservative powers. Prussia gained the Rhineland, becoming France's eastern bulwark. Austria secured dominance in northern Italy and influence over the German Confederation. Russia expanded westward, gaining most of Poland. A ring of buffer states, including the Kingdom of the Netherlands, Piedmont-Sardinia, and an enlarged Switzerland, surrounded France itself. These arrangements reflected no underlying principle except balance of power: "geographic determinism," as one diplomat cynically remarked, "follows the interests of the strongest."

Beyond territorial adjustments, the Congress established an unprecedented system of international cooperation that became known as the "Concert of Europe." Through regular consultations and occasional military interventions, the great powers committed to maintaining the Vienna settlement against revolutionary challenges. This system, largely engineered by Metternich, recognized that no single power could ensure stability; only collective action could contain revolutionary forces. For the first time, European powers institutionalized their relationships through regular conferences and coordinated diplomatic efforts, a significant innovation that would influence international relations for generations.

The Vienna system represented a deliberate attempt to halt the historical momentum unleashed by the revolutionary era. Its architects, particularly Metternich, believed that revolutionary ideas threatened not just particular regimes but the very fabric of civilized society. "The first and greatest concern for the immense majority of every nation," Metternich wrote, "is the stability of laws, never their change." In his view, revolutionary change inevitably led to chaos, violence, and tyranny; only by anchoring society in traditional authority could peace and prosperity be secured. This perspective, shaped by the traumatic experience of revolutionary excess, would guide European governance for decades to come.

The conservative reaction went beyond power politics to develop intellectual foundations that directly challenged revolutionary principles. Edmund Burke, the Anglo-Irish statesman and philosopher, provided the most influential framework for this conservative worldview in his *Reflections on the Revolution in France*, published in 1790. Though Burke died in 1797, well before the Congress of Vienna, his ideas profoundly shaped the conservative response to revolutionary upheaval.

Burke rejected the French revolutionaries' abstract rationalism and their attempt to rebuild society based on theoretical principles. "The science of constructing a commonwealth," he wrote, "is not to be taught a priori." Instead, Burke championed the wisdom embedded in existing institutions that had evolved over centuries to address human needs and circumstances. He viewed society as an organic entity developing through gradual adaptation rather than radical reconstruction. "The individual is foolish, but the species is wise," he declared, arguing that traditional institutions contained wisdom beyond any single generation's understanding.

For Burke, the revolutionaries' fatal error was their willingness to destroy existing social structures before understanding their essential functions. He famously described society as "a partnership not only between those who are living, but between those who are living, those who are dead, and those who are to be born." By severing this partnership through revolutionary rupture, the French had, in Burke's view, condemned themselves to instability and eventual tyranny. His predictions of the Terror and Napoleon's rise seemed prophetic to many post-Napoleonic conservatives, confirming his central insight that revolution leads to outcomes worse than the problems it claims to solve.

The ultraconservative Joseph de Maistre developed an even more radical critique of revolutionary principles. Where Burke acknowledged the need for gradual reform, de Maistre rejected the very notion of human-designed political systems. Writing from exile after the French Revolution consumed his native Savoy, de Maistre argued that legitimate authority came only from God, not from social contracts or popular consent. "Every nation gets the government it deserves," he asserted, seeing political arrangements as divinely ordained reflections of national character rather than conscious human creations.

De Maistre's vivid descriptions of the Revolution's horrors, particularly public executions, led him to emphasize humanity's violent tendencies and need for restraint. "All grandeur, all power, all subordination rests on the executioner," he wrote with characteristic bleakness. "He is the horror and the bond of human association. Remove this incomprehensible agent from the world, and at that very moment order gives way to chaos, thrones topple and society disappears." This dark view of human nature contrasted sharply with revolutionary optimism about perfectible humans and rational self-governance.

Religious authority formed a central pillar of post-Napoleonic conservatism. While revolutionaries had attacked the Church as an obstacle to freedom, conservatives viewed religion as essential to social order. "Man must have a master," wrote Louis de Bonald, another leading conservative thinker, "and when he is not willing to obey God, he is compelled to obey the forcible man... that is to say, the despot." The alliance between throne and altar became a defining feature of the restoration period, with religious revival movements supporting conservative political aims across Europe.

This philosophical conservatism offered a comprehensive alternative to revolutionary ideals. Instead of natural rights, conservatives emphasized customary rights developed through historical experience. Instead of equality, they advocated natural hierarchies and organic social relationships. Instead of popular sovereignty, they championed authority derived from tradition, religion, and historical legitimacy. Instead of revolutionary transformation, they promoted gradual, evolutionary change that preserved essential social structures while addressing specific problems.

The most sophisticated conservatives were not simply reactionaries seeking to restore the past. They recognized that some revolutionary changes, including administrative reforms, legal equality, and dismantling feudal restrictions, had addressed real problems and could not be entirely reversed. Their aim was not to return to 1789 but to stabilize European society on foundations that balanced traditional authority with necessary modernization. As Metternich explained,

"The art of statesmanship is to recognize the direction of things and to direct them toward fruitful paths" rather than simply opposing all change.

The battle for Europe's future was fought not only in diplomatic chambers and philosophical treatises but in the rapidly evolving media landscape of the early nineteenth century. The revolutionary era had witnessed an explosion of newspapers, pamphlets, books, and journals that continued to shape public opinion during the restoration period. Both conservative and liberal forces recognized the power of print culture in mobilizing support and legitimizing their visions for post-revolutionary society.

Rising literacy rates transformed political communication during this period. While only a small percentage of Europeans could read at the century's beginning, educational expansion steadily increased literacy, particularly in urban areas and among the middle class. In Britain, literacy rates approached 60% by 1830, creating a substantial reading public. France, despite revolutionary disruptions, also saw literacy growth, with rates reaching about 40% by 1820. German states varied widely, but areas like Prussia invested heavily in education, achieving literacy rates above 70% in some regions. This expanding literacy created new possibilities for circulating ideas beyond elite circles.

Conservative governments moved to control information flow, recognizing its potential power. Censorship became a central feature of the restoration period, with varying degrees of strictness across Europe. The Habsburg Empire under Metternich developed perhaps the most comprehensive system, employing an army of censors to review all publications. As one censor explained their approach: "When in doubt, strike it out." Austrian authorities categorized books as "forbidden," "tolerated," or "approved," with most foreign political works falling into the first category. Even classic works of literature faced censorship if they contained politically suspect ideas.

France's approach to press regulation fluctuated with political circumstances. The restored Bourbon monarchy initially allowed relatively free expression, but after the assassination of the Duke of Berry in 1820, it imposed stricter controls, including pre-publication censorship and hefty financial deposits required to publish newspapers. The resulting system created what one historian calls a "cautious press" that avoided direct criticism of the monarchy while sometimes employing allegory and historical references to convey political messages.

Despite these restrictions, critical voices found ways to circulate their ideas. Publishers developed sophisticated methods to evade censorship, including allegorical writing, fictional dialogues, and historical analyses with obvious contemporary parallels. Some authors published anonymously or under pseudonyms, while others established printing operations in more liberal territories like Switzerland or the United Kingdom. Smuggling networks transported banned materials across borders, creating what one contemporary called "a literary black market" throughout the continent.

Conservative media developed its own persuasive strategies, particularly warning about the dangers of revolutionary chaos. Newspapers friendly to restoration governments regularly featured stories about revolutionary atrocities, emphasizing the Terror's victims and the destruction wrought by Napoleonic wars. Religious publications portrayed revolution as moral decay, linking political upheaval to religious decline. Historical works presented conservative readings of recent events, portraying revolutionaries as misguided idealists whose abstract theories had produced practical disasters.

Visual media played an increasingly important role in shaping public perception. Political caricatures and engravings reached audiences regardless of literacy, depicting complex political situations through powerful imagery. Conservative artists portrayed revolutionaries as demonic figures or naive dreamers, while liberal cartoonists depicted rulers as corpulent oppressors and their supporters as mindless puppets. These images circulated widely, sometimes reaching audiences that written propaganda could not penetrate.

Public spaces provided additional venues for ideological conflict. Coffeehouses, salons, reading societies, and lecture halls became forums where ideas could be discussed with varying degrees of openness. While authorities monitored these gatherings, they proved difficult to control completely. As one police informant in Vienna reported: "They speak in whispers but think in shouts." These semi-private spaces allowed for the development of what historians have called "counter-publics," alternative discourse communities that challenged official narratives while avoiding direct confrontation with authorities.

While political authorities worked to restore stability after the revolutionary era, another revolution was transforming European society with equal force: the rise of industrial production. Beginning in Britain and gradually spreading to the continent, this technological revolution reordered economic relationships, transformed physical landscapes, and challenged traditional ways of life. Like political revolution, industrialization provoked both excitement and apprehension, creating new possibilities while threatening established patterns of work and community.

The technological innovations driving this transformation had been developing gradually through the eighteenth century, but accelerated dramatically in the post-Napoleonic period. Steam power, first harnessed effectively by James Watt's improved engine in the 1770s, became increasingly efficient and widespread in the early nineteenth century. By 1830, Britain alone had approximately 15,000 steam engines operating in factories, mines, and transportation. The power these engines generated, unconstrained by weather or season, capable of running continuously, created unprecedented productive capacity while freeing industry from geographic limitations imposed by water power.

Textile manufacturing exemplified the industrial transformation. Traditional production had involved household-based spinning and weaving, often performed as supplementary family income. The mechanical innovations of the late eighteenth century, including the spinning jenny, water frame, and power loom, shifted production to centralized factories where machines could be operated by less-skilled workers under direct supervision. As one Lancashire weaver observed: "What once employed a hundred hands can now be done by a dozen children." The result was dramatically increased output; British cotton production grew nearly tenfold between 1800 and 1830, while prices fell steadily.

Factory organization represented a fundamental shift in working patterns. Pre-industrial labor had typically followed irregular rhythms governed by daylight, seasons, and traditional practices including frequent holidays. Workers often controlled their own pace and methods within the broad requirements of their craft. Industrial discipline imposed strict timekeeping, continuous labor, and standardized methods. Factory bells and clocks regulated the workday, while supervisors enforced consistency and pace. One factory owner explained the change bluntly: "Workers must be made to understand that they sell not just their craft but their time, and that time belongs to those who purchase it."

The physical environment of industrialization generated both wonder and concern. Factory towns grew rapidly, often with minimal planning or infrastructure. Manchester's population tripled between 1801 and 1831 as rural workers migrated to find employment in its cotton mills. Similar growth occurred in Leeds, Sheffield, and Birmingham. These industrial centers typically featured stark divisions between working-class districts, characterized by overcrowding, poor sanitation, and industrial pollution, and the more spacious neighborhoods of factory owners and managers. As one observer noted: "Two nations are forming within England, between whom there is little sympathy and less understanding."

Environmental impacts of early industrialization were severe but often localized. Factory emissions blackened buildings, damaged vegetation, and caused respiratory ailments among nearby residents. Mining operations scarred landscapes and polluted waterways. Urban crowding created conditions for disease outbreaks, particularly cholera and typhoid. Yet these externalities remained largely unregulated, considered acceptable costs of progress. "The smoke of industry is the breath of prosperity," declared one manufacturer defending his factory's emissions against local complaints.

Continental industrialization lagged behind Britain, constrained by wartime disruptions and less developed commercial infrastructure. France, despite possessing technical knowledge comparable to Britain's, industrialized more gradually and selectively, with traditional craft production remaining important alongside newer factories. The German states began significant industrialization only in the 1830s and 1840s, with regions like the Rhineland and Saxony leading the transition. This developmental gap gave continental observers opportunity to study the British experience, learning from both its achievements and problems.

Transportation innovations accelerated industrial development while reshaping relationships between regions. Road improvements through macadamization (using compressed gravel for all-weather surfaces) significantly reduced travel times and freight costs over traditional dirt roads. Canal networks expanded dramatically, with Britain's navigable waterways tripling between 1760 and 1830. Railways, the most transformative transportation technology, began commercial operation in the 1820s and expanded rapidly thereafter. The Liverpool and Manchester Railway, completed in 1830, demonstrated the revolutionary potential of steam locomotion, moving passengers and freight at unprecedented speeds that "annihilated distance" in contemporary accounts.

The human cost of industrialization fell heaviest on skilled craftspeople whose traditional practices faced obsolescence from mechanical production. These artisans, the hand-loom weavers, framework knitters, croppers, and other specialized workers, experienced not only economic hardship but existential threat to identities and communities built around craft traditions developed over generations. Their struggle to maintain dignity and livelihood amidst technological change reveals both the personal trauma of industrial transition and the broader social tensions it generated.

Hand-loom weavers represented the largest and most severely affected group. Before mechanization, weaving provided relatively comfortable livelihoods for skilled practitioners who typically worked from home workshops. These artisans controlled their production process, set their own hours, and took pride in their specialized knowledge passed down through family and apprenticeship networks. The weaver's home-workshop symbolized independence: "A man's cottage was his castle," recalled one Yorkshire weaver, "where he answered to none but himself and could hold his head high in the community."

The introduction of power looms operated in factories by less-skilled workers transformed this landscape rapidly. A single power loom could produce as much cloth as two to three hand-loom weavers, while requiring less skill to operate. The economic consequences were devastating. In Lancashire, weekly wages for hand-loom weavers collapsed from about 15 shillings in 1800 to less than 6 shillings by 1830, far below subsistence level. The number of hand-loom weavers actually increased during this period as displaced agricultural workers and others sought entry to a trade requiring minimal capital investment, creating a desperate oversupply of labor that further depressed wages.

The personal testimonies of affected weavers reveal both material suffering and psychological distress. One Manchester weaver described working "from five in the morning till nine at night" yet still finding "my children crying for food with none to give them." A parliamentary report documented weavers subsisting on "water porridge, with a little salt" for days at a time. Beyond physical deprivation, many expressed grief over lost independence and dignity. "We were masters once," lamented a Spitalfields silk weaver, "but now are slaves in all but name, dependent on the factory and its machines."

Framework knitters, who produced stockings and other hosiery items using specialized frames, faced similar pressures through different mechanisms. Rather than competing directly with mechanized production, these craftsmen increasingly lost autonomy through the "putting-out" system, where merchant capitalists owned the frames and rented them to workers who became effectively wage laborers rather than independent artisans. Frame rents rose while piece rates fell, creating what workers called "slavery in the midst of freedom." By the 1810s, framework knitting families in Nottinghamshire regions often worked fourteen-hour days yet remained in perpetual debt to frame owners and landlords.

Croppers, skilled workers who finished woolen cloth by raising and cutting the nap to create a smooth surface, saw their entire profession threatened by the introduction of shearing frames that could be operated by unskilled laborers. This tightly knit occupational community, concentrated in Yorkshire's West Riding, faced particularly abrupt displacement. The cropper's specialized hand shears, which had represented significant investment and years of skill development, became virtually worthless as mechanical alternatives spread. "My shears were my inheritance," one cropper testified, "passed from my father and worth twenty pounds in better days. Now they would not fetch the price of scrap metal."

The economic devastation extended beyond individual craftsmen to entire communities built around traditional production. Villages and small towns specialized in particular crafts entered severe decline as work shifted to mechanized urban factories. Family structures strained as traditional patterns of fathers teaching sons their craft became untenable. Community mutual aid systems collapsed under the weight of widespread poverty. Religious and cultural institutions that had provided social cohesion struggled as their economic foundations eroded. These communal losses intensified the trauma of industrial transition beyond mere financial hardship.

As traditional social systems faced disruption from both political and technological changes, conservative regimes developed sophisticated control mechanisms to maintain stability. These methods extended beyond conventional censorship to include surveillance, educational control, legal restrictions, and coordinated international action against perceived threats. While these mechanisms successfully suppressed revolutionary activity in the short term, they also revealed the underlying insecurity of the conservative order and its reliance on coercion rather than genuine consent.

Surveillance networks expanded dramatically during the restoration period. Metternich's Austria developed the most comprehensive system, employing hundreds of police spies and informants to monitor potential dissidents. These agents infiltrated universities, literary societies, coffee houses, and other gathering places where dangerous ideas might circulate. Their reports, meticulously archived, provided authorities detailed information about private conversations, unpublished manuscripts, and even personal relationships that might indicate political unreliability. The scale of this surveillance created what one historian calls a "culture of suspicion" that permeated society and discouraged open political discussion.

The Russian Empire under Tsar Nicholas I institutionalized similar surveillance through the Third Section, a political police force established in 1826 after a failed military revolt. This organization monitored suspected revolutionaries, intercepted private correspondence, and compiled detailed reports on public opinion. Count Alexander Benckendorff, its first chief, described the Third Section's mission as "drying the tears of the unfortunate and ensuring that the powerful do not abuse their power," but its primary function remained protecting the autocratic system from internal challenge. The Third Section's reach extended beyond Russian borders through networks of agents monitoring Russian subjects abroad, particularly students exposed to Western liberal ideas.

Educational institutions faced particular scrutiny as potential sources of dangerous thinking. The Carlsbad Decrees of 1819 specifically targeted German universities, establishing government commissioners to monitor teaching and student activities. Professors deemed politically unreliable faced dismissal, while student organizations suspected of nationalist or liberal leanings were banned. Similar restrictions affected universities across Europe, with philosophy, history, and literature departments receiving special attention due to their potential for fostering critical thought. "The university must form good subjects, not independent thinkers," declared one Prussian education minister, capturing the conservative approach to higher education.

Lower education similarly aimed to produce obedient subjects rather than engaged citizens. Religious instruction received prominent place in curricula, emphasizing moral obligations to divinely ordained authority. History teaching stressed continuity and tradition rather than revolutionary moments. Reading selections carefully excluded materials that might provoke questioning of established institutions. In some regions, schooling intentionally remained limited for lower classes, reflecting the sentiment expressed by a French aristocrat that "teaching the poor to read has caused nothing but trouble."

Legal systems provided additional control mechanisms. Political offenses received increasingly broad definition during this period, with "sedition," "disrupting public order," and "insulting sovereignty" applied to a widening range of expressions. Procedural protections for the accused in political cases were often minimal, with secret trials, limited defense rights, and harsh sentences creating deterrent examples. Austria, Prussia, and Russia maintained networks of fortresses and remote outposts where political prisoners could be held indefinitely without public knowledge. The threat of these punishments helped suppress open opposition to the conservative order.

From a celestial perspective, one might observe how the pendulum of history had swung from revolutionary excess toward conservative reaction. Yet this pendulum never returns precisely to its starting point; instead, it traces a spiral path that integrates elements of both movements. The conservative order could not simply erase the revolutionary experience; it had to incorporate certain changes while controlling their effects. Similarly, the industrial transformation could neither be wholly embraced nor entirely rejected, but required frameworks that could harness its productive potential while mitigating its human costs. These dual challenges, political restoration amid revolutionary aftershocks and technological advancement amid social disruption, marked this historical cycle with a particular tension between preservation and transformation.

NO MAN'S LAND: TRADITION VS. INNOVATION

Traditional ways of life embody accumulated wisdom and provide stability, meaning, and social cohesion that should be preserved.

Pause. Notice what arises in you.

Technological and social innovation drives material progress, solves problems, and opens new possibilities that improve human welfare.

Pause. Notice what arises in you.

You do not have to agree with or justify either statement. Simply hold them both in your mind and observe what comes up.

This fundamental tension defined the post-Napoleonic era, as societies sought balance between preserving valuable traditions and embracing beneficial changes. Conservative thinkers like Edmund Burke emphasized the wisdom embedded in traditional institutions that had evolved over generations to address human needs. "Prejudice renders a man's virtue his habit," Burke wrote, arguing that established practices provide stability and meaning that abstract reasoning alone cannot supply. The social fabric woven through family structures, religious communities, craft guilds, and local traditions offered essential continuity amidst disruption.

Yet innovation brought undeniable benefits that even the most tradition-minded recognized. The industrial advances transforming Britain had doubled per capita income between 1780 and 1840, producing material abundance previously unimaginable. New technologies solved pressing problems from transportation limitations to communication barriers. Even conservative governments embraced innovation when it strengthened state capacity or military power. Administrative reforms introduced during the revolutionary era improved governance efficiency across Europe, regardless of political orientation.

For craftspeople facing technological displacement, this tension was lived rather than theoretical. Hand-loom weavers witnessed both the destruction of their way of life and the production of more affordable cloth for working-class consumers. Framework knitters saw their independence erode while total hosiery output increased dramatically. The same machines that threatened livelihoods also created new possibilities for human flourishing through increased productivity and material abundance.

Neither simplistic progressivism nor reflexive traditionalism adequately addresses this complex relationship between preservation and innovation. Societies that have navigated technological transitions most successfully have found ways to incorporate valuable innovations while preserving essential human and community needs, adapting at a pace that allows for genuine integration rather than destructive disruption. This balance requires recognizing both the wisdom embedded in tradition and the possibilities offered by thoughtful innovation.

The question is not whether to embrace change, but how to manage its pace and direction to serve human flourishing. As one framework knitter testified: "We ask not to stop the machine, but to be allowed to travel with it." This distinction between resisting all change and seeking more equitable participation in its benefits remains central to navigating technological transitions from the industrial revolution to the present day.

Chapter Eight

When Workers Broke the Gears

In a small stone cottage on the outskirts of Nottingham in 1810, Samuel Marsden sat at his frame loom, his practiced hands moving with subtle precision as they had for three decades. Morning light filtered through the window, illuminating the intricate pattern taking shape on his loom. The sound of his shuttle passing back and forth created a meditative rhythm, punctuated by quiet adjustments as he periodically examined his work. On the wall hung the tools of his trade, inherited from his father, who had received them from his father before him. A small garden visible through the window provided vegetables for his family, while the loom provided income. His ten-year-old son watched from the corner, absorbing the techniques he would someday employ as the next generation in an ancient craft.

Ten miles away, in a newly constructed brick factory beside the River Trent, a very different scene unfolded. Dozens of mechanical looms operated in thunderous concert, their iron frames clanking and vibrating as they produced yard after yard of cotton cloth. The air hung heavy with cotton dust and the smell of machine oil. Pallid workers, many of them women and children, tended the machines in twelve-hour shifts, monitored by supervisors who paced the aisles with pocket watches. No natural light penetrated the workroom; instead, the space was illuminated by gas lamps that allowed production to continue regardless of the hour. A steam engine in the adjoining room powered the entire operation, its steady chug providing the heartbeat of industrial production.

These contrasting settings, separated by mere miles but representing radically different worlds, embodied the wrenching transformation reshaping early nineteenth-century society. For craftsmen like Marsden, the mechanized factory represented not just economic competition but an existential threat to an entire way of life built around skill, independence, and community. As mechanical looms spread across the textile districts of England, these artisans faced an impossible choice: adapt to a system that reduced them from skilled craftsmen to machine operators, or resist changes that seemed poised to erase generations of tradition and expertise. Their response, organized campaigns of machine-breaking under the mythical leader "Ned Ludd," would echo through history as an emblematic struggle between traditional life and technological transformation.

This tension between preserving valuable traditions and embracing necessary change extended far beyond English textile districts. Across Europe, societies grappled with similar questions about the pace and nature of transformation. Should change occur gradually through careful evolution, or rapidly through revolutionary rupture? Who should control these processes, established authorities or popular movements? How could the benefits of progress be balanced against the human costs of disruption? These questions would find dramatic expression not only in the Luddite movement but in the revolutionary wave that would sweep Europe in 1848, challenging the conservative order established after Napoleon's defeat.

The stars that had witnessed the conservative restoration after Napoleon's fall now looked down upon a Europe experiencing the first tremors of industrial transformation. From their celestial vantage point, these distant observers might notice how the pendulum of human affairs continued its perpetual swing, this time between the stability of traditional craftsmanship and the disruptive power of mechanization, between the order imposed by conservative governments and the revolutionary aspirations of those who felt excluded from power. The spiral of history continued its turn, not returning to exactly the same position but revisiting familiar tensions between stability and change, authority and liberty, tradition and innovation.

On a March night in 1811, a group of men with blackened faces slipped silently through the darkness of Nottinghamshire. Their destination: a workshop containing several wide stocking frames that had been adapted to produce lower-quality hosiery operated by unskilled workers. Armed with hammers, axes, and a few pistols, they broke into the workshop, smashed the frames into useless fragments, and disappeared into the night. Days later, a letter appeared in a local newspaper signed by "Ned Ludd, King of the Frame Breakers," warning that more destruction would follow unless employers returned to traditional quality standards and fair wages.

This first organized attack marked the birth of what would become known as the Luddite movement, though the grievances driving it had been simmering for years. The English textile industry had been undergoing gradual mechanization since the late eighteenth century, but several factors converged around 1811 to create a perfect storm of worker distress. The Napoleonic Wars had disrupted export markets, creating economic hardship throughout manufacturing regions. Simultaneously, a severe economic depression compounded by poor harvests had increased food prices while depressing wages. Against this backdrop, technological changes that might have been tolerated in better times became lightning rods for worker resentment.

The movement's mysterious leader, "General" or "King" Ned Ludd, was most likely a fiction, a symbolic figure behind whom workers could unite while distributing responsibility for illegal actions. The name possibly derived from a local legend about an apprentice named Ned Ludd who had allegedly smashed a stocking frame in a fit of rage years earlier. By creating this mythical leader, the actual organizers gained both protective anonymity and a powerful symbol that personified their resistance. Letters and proclamations issued in Ludd's name often displayed surprising sophistication, mixing traditional ballad forms with legal language and biblical references that resonated with working class communities.

The movement spread rapidly through the textile districts of central England, first concentrating in Nottinghamshire before expanding to Yorkshire and Lancashire. Each region had its own economic specialization and particular grievances. In Nottinghamshire, framework knitters primarily objected to "cut-ups," inferior goods produced on adapted frames by unskilled workers that undermined quality standards and wages. Yorkshire croppers, who finished woolen cloth using heavy shears, targeted the new shearing frames that threatened to eliminate their highly skilled profession entirely. Lancashire cotton weavers attacked power looms that could produce exponentially more cloth while requiring minimal skill to operate.

Despite their regional differences, these groups shared certain characteristics. They consisted primarily of skilled artisans defending craft traditions and community standards against changes they viewed as degrading both their products and their way of life. Their actions, while illegal and sometimes violent, followed specific patterns that demonstrated discipline and purpose rather than blind rage. They typically targeted only machinery they considered unfair, sparing frames owned by employers who maintained fair wages and quality standards. They issued warnings before attacks, often giving employers opportunities to address grievances peacefully. When they did destroy frames, they did so methodically, damaging only the objectionable machinery while carefully protecting other property.

The name "Luddite" would later become synonymous with mindless opposition to technology, but historical evidence reveals a more nuanced reality. The original Luddites did not oppose all machinery or technological progress. Instead, they objected to specific implementations of technology that threatened their communities without providing commensurate benefits. As one Luddite letter made clear: "We will never lay down our arms until the House of Commons passes an Act to put down all machinery hurtful to the commonality." This distinction between beneficial and harmful applications of technology reveals a sophisticated analysis of industrialization's social impacts rather than reflexive technophobia.

Economic desperation drove much of the movement. Mechanical innovations had dramatic effects on worker livelihoods. In cotton weaving, where power looms competed directly with hand-loom weavers, wages collapsed catastrophically. A parliamentary committee reported that weekly earnings fell from around 15 shillings in 1800 to less than 6 shillings by 1811, an income insufficient for even basic subsistence. One observer reported seeing "weavers, once respectable men, pulling up nettles from the roadside to boil for their children's dinner, having nothing else to feed them." Similar wage collapses affected framework knitters and other textile workers, creating conditions where desperate action seemed the only recourse.

Beyond economic motives, Luddism represented resistance to the changing relationship between capital and labor. Traditional production had operated under a quasi-paternal model where masters maintained responsibilities toward workers and communities, often regulated by guild standards. New industrial organizations prioritized profit maximization with minimal concern for worker welfare or community cohesion. As economist E.P. Thompson later observed, Luddism represented "collective bargaining by riot," a desperate attempt to enforce community standards when other regulatory mechanisms had collapsed. Their machine-breaking constituted not rejection of technology itself but resistance to technology deployed within exploitative social arrangements.

By January 1812, Luddite activity had spread beyond its Nottinghamshire origins to the woolen districts of Yorkshire and the cotton country of Lancashire. Each region saw distinct patterns of machine-breaking adapted to local conditions, but all experienced an intensification of both Luddite actions and government response. What had begun as targeted attacks against specific types of machinery evolved into a broader confrontation that reflected deepening social divisions and increasingly desperate economic conditions.

Yorkshire witnessed particularly dramatic escalation. The West Riding's woolen industry centered around Leeds and Huddersfield had traditionally employed specialized craftsmen called croppers, who used massive hand shears to trim the surface of woolen cloth to create a smooth finish. The introduction of shearing frames threatened to eliminate this skilled profession entirely. Under the leadership of a man known as "General Ludd's nephew," Yorkshire croppers organized nighttime raids on mills where these frames had been installed. Unlike Nottinghamshire Luddites, who had primarily targeted smaller workshops, Yorkshire croppers attacked larger mills, requiring more significant organization and firepower.

The most notorious Yorkshire incident occurred at Rawfolds Mill near Huddersfield in April 1812. The mill's owner, William Cartwright, had received threatening letters demanding he remove his shearing frames. When he refused and instead fortified his mill with armed guards, approximately 150 Luddites mounted a midnight attack. The ensuing battle lasted nearly twenty minutes, with the attackers smashing windows and attempting to breach the doors using hammers and axes while those inside fired upon them. Two Luddites were fatally wounded, and the attack ultimately failed. The incident demonstrated both the increasing violence of the conflict and the growing determination of mill owners to protect their machinery at all costs.

Violence escalated further two weeks later when William Horsfall, another mill owner known for his vocal opposition to the Luddites, was assassinated while returning from a business trip to Huddersfield. Horsfall had reportedly boasted that he would "ride up to his saddle girths in Luddite blood" and had installed particularly hated machinery in his mill. Four men ambushed and shot him in a planned attack that marked a significant escalation beyond machine-breaking to targeted killing. This assassination shocked authorities and the public, strengthening support for harsh measures against the movement.

Lancashire's cotton district experienced parallel developments, though focused primarily on power looms rather than finishing machinery. The economic context was particularly dire, as the region suffered severely from American trade embargoes during the War of 1812, which restricted cotton imports. Manchester and surrounding towns saw increasing attacks on factories containing power looms. In April 1812, a large-scale attack on Burton's Mill in Middleton led to a violent confrontation in which soldiers fired on a crowd of several thousand people who had gathered around the mill, killing at least three protesters and wounding many more. The next day, outraged community members burned the home of Emmanuel Burton, the mill owner, though he and his family escaped unharmed.

The systematic suppression of Luddism represented one of the most extensive domestic security operations in British history to that point. Beyond the immediate military response, authorities developed a comprehensive strategy combining legal prosecution, intelligence gathering, and public messaging designed not merely to halt machine-breaking but to utterly discredit the movement and its underlying grievances. This multi-pronged approach revealed both the government's determination to protect industrial capitalism and its fear that worker resistance might escalate into broader revolutionary activity.

Special legal commissions were established in affected regions to try Luddite cases, operating with extraordinary powers and procedural advantages for the prosecution. These commissions allowed cases to be tried away from local communities where sympathy for defendants might influence jurors. They also permitted relaxed standards of evidence, with convictions secured based on circumstantial evidence or testimony from paid informants that would have been inadmissible in ordinary courts. The government's goal was not merely to punish machine-breakers but to make examples that would deter others.

The York Special Commission of January 1813 exemplified this approach. Sixty-four men faced charges ranging from machine-breaking to administering illegal oaths to murder. The proceedings lasted two weeks and featured elaborate security measures, including soldiers surrounding the courthouse. Prosecutors presented evidence ranging from seized weapons and disguises to testimony from paid informants who had infiltrated Luddite meetings. The standards of evidence appeared notably flexible; when direct proof was lacking, prosecutors emphasized the general atmosphere of unrest and defendants' known associations with others involved in Luddite activities.

Sentencing reflected the government's determination to crush the movement through terror. Of those tried at York, seventeen men were executed on various charges, including the assassination of William Horsfall. Their public hangings were staged as elaborate spectacles designed to maximize deterrent effect. The condemned men mounted the scaffold before large crowds, with their families often present. Officials ensured these executions received extensive newspaper coverage, including details of the men's final moments. Beyond those executed, many others received transportation sentences to penal colonies in Australia, a punishment that typically meant permanent separation from family and community.

The human cost of this repression extended far beyond those formally prosecuted. Hundreds were imprisoned without trial under various emergency powers, often held in appalling conditions for months before being released without charges. Military raids on suspected Luddite homes occurred throughout affected regions, traumatizing families and communities. Economic punishment complemented legal measures, with known Luddite sympathizers blacklisted from employment. The collective trauma inflicted on textile communities created lasting psychological impacts that survivors described in letters and memoirs for decades afterward.

By late 1813, the combination of military suppression, legal prosecution, economic pressure, and propaganda had largely broken organized Luddism in its original form. Sporadic machine-breaking incidents continued through 1814 and 1815, but the coordinated movement under the Ludd banner had effectively been crushed. Government officials congratulated themselves on successful suppression, with one Home Office circular declaring: "The firmness of His Majesty's Government, the vigilance of the magistracy, and the active exertions of the military... have successfully accomplished the restoration of tranquility."

Yet this "tranquility" came at significant cost, not only to the executed, transported, and imprisoned Luddites and their families, but to Britain's evolving relationship between governors and governed. The massive deployment of military force against citizens, exceptional legal procedures, and the government's refusal to address legitimate grievances established a precedent of treating industrial disputes as matters of state security rather than economic policy. This approach would influence British responses to labor unrest throughout the nineteenth century, contributing to the adversarial character of British industrial relations for generations to come.

On February 22, 1848, Parisians awoke to news that the government had banned a planned political banquet, one of a series of opposition gatherings demanding electoral reform. By evening, crowds had gathered in protest, erecting impromptu barricades in narrow streets. Two days later, King Louis Philippe, the "Citizen King" who had ruled France since the 1830 revolution, abdicated and fled to England. A provisional government was hastily formed, declaring France a republic and promising universal male suffrage. Within weeks, this seemingly localized Parisian uprising had triggered a continental chain reaction that would challenge the conservative order established at the Congress of Vienna three decades earlier.

The revolution spread with astonishing speed. News traveled faster than in previous eras thanks to improved transportation and communication networks, including the telegraph recently installed between some major cities. By March 13, Vienna erupted in student demonstrations demanding constitutional reforms. Chancellor Metternich, architect of the post-Napoleonic conservative system and symbol of resistance to political change, resigned and fled the city, disguised and under cover of darkness. Emperor Ferdinand I promised a constitution and agreed to abolish censorship. Five days later, revolution reached Berlin, where street fighting forced King Frederick William IV of Prussia to order his troops to withdraw and agree to a constituent assembly. Similar uprisings followed in Milan, Venice, Prague, and dozens of smaller German states.

This revolutionary wave represented the most comprehensive challenge to European political order since the French Revolution of 1789. Unlike earlier revolts that had been largely confined to individual countries, the 1848 movements crossed national boundaries with unprecedented speed and coordination. Contemporary observers noted the almost viral nature of revolution's spread. "It is as if an electric current were running through the continent," wrote one journalist, "energizing populations long held in check by the machinery of repression." Even areas that had seen little previous revolutionary activity, like the Habsburg Empire's Hungarian provinces, suddenly produced fully formed revolutionary movements with detailed political programs.

The revolutionaries presented diverse demands reflecting local conditions but showing remarkable commonalities across borders. Political liberalization stood at the forefront, with calls for written constitutions, expanded suffrage, freedom of press and assembly, and responsible ministerial government. National self-determination emerged as a powerful theme, particularly in multi-ethnic empires like Austria, where Hungarian, Czech, Italian, and Slavic nationalists demanded autonomy or independence. Social and economic reforms featured prominently, with workers demanding labor protections and peasants seeking abolition of remaining feudal obligations. These varied strands created revolutionary coalitions uniting middle-class professionals, students, workers, and peasants, temporary alliances that would prove difficult to maintain.

The February Revolution in France epitomized both the hopes and contradictions of 1848. The provisional government established after Louis Philippe's flight included both moderate republicans like poet Alphonse de Lamartine and socialists like Louis Blanc. This coalition produced dramatic reforms including universal male suffrage, abolition of slavery in French colonies, and establishment of "national workshops" to provide employment for Parisian workers. Yet tensions quickly emerged between middle-class liberals focused on political reforms and workers demanding economic restructuring. Bloody street fighting between workers and the National Guard in June revealed the revolutionary coalition's fragility and foreshadowed similar divisions across Europe.

The initial revolutionary victories created unprecedented public spaces for political expression. Censorship collapsed across much of Europe, leading to an explosion of newspapers, political clubs, and public meetings. In Vienna, more than 150 newspapers began publication in the months following March, compared to three permitted before the revolution. Political societies formed in every district of major cities, allowing ordinary citizens to engage in political debate for the first time. Elections with expanded suffrage took place in France, German states, and parts of the Habsburg domains. These developments represented a dramatic shift from the controlled public sphere of the restoration period, creating what one historian calls a "rehearsal for democracy" even where revolutionary regimes ultimately failed.

Women's participation marked another distinctive feature of 1848, though their contributions received ambivalent recognition from male revolutionaries. In Paris, women organized clubs advocating political rights and economic protections for female workers. Viennese women formed aid societies supporting revolutionary causes while also advocating educational access. In Berlin, Louise Aston and other feminist writers published revolutionary journals addressing women's status. Despite these efforts, when the French provisional government established universal suffrage, it explicitly excluded women, a pattern repeated across revolutionary territories. This contradiction between revolutionary principles of equality and continued gender exclusion highlighted the movement's limitations even at its most radical.

The initial revolutionary tide began receding by summer 1848, as conservative forces reorganized and revolutionary coalitions fractured. Austrian imperial forces under General Windischgrätz recaptured Prague in June after nationalist tensions between Czechs and Germans provided pretext for military intervention. In France, General Cavaignac suppressed the June workers' uprising in Paris, signaling the revolution's rightward shift. By fall, counter-revolutionary armies moved against Vienna, capturing the city in October after heavy fighting. Hungarian revolutionaries under Lajos Kossuth continued resistance into 1849 but faced eventual defeat when Russian Tsar Nicholas I sent 300,000 troops to support Austrian restoration, a dramatic example of the international counter-revolutionary coordination Metternich had established decades earlier.

The initial revolutionary successes of 1848 stunned conservative powers, but their recovery proved remarkably swift. Within a year, most revolutionary regimes had collapsed under coordinated counter-revolutionary pressure combining military force, political maneuvering, and social division. This conservative counterattack demonstrated both the resilience of traditional authority structures and their capacity to adapt tactics to meet the revolutionary challenge. The pattern of revolutionary advance followed by reactionary restoration that had characterized the post-Napoleonic period repeated itself, albeit with important differences reflecting changed conditions.

Military force provided the most direct conservative response. The armies of major European powers had remained largely loyal to traditional authorities despite initial confusion. In the Habsburg Empire, Field Marshal Joseph Radetzky maintained control of his army in northern Italy even as Vienna fell to revolutionaries. From this base, he methodically recaptured Milan and defeated Piedmontese forces attempting to support Italian nationalism. His success demonstrated a crucial conservative advantage: while revolutionaries struggled to create unified command structures for improvised forces, conservative powers possessed professional military organizations with established chains of command, disciplined troops, and substantial resources.

Military suppression came alongside shrewd political maneuvering that exploited divisions within revolutionary movements. Conservative leaders recognized that the broad coalitions formed during initial revolutionary phases contained inherent contradictions between liberal, nationalist, and social revolutionary elements. By selectively addressing some revolutionary demands while rejecting others, they could fragment opposition and isolate the most radical elements. In the Habsburg Empire, officials encouraged ethnic tensions between revolutionary groups, supporting Croatian opposition to Hungarian nationalism and Slovak resistance to Magyar dominance. These divide-and-rule tactics prevented unified opposition to imperial authority.

Prussia's Frederick William IV exemplified this political approach. After initially agreeing to constitutional concessions during Berlin's March revolution, he gradually reasserted royal authority while maintaining selected reforms. He rejected the Frankfurt Parliament's offer of a German imperial crown based on popular sovereignty, but simultaneously pursued his own version of German unification under Prussian leadership. By appropriating nationalist sentiment while rejecting democratic principles, he drew middle-class liberals away from more radical elements. When he eventually dissolved Prussia's constitutional assembly and imposed his own more conservative constitution in December 1848, opposition had been sufficiently fragmented to prevent effective resistance.

Social divisions proved particularly useful to counter-revolutionary strategy. As revolutions progressed, tensions frequently emerged between middle-class liberals focused on political reforms and working-class participants demanding economic transformation. Conservative forces exploited these divisions by appealing to middle-class fears of social disorder. In France, the June Days uprising saw middle-class National Guard units suppressing worker demonstrations, violence that claimed over 3,000 lives. This class conflict paved the way for Louis Napoleon's election on a platform promising order and stability. Throughout Europe, property owners who had initially supported constitutional demands increasingly aligned with conservative forces against perceived threats to economic order, demonstrating the limits of revolutionary coalition.

By 1851, conservative restoration appeared complete across Europe. Louis Napoleon's coup transforming the French Second Republic into an empire provided final confirmation that the revolutionary movement had been contained. Yet this restoration differed significantly from the post-1815 settlement. The restored regimes maintained aspects of revolutionary programs, particularly regarding administrative modernization and limited constitutionalism. They increasingly embraced nationalism as a potential conservative force rather than treating it exclusively as revolutionary threat. Most significantly, the social and political consciousness awakened in 1848 could not simply be extinguished by repression. The revolutionary experience had transformed European political culture in ways that would shape subsequent developments toward national consolidation and gradual democratization.

Looking down upon these tumultuous events, the stars might have observed familiar patterns repeating in new forms. Just as the Luddites had fought against technological changes that threatened their way of life, the revolutionaries of 1848 challenged political arrangements that limited their participation in governance. Both movements represented human attempts to assert control over forces that seemed to be reshaping society without consent from those most affected. Both ultimately faced suppression by established powers determined to maintain control over the pace and direction of change. Yet both left enduring legacies that continued to influence social development long after the immediate conflicts had subsided. The celestial perspective reveals not simply cycles of resistance and repression, but a spiral of human development where each confrontation, even when seemingly defeated, advances the conversation about how societies should manage change.

Both the Luddite movement and the 1848 revolutions, despite their significant differences in scale and focus, exhibited similar psychological patterns characteristic of reactive resistance to rapid change. These movements emerged during periods when established social systems faced dramatic disruption, generating deep anxiety among affected populations. Understanding these psychological dimensions helps explain both the emotional intensity that drove participants and the specific forms their resistance took. Beyond their historical significance, these movements reveal enduring patterns in human responses to perceived existential threats to identity and livelihood.

Fear served as the primary emotional driver for both movements, though this operated through different mechanisms. For Luddites, fear centered on immediate threats to economic survival and craft identity as mechanization undermined traditional skills and livelihoods. Contemporary accounts describe weavers' "dread and alarm" upon learning of new mechanical looms being installed nearby. This represented not abstract anxiety but concrete threat, as wages had already fallen below subsistence levels in many districts. For revolutionaries in 1848, fear often focused on political repression, economic stagnation, and perceived threats to national identity. In both cases, these fears triggered what modern neuroscience identifies as threat responses, physiological and psychological reactions designed to address dangers to survival or core identity.

The specific fears driving reactive movements typically combined material and psychological components. Luddites faced not just economic hardship but loss of autonomy, skill recognition, and community standing. One cropper's testimony captured this dual threat: "It is not just bread I am losing, but my place in the world." Similarly, 1848 revolutionaries responded to both concrete grievances (censorship, food prices, limited political rights) and psychological threats to dignity and identity. Austrian revolutionaries demanded not only constitutional government but recognition of national communities that imperial administration had suppressed. These combined threats to material welfare and core identity created particularly potent motivation for resistance.

Uncertainty magnified these fear responses in both contexts. Research in behavioral economics and psychology demonstrates that humans generally find uncertainty more stressful than known negative outcomes. For traditional craftsmen, mechanization created profound uncertainty about future livelihoods, as established career paths and intergenerational knowledge transfer suddenly lost reliability. Similarly, in pre-revolutionary 1848, economic recession combined with political stagnation created uncertainty about whether existing systems could address mounting problems. This uncertainty generated what psychologists call "anticipatory anxiety," stress responses to imagined future threats that can produce more severe reactions than immediate dangers.

The importance of dignity and agency emerges as a common psychological thread across these reactive movements. Both Luddites and revolutionaries expressed determination to assert control over conditions affecting their lives rather than passively accepting changes imposed from above. Machine-breaking represented not mere destruction but an attempt to reassert worker influence over production conditions when other channels proved unavailable. As one framework knitter expressed: "If we cannot control our lives through fair wages, we shall control them through fear." Similarly, 1848 revolutionaries across Europe demanded constitutions and representative institutions that would give ordinary citizens voice in governance. This psychological need for agency, what psychologists call "self-efficacy," appears fundamental to human wellbeing across cultures and historical periods.

These psychological dynamics help explain why reactive movements often employed symbolic actions alongside practical tactics. Luddites developed elaborate rituals around machine-breaking, including oath-taking ceremonies, military-style organization, and formal communications in "General Ludd's" name. These symbolic elements provided psychological benefits beyond their practical utility, creating what sociologists call "collective effervescence," emotional reinforcement through shared ritual that strengthens group solidarity and individual resolve. Revolutionary movements in 1848 similarly employed rich symbolism, from flag-raising ceremonies to public tree-planting representing liberty. These symbolic dimensions addressed psychological needs for meaning and solidarity that complemented material grievances.

NO MAN'S LAND: MANAGED VS. DISRUPTIVE CHANGE

Societal change should be gradual, controlled, and managed to prevent chaos and preserve valuable institutions.

Pause. Notice what arises in you.

Deeply entrenched problems sometimes require rapid, disruptive change to overcome powerful resistance to reform.

Pause. Notice what arises in you.

You do not have to agree with or justify either statement. Simply hold them both in your mind and observe what comes up.

The early nineteenth century crystallized this tension between evolutionary and revolutionary approaches to change. Conservative thinkers like Edmund Burke championed gradual development, arguing that societies function as complex organic systems where hasty alterations risk unforeseen damage. "A state without the means of some change," Burke acknowledged, "is without the means of its conservation." Yet he insisted changes should occur through careful evolution, preserving essential continuities while addressing specific problems. This perspective found expression in reform-minded conservatives who recognized industrialization's inevitability but sought to manage its pace and mitigate its human costs.

Revolutionary movements offered a contrasting vision. After decades of suppressed grievances under Metternich's system, 1848 revolutionaries argued that significant transformation required breaking existing power structures. As one Hungarian revolutionary declared: "When those who benefit from injustice control the mechanisms of change, true reform becomes impossible without disruption." This perspective maintained that gradual approaches often preserve underlying injustices while creating illusions of improvement. The revolutionary experience in Paris, Vienna, and Berlin demonstrated how rapid mobilization could achieve reforms in weeks that had been blocked for decades.

Both approaches contained wisdom and limitations. Managed change preserves social fabric, utilizes accumulated experience, and minimizes transitional suffering. The British parliamentary reform process, though painfully slow, eventually expanded suffrage without the traumatic ruptures experienced on the continent. Yet conservative management often preserved fundamental inequalities while making superficial adjustments. Metternich's "stability above all" approach maintained peace between states while suppressing legitimate aspirations within them, creating pressure that eventually erupted more dramatically.

Disruptive change can overcome entrenched resistance and address fundamental problems when incremental approaches fail. The 1848 revolutions, despite their ultimate suppression, achieved lasting gains in peasant emancipation and constitutional development that previous reform efforts had not secured. Yet revolutionary processes frequently unleashed forces their initiators couldn't control, sometimes replacing old problems with new ones, as demonstrated when French workers who helped establish the Second Republic found themselves under fire from that same republic during the June Days.

The craftsmen facing industrialization lived this tension directly. Some advocated destroying machines to halt disruptive change, while others sought accommodation through gradual adaptation. Ultimately, neither approach alone proved sufficient. The Luddites could not prevent mechanization through resistance, yet unmanaged industrial transformation created unnecessary suffering that wiser transitions might have mitigated. The question was not whether change would occur, but how to navigate it while preserving essential human values.

Chapter Nine

When Steam Made Peace with Steel

Oil lamps cast flickering shadows across the crowded back room of the King's Arms tavern in Manchester on a winter evening in 1845. Several dozen men, their hands bearing the calluses and stains of industrial labor, gathered in hushed concentration as William Benson, a graying cotton spinner with thirty years in the mills, called the meeting to order.

"Brothers," Benson began, his voice carrying the weight of experience, "we gather not to break machines or threaten masters, but to build something that may outlast us all." Around him sat not random protesters but elected delegates from cotton mills across Manchester, each wearing a small pin identifying his factory. On the table before them lay account books, membership rolls, and a draft constitution for the newly forming Lancashire Spinners' Association.

"Ten years ago, many of us followed different paths," Benson continued, referencing the machine-breaking and riots that had once seemed the only recourse against industrial transformation. "Today we seek not to destroy the machinery that has come to stay, but to ensure that those who operate it may live in dignity." The meeting proceeded with remarkable order: motions proposed, seconded, debated, and voted upon. Subscription rates were established, benefit schedules for injured or unemployed members determined, and representatives appointed to negotiate with mill owners. These were men adapting to the industrial era not through desperate resistance but through organized engagement, creating institutions that would provide workers voice within the new industrial order rather than futilely opposing it.

Across Europe and beyond, similar adaptations were unfolding, not just among workers forming unions, but throughout societies coming to terms with industrial transformation. Conservative governments that had once responded to change with reflexive repression gradually recognized the need for reform and accommodation. Factory owners who had initially resisted all regulation began discovering that improved conditions could increase productivity and stability. And the machines themselves, once objects of fear and targets of sabotage, became accepted components of a new economic landscape that, despite its harshness, steadily generated unprecedented material prosperity.

This process of adaptation represented neither simple acceptance of industrialization's harsh realities nor continued resistance to technological progress, but something more complex: the gradual construction of new social, political, and economic arrangements that could harness industrial power while mitigating its human costs. Through labor organization, political reform, regulatory legislation, and cultural adaptation, societies found ways to navigate technological transformation without abandoning either progress or human welfare, creating models of adaptive response that would prove valuable across subsequent periods of disruptive change.

The stars that had witnessed the desperate machine-breaking of the Luddites and the revolutionary upheavals of 1848 now looked down upon a different kind of response. From their celestial vantage point, these distant observers might notice how the pendulum swing between resistance and adaptation had produced not a return to the pre-industrial past but a new synthesis, one that accepted technological change while seeking to shape its implementation. This spiral of historical development, neither circular repetition nor linear progress, revealed humanity's capacity to learn from both the desperate resistance and rigid enforcement that had characterized earlier phases of industrialization. As societies found ways to accommodate change without surrendering essential human values, they demonstrated a resilience that would serve future generations facing their own technological revolutions.

By the mid-nineteenth century, the pattern of response to industrialization was shifting decisively from resistance toward adaptation. This transition occurred neither suddenly nor uniformly, but through gradual accommodations across multiple dimensions of social and economic life. The very communities that had once produced machine-breakers increasingly produced machine operators, as new generations grew up with industrial technology as a familiar rather than alien presence in their lives.

The material benefits of industrialization, initially concentrated among factory owners and investors, gradually extended to broader segments of society. While early industrial development had frequently depressed working-class living standards, evidence from the 1840s onward showed steady improvements in real wages. British cotton textile workers, who had faced catastrophic wage declines during the transition to power looms, saw their average weekly earnings rise approximately 20 percent between 1850 and 1870. Similar patterns emerged in other industrial sectors and countries, though with significant variations across regions and occupations. As economist Arnold Toynbee observed, "The characteristic of our age is improvement in the conditions of the working class combined with accumulation of capital."

This material improvement manifested in various aspects of daily life. Working-class diets gradually improved, with increased consumption of meat, dairy products, and previously luxury items like tea and sugar. Housing conditions, though remaining severely inadequate by modern standards, showed incremental improvements in newer industrial developments. Mass production reduced the price of manufactured goods, bringing previously inaccessible items within working-class reach. By the 1860s, items like cotton clothing, metal cookware, and even modest furniture had become standard possessions in working-class households across industrialized regions, representing a significant change from pre-industrial conditions when such goods remained beyond reach for most families.

Technological innovation continued and even accelerated despite early resistance. The machines that had provoked Luddite attacks grew steadily more sophisticated and efficient, while new technologies transformed industries beyond textiles. The Bessemer process for mass-producing steel (patented in 1856) revolutionized metalworking industries. Chemical innovations created synthetic dyes that transformed textile finishing and opened new industrial pathways. Electromagnetic discoveries led to practical generators and motors by the 1870s, laying groundwork for electrical industrialization. These developments represented what historians would later call the "Second Industrial Revolution," a wave of innovation building upon rather than replacing earlier mechanical advances.

Transportation technologies created perhaps the most visible manifestation of industrial acceptance. Railways, initially viewed with suspicion and fear, became objects of civic pride and economic hope. Communities that had once resisted industrialization now campaigned desperately to ensure railway connections, recognizing that economic viability increasingly depended on integration into expanding transportation networks. Britain's railway network grew from 98 miles in 1830 to over 13,500 miles by 1870, physically integrating the nation through industrial technology. Similar expansions occurred across Europe, with France developing over 11,000 miles of track by 1870 and German states constructing nearly 12,000 miles. These networks not only transported goods and people but symbolized integration into the new industrial order.

Labor patterns shifted as the industrial workforce stabilized and developed intergenerational continuity. Unlike early industrial workers who had experienced traumatic transition from craft or agricultural work, second and third generations grew up with factory employment as their expected occupation. "My grandfather broke frames," recalled one Lancashire mill worker in the 1860s, "my father fought for shorter hours, and I operate a power loom without thinking twice about it." This familiarity reduced psychological resistance while creating communities adapted to industrial rhythms and requirements. Factory neighborhoods developed institutions, including churches, schools, pubs, and friendly societies, that accommodated industrial schedules and addressed industrial needs.

Cultural representations reflected this shifting relationship with industrialization. Early industrial literature had often emphasized the alien, monstrous quality of factories and machinery. By mid-century, industrial settings and technologies increasingly appeared as normal backdrops in fiction, poetry, and visual arts. Charles Dickens's novels, while criticizing industrial abuses, nevertheless portrayed industrial settings as familiar social landscapes rather than alien intrusions. Visual artists including J.M.W. Turner incorporated industrial elements like steamships and railways into Romantic landscapes, integrating technology with natural beauty. Popular prints and later photographs presented industrial achievements with pride rather than alarm. These cultural productions both reflected and reinforced growing accommodation with industrial reality.

From the ashes of failed machine-breaking emerged a more enduring response to industrial transformation: organized labor movements that sought to improve workers' conditions within the industrial system rather than opposing industrialization itself. This transition from resistance to organization represented not surrender to industrial realities but strategic adaptation, creating institutions capable of advancing worker interests in an industrial economy that had clearly come to stay.

Early labor organizations developed from preexisting mutual aid traditions. Friendly societies, which provided financial support during illness, unemployment, or funeral expenses, had existed for generations before industrialization. By 1815, over 925,000 British workers belonged to such organizations. As industrialization concentrated workers in factories and undermined traditional craft protections, these mutual aid networks gradually developed more explicitly economic functions, establishing standard wages, regulating working conditions, and creating collective rather than individual relationships with employers. This evolution occurred gradually and often covertly, as legal restrictions initially suppressed explicit labor combinations.

Legal barriers to worker organization gradually diminished, though the process varied across countries. Britain's Combination Acts, which had prohibited worker associations, were repealed in 1824-1825, though significant legal obstacles remained until the Trade Union Act of 1871 provided full recognition. French law prohibited worker combinations until 1864, while German states maintained various restrictions until the 1860s. Despite these legal constraints, workers found numerous ways to organize, often disguising labor associations as friendly societies, educational groups, or cultural organizations to avoid prosecution. These adaptive strategies reflected growing organizational sophistication and determination to create lasting institutions rather than temporary protest movements.

The contrast between earlier resistance and emerging organization appeared clearly in specific movements like British Chartism (1838-1857). Though often remembered primarily as a political movement demanding democratic reforms, Chartism emerged directly from workers' economic grievances and maintained close connections with early labor organizations. Unlike Luddites who had attacked machines, Chartists created sophisticated organizational structures including local branches, regional federations, a national convention, and specialized committees. They collected over three million signatures on their petitions, published newspapers, organized mass meetings, and developed coordinated national strategies. Though ultimately unsuccessful in achieving immediate political reforms, Chartism demonstrated workers' capacity for disciplined, sustained organization rather than spontaneous protest, a capacity that would prove crucial for subsequent labor movements.

The 1834 case of the Tolpuddle Martyrs illustrated both the challenges facing labor organization and growing worker solidarity. When six agricultural laborers from Dorset were sentenced to transportation to Australia for swearing a union oath, widespread protests erupted across Britain. Over 800,000 people signed petitions demanding their pardon, and union organizations collected funds to support the men's families. This response demonstrated an emerging class consciousness that transcended particular trades or localities. Though the government maintained the convictions, public pressure secured pardons by 1836, allowing the men to return home as labor movement heroes. The episode became a foundation story for British unionism, symbolizing both official hostility and the power of organized worker solidarity.

The nature of labor demands evolved alongside organizational structures. Where machine-breakers had sought to preserve pre-industrial production methods, unions increasingly accepted industrialization while demanding improved conditions within it. Standard wage rates, maximum working hours, workplace safety regulations, apprenticeship protections, and unemployment benefits became typical union objectives rather than the elimination of machinery. This shift reflected growing recognition that industrial technology itself was not inherently exploitative; rather, the social relations surrounding its implementation determined whether it enhanced or degraded worker welfare. As one union pamphlet expressed: "We do not oppose the machine, but demand just share in the wealth it creates."

While workers adapted to industrialization through organization from below, political elites developed parallel adaptive strategies from above. Traditional ruling classes, initially inclined toward simple repression of both technological resistance and democratic aspirations, gradually recognized that maintaining authority required more sophisticated approaches. This recognition produced what historians would later call "revolution from above," preemptive reforms designed to address genuine grievances while preserving fundamental power structures. This approach represented conservative adaptation to changing conditions rather than mere reaction against them.

Factory legislation exemplified this reformist conservatism. Britain's Factory Acts, beginning modestly with the 1833 act restricting child labor and expanding through subsequent legislation, came not from radical reformers but from conservative aristocrats including Lord Ashley (later Earl of Shaftesbury). These paternalistic conservatives viewed unregulated industrialization as threatening traditional social order through its disruption of family structures and moral development. The 1833 act prohibited employment of children under nine in textile factories, limited children aged 9-13 to eight-hour workdays, and required factory schooling. Subsequent legislation including the 1844 Factory

Act, 1847 Ten Hours Act, and 1867 extension acts gradually expanded protections to women, additional industries, and smaller workshops.

Implementation mechanisms proved as important as legislation itself. Britain established factory inspectors authorized to enter workplaces, investigate conditions, and prosecute violations. Though initially limited in number and authority, these inspectors created unprecedented state involvement in previously private employment relationships. Their detailed reports provided empirical foundation for subsequent reforms while establishing expectation of public accountability for industrial conditions. This administrative apparatus represented significant expansion of state capacity, developed not through revolutionary rupture but through pragmatic conservative reform addressing specific problems rather than comprehensive ideological programs.

Conservative reformism found its most sophisticated practitioner in Otto von Bismarck, who engineered German unification under Prussian leadership while implementing social reforms that mitigated industrialization's harshest effects. After establishing the German Empire in 1871, Bismarck initiated ambitious social insurance programs including health insurance (1883), accident insurance (1884), and old-age pensions (1889), creating the world's first national social security system. Yet these reforms accompanied repressive measures against political opponents, particularly the Anti-Socialist Laws targeting the Social Democratic Party. Bismarck explicitly framed social welfare as alternative to revolution, declaring, "Whoever has a pension for his old age is far more content and far easier to handle than one who has no such prospect."

Electoral reforms similarly reflected conservative adaptation rather than democratic conviction. Britain's Reform Act of 1867, though doubling the electorate by extending voting rights to urban working-class householders, passed under Conservative government led by Benjamin Disraeli. This apparent paradox reflected strategic calculation that controlled democratization could strengthen rather than undermine traditional authority by incorporating new social forces within existing institutions. Disraeli's colleague Lord Derby aptly described the reform as "a leap in the dark," but one calculated to channel democratic pressures through established parliamentary structures rather than revolutionary upheaval. Similar conservative-led electoral reforms occurred across Europe, typically extending suffrage incrementally while maintaining property qualifications, plural voting for propertied classes, or undemocratic upper houses.

The mid-nineteenth century witnessed transformation not only in economic and social organization but in the fundamental structure of political authority. Traditional political forms, including dynastic empires, city-states, and loosely integrated kingdoms, increasingly gave way to nation-states defined by territorial boundaries, centralized administration, and claimed connection between state institutions and national identity. This emergent nation-state model represented adaptation to industrial conditions rather than mere continuation of previous political evolution, as industrial development required levels of standardization, integration, and administration that older political forms struggled to provide.

German unification exemplified this nation-state development, transforming dozens of separate German-speaking territories into a unified federal empire. The process combined economic integration through the Zollverein (customs union) established in 1834, military power through Prussia's modernized army, and nationalist sentiment cultivated through educational and cultural institutions. Otto von Bismarck, appointed Prussian Minister-President in 1862, orchestrated this unification through three carefully managed wars, against Denmark (1864), Austria (1866), and France (1870-1871). These conflicts enabled Bismarck to unite German territories under Prussian leadership while managing the process to maintain monarchical authority rather than implementing the democratic nationalism advocated during the failed 1848 revolutions.

The resulting German Empire, proclaimed in 1871, exemplified modern nation-state characteristics while preserving traditional authority. Its federal structure balanced national integration with regional autonomy. Its constitution combined democratic elements including universal male suffrage for the Reichstag (parliament) with authoritarian features including ministerial responsibility to the emperor rather than parliament. Its administrative apparatus featured professional civil service, standardized legal codes, and centralized statistical gathering. Its educational system combined technical training with nationalist curriculum. Most crucially, it integrated industrial development with state power, using economic strength to support military capability while employing military prestige to reinforce political legitimacy.

Italian unification paralleled German developments, though with distinctive features reflecting different conditions. The Risorgimento (resurgence) movement transformed the Italian peninsula from collection of separate states, many under foreign control, into unified kingdom. Unlike Germany's Prussian-led unification, Italy's process combined Piedmont-Sardinia's state power under Count Camillo Benso di Cavour with Giuseppe Garibaldi's revolutionary nationalist movement. Cavour employed diplomatic maneuvering, alliance with France, and strategic military engagements to secure northern territories, while Garibaldi's 1860 expedition conquered southern regions with volunteer forces. The Kingdom of Italy's 1861 proclamation (completed with Rome's incorporation in 1870) created another modern nation-state, though one suffering significant regional disparities between industrializing north and predominantly agricultural south.

Nation-state development featured certain common institutional characteristics across different national contexts. Standardized national languages received official promotion through education systems, publishing policies, and administrative requirements, often marginalizing regional dialects and minority languages. Legal codes underwent rationalization and national standardization, replacing local customary law and jurisdictional complexity. Taxation systems became more comprehensive and centralized, funding expanded state functions. Citizenship definitions clarified national membership, distinguishing citizens from foreigners through official documentation. Military service became nationalized through conscription systems that simultaneously provided defense capabilities and socialized young men into national identity.

Alongside industrial adaptation and nation-state formation, the mid-nineteenth century witnessed significant expansions of democratic participation, though with important limitations that maintained distance between theoretical democratic principles and practical political power. This period saw transition from governance systems based primarily on hereditary privilege, property ownership, and traditional authority toward systems incorporating broader popular participation through representative institutions, expanded suffrage, and civil liberties protections. However, this democratization remained partial and constrained, as traditional elites developed strategies to maintain influence within nominally democratic structures.

Britain's Reform Acts illustrated this gradual, controlled democratization. The 1832 Reform Act, though modest by later standards, marked significant departure from previous arrangements by eliminating "rotten boroughs" (constituencies with tiny electorates controlled by landowners), redistributing parliamentary seats to reflect population, and modestly expanding franchise to middle-class property owners. The electorate increased from approximately 366,000 to 650,000, still representing less than 7% of the total population but significantly broadening representation beyond landed aristocracy. Subsequent Reform Acts in 1867 and 1884 progressively expanded the franchise, with the 1867 act enfranchising urban working-class householders and the 1884 act extending similar provisions to rural areas. By 1885, approximately 60% of adult males could vote, a dramatic expansion from 1832 though still excluding substantial populations including all women.

Continental democratization followed more volatile trajectories, often featuring dramatic expansions followed by retractions or limitations. France established universal male suffrage following the 1848 revolution, creating the world's most democratic major state at that moment. However, Louis Napoleon's 1851 coup transformed the Second Republic into the Second Empire, maintaining universal male suffrage but within semi-authoritarian framework emphasizing plebiscitary approval rather than parliamentary governance. The Third Republic established after 1870 created more stable democratic institutions, though influential Senate, administrative centralization, and military autonomy limited democratic control. German unification paradoxically combined universal male suffrage for the Reichstag with constitutional provisions ensuring elite control over key government functions.

Women's exclusion from formal political participation represented the most significant limitation on nineteenth-century democratization. Despite women's active participation in various reform movements and growing educational access, virtually no nineteenth-century state granted women voting rights before the century's end (with limited exceptions like some western American territories). Early women's suffrage movements emerged in both Britain and the United States during the 1860s, but faced opposition from conservatives defending traditional gender roles and even from male reformers who prioritized other democratic advances. This exclusion from formal political participation limited democracy's practical scope while establishing precedent for other categorical exclusions based on identity rather than civic capacity.

If we could view this historical period from among the stars, we might perceive a fascinating pattern in humanity's response to technological disruption. The initial resistance to industrialization had given way not to passive acceptance but to active adaptation, creating new institutions, adjusting political structures, and developing cultural frameworks that could accommodate technological change without surrendering essential human values. This adaptive process revealed the spiral pattern of history, where societies do not simply repeat past experiences or progress in straight lines, but integrate elements of continuity and change as they navigate new challenges. From the desperate machine-breaking of the Luddites to the organized labor movements, from reactionary repression to conservative reform, from fragmented territories to integrated nation-states, this cycle of industrial adaptation demonstrated humanity's capacity to learn from both resistance and acceptance, finding a middle path that would guide future responses to technological transformation.

The mid-nineteenth century transition from resistance to adaptation offers valuable insights into managing significant technological and social transformation. Neither unthinking acceptance nor reflexive rejection proved sustainable; instead, societies developed adaptive strategies that acknowledged irreversible change while shaping its implementation to preserve human welfare. These adaptations occurred across multiple domains, economic, political, social, and cultural, and involved various actors from elite reformers to worker organizations. Their collective experience suggests broader patterns applicable beyond their specific historical context.

Pace emerged as crucial variable in managing disruptive change. Rapid, unmanaged transformation generated severe dislocation and resistance, while gradual, phased implementation allowed adaptation of social systems and individual expectations. Britain's transition to industrialization, while traumatic even at its measured pace, generated less violent resistance than might have occurred with even faster implementation. Similarly, political reforms introduced gradually through Britain's Reform Acts produced more stable outcomes than France's oscillation between revolutionary expansion and authoritarian contraction. As economist Karl Polanyi would later observe, "The rate of change is often of no less importance than the direction of the change itself." Successful management of transformation required attention not just to ultimate objectives but to transitional processes and their human impact.

Institutional channels for expressing grievances proved critical for constructive adaptation. When legitimate mechanisms existed for addressing concerns, affected populations typically pursued reform through these channels rather than resorting to destructive resistance. Labor movements' evolution from machine-breaking to union organization exemplified this pattern, as workers developed institutional structures for collective bargaining when legal restrictions diminished. Similarly, political reforms establishing representative institutions directed potential revolutionary energy toward electoral competition rather than insurrection. These institutional channels did not eliminate conflict but transformed its expression from destructive confrontation to structured negotiation within established parameters.

Distributional considerations significantly influenced adaptive outcomes. Where industrial benefits remained narrowly concentrated among entrepreneurs and investors while costs fell disproportionately on workers and communities, resistance proved more intense and sustained. Conversely, when productivity gains translated into broadly improved living standards through wage increases, price reductions, and expanded consumption opportunities, acceptance grew more rapidly. This pattern appeared clearly in the contrast between early industrialization's harshness and later industrialization's broader prosperity. As economist Arnold Toynbee noted, "It is not so much the growth of the factory system as the delay in the adaptation of society to it that causes the suffering." Successful adaptation required attention to distributional outcomes alongside aggregate economic gains.

Leadership approaches substantially influenced adaptive success. Reformist conservative leaders like Disraeli and Bismarck achieved greater stability than rigid reactionaries through strategic concessions addressing genuine grievances while preserving fundamental authority structures. Similarly, pragmatic labor leaders focused on achievable improvements rather than comprehensive transformation typically secured more concrete benefits than revolutionary purists. These effective leaders demonstrated capacity to distinguish between essential principles requiring steadfast defense and secondary matters allowing flexibility and compromise. Their adaptive leadership navigated between dogmatic rigidity that rejected necessary change and unprincipled opportunism that abandoned core values amid changing circumstances.

Cultural integration of technological change influenced its acceptance and implementation. Industrial innovations initially appeared as alien intrusions into traditional lifeways, generating psychological resistance beyond specific economic impacts. As industrial elements became incorporated into cultural expression, education, and identity formation, their alienating quality diminished. The contrast between early industrial literature emphasizing machinery's monstrous aspects and later works treating industrial settings as normal backgrounds illustrated this cultural integration process. Similarly, as national education systems incorporated industrial knowledge and values, new generations grew up with industrialization as familiar rather than foreign element in their worldview. This cultural dimension of adaptation highlighted the importance of meaning and identity alongside material considerations in managing significant change.

These historical insights remain relevant for managing subsequent technological transitions. The pattern of initial resistance yielding to adaptive engagement has recurred through various technological waves, from electrification and automobile adoption to computerization and digital transformation. In each case, successful adaptation has required attention to implementation pace, institutional channels, distributional outcomes, leadership approaches, cultural integration, pragmatic experimentation, continuity balancing change, and multidimensional responses. The mid-nineteenth century experience thus offers enduring lessons about human societies' capacity to navigate disruptive change through adaptive strategies that neither reject innovation nor accept its unmanaged implementation.

NO MAN'S LAND: ELITE GOVERNANCE VS. POPULAR SOVEREIGNTY

Effective governance requires expertise, stability, and long-term thinking best provided by educated elites.

Pause. Notice what arises in you.

Legitimate political authority comes from the consent of ordinary citizens who should directly shape their governance.

Pause. Notice what arises in you.

You do not have to agree with or justify either statement. Simply hold them both in your mind and observe what comes up.

The mid-nineteenth century witnessed this tension playing out across industrializing societies. Conservative leaders like Metternich argued that social complexity required elite governance: "The great mass of people requires guidance; like children who must have guardianship if they are not to suffer harm." From this perspective, effective governance required specialized knowledge, historical awareness, and strategic thinking that came only through elite education and experience. Democracies risked impulsive decision-making, short-term thinking, and susceptibility to demagogues.

Yet democratic reformers countered that governance without popular consent lacked both legitimacy and necessary information. "The humblest citizen's experience contains wisdom no minister can access from his office," argued British Chartist leader Feargus O'Connor. Democratic participation provided not just moral authority but practical knowledge about conditions requiring government attention. Without this input, even well-intentioned elites would make decisions based on abstract principles rather than lived reality.

The most successful political systems of this period neither fully embraced nor completely rejected either principle. Britain's gradual democratization maintained significant elite influence through the House of Lords, educational advantages, and social networks while expanding popular participation through electoral reform. Bismarck's Germany combined universal male suffrage with constitutional provisions ensuring elite control over key government functions. These hybrid systems acknowledged legitimate insights from both perspectives, recognizing both expertise's value and consent's necessity.

This tension reflects deeper questions about governance that transcend specific historical contexts. Elite governance typically provides continuity, expert administration, and protection against momentary popular passions. Popular sovereignty offers legitimacy, accountability, and broader perspective incorporating ordinary citizens' experiences. Both contain wisdom; both present challenges. The most sustainable political arrangements have typically found ways to incorporate elements of both approaches, creating systems that neither sacrifice expertise to populism nor subordinate popular consent to elite domination.

The contrast is not merely academic. Different societies have made different choices about this balance, with significant consequences for their development. Understanding both perspectives helps us recognize that neither pure technocracy nor unfiltered majority rule provides complete solution to governance challenges. The tension between expert guidance and popular control represents not a problem to solve but a balance to maintain, a continuous conversation rather than a final resolution.

Cycle 4: When Darwin Met Prejudice

Chapter Ten

When Blood Told Stories

The children fell silent as Dr. Francis Galton addressed the audience at London's 1884 International Health Exhibition. An imposing figure with piercing eyes beneath bushy eyebrows, the distinguished scientist gestured toward an array of instruments and charts dominating the central display.

"Ladies and gentlemen," he announced with measured authority, "I present to you the Anthropometric Laboratory, where we shall precisely measure the physical and mental qualities of our citizens." Visitors watched with fascination as volunteer subjects had their heads measured with calipers, reaction times tested with electric instruments, and visual acuity quantified through standardized tests. Attendants in crisp white coats meticulously recorded each measurement on standardized forms, building what Galton proudly described as "a scientific catalog of human variation."

Galton, a cousin of Charles Darwin and respected polymath in Victorian scientific circles, explained to the gathered crowd how these measurements would advance his new science of "eugenics," a term he had coined just a year earlier. "Just as we have improved cattle and roses through selective breeding," he explained, "we may improve the human race by encouraging reproduction among those with superior qualities and discouraging it among the unfit."

What made this moment extraordinary was not the technical apparatus or the boldness of Galton's ambition, but how unremarkable most visitors found his proposal. By 1884, the application of scientific principles to human populations seemed not only reasonable but necessary to many educated Victorians. In an era of rapid industrialization, urbanization, and immigration, the idea that science might manage human development as efficiently as it had transformed industry appeared a natural progression. As one newspaper account described the exhibition: "Dr. Galton's laboratory offers the promise that human improvement may be achieved with the same precision that has revolutionized our factories and railways."

Over the nine months of the exhibition, more than 9,000 visitors paid the small fee to be measured in Galton's laboratory, each receiving a card with their personal metrics compared to population averages. Many left with a sense of having participated in scientific progress, few with any premonition of where such thinking might ultimately lead.

This scene captured a pivotal moment in the late nineteenth century when scientific authority, technological confidence, and social anxiety converged. The industrial transformations that had reshaped economic life now extended to human biology and society itself. A generation that had witnessed steam power replace muscle, electric lights banish darkness, and telegraph signals collapse distance placed extraordinary faith in technical solutions to social problems. Against a backdrop of unprecedented urban growth, massive immigration, and growing class consciousness, elites and reformers alike sought scientific approaches to manage a society changing more rapidly than at any previous time in human history.

Yet this moment also contained deep tensions. The same tools being developed to improve human welfare could easily serve to reinforce existing hierarchies and prejudices. The emerging sciences of human difference might be used either to understand humanity's common needs or to justify discrimination. The new mass communication technologies could inform public debate or manipulate public opinion. As societies navigated the transition from industrial to scientific modernity, they faced choices about how to apply new capabilities, choices that would ultimately determine whether scientific advancement would enhance human dignity or subordinate it to supposed biological imperatives.

The stars that had witnessed the adaptation to industrial change now looked down upon a world being transformed by new forces. From their celestial vantage point, these silent observers might have noticed how the pendulum of human affairs continued its perpetual swing, this time between traditional social structures and the disruptive power of scientific authority, between homogeneous communities and the diversity created by mass migration, between understanding humans as spiritual beings and reducing them to measurable biological specimens. The spiral of history continued its turn, not returning to exactly the same position but revisiting familiar tensions between stability and change, tradition and innovation, unity and diversity. This new cycle would test humanity's capacity to harness scientific advancement for genuine progress while avoiding the temptation to use new knowledge as justification for age-old prejudices.

The evening newspaper seller at the corner of Broadway and Fulton Street in New York City stared up at the looming structure before him. The New York World Building, completed in 1890, rose an unprecedented 309 feet into the Manhattan skyline, briefly the tallest building in the city. This architectural marvel housed not government offices or a financial institution, but a newspaper. The imposing dome crowning the structure made its purpose unmistakable: in the new industrial era, the production and distribution of information had become a power rivaling government and industry.

Inside this journalistic fortress, publisher Joseph Pulitzer had assembled the most sophisticated news-gathering operation in American history. Telegraph wires transmitted dispatches from correspondents across the globe. The basement housed massive printing presses capable of producing 48,000 complete newspapers per hour. By 1890, the World's circulation exceeded 250,000 copies daily and approached 500,000 on Sundays, reaching more New Yorkers than any other publication in the city's history. Pulitzer's competitor William Randolph Hearst built a similar empire around the New York Journal, while Alfred Harmsworth (later Lord Northcliffe) transformed British journalism with the

Daily Mail, which reached one million circulation by 1900. These publishing titans created the world's first true mass media, communications channels reaching unprecedented audiences with unprecedented speed.

The technological foundations for this media revolution had been building throughout the nineteenth century. Steam-powered printing presses replaced hand-operated equipment, dramatically increasing production speed and reducing costs. The invention of the linotype machine in 1884 revolutionized typesetting, allowing operators to cast entire lines of type simultaneously rather than placing individual letters. Wood pulp paper, significantly cheaper than traditional rag-based paper, reduced material costs. Telegraph networks transmitted news almost instantly across continents and undersea cables connected continents. These technical innovations transformed newspapers from expensive products for elite audiences into affordable commodities for mass consumption.

Concurrent social changes expanded potential readership. Rising literacy rates meant larger portions of the population could consume written content. In Britain, the Education Act of 1870 established universal elementary education, while similar efforts across industrialized nations dramatically increased literacy rates. By 1900, literacy exceeded 90 percent in most industrialized regions, creating an unprecedented market for printed materials. Urbanization concentrated potential readers in dense settlements where distribution costs remained minimal. Growing middle and working classes with modest disposable income and limited leisure time found newspapers an affordable and convenient information source.

The economic model supporting mass media fundamentally changed during this period. Traditional newspapers had derived primary revenue from high subscription prices and political subsidies. New mass-circulation papers dramatically reduced cover prices, some to as little as one cent, making them affordable to working-class readers. Instead of reader payments, these publications increasingly relied on advertising revenue. This shift created what media historians call the "advertising-circulation spiral": lower prices increased circulation, which attracted more advertising, which funded further price reductions and content improvements, driving circulation still higher. By 1900, advertising typically provided more than two-thirds of newspaper revenue, transforming readers from customers into products delivered to advertisers.

Content evolved to attract the largest possible audience rather than serving particular political constituencies. Human interest stories, sensational crime coverage, sports, entertainment features, and visual elements including political cartoons, illustrations, and eventually photographs gained prominence alongside traditional political reporting. The resulting mix appealed across class boundaries while demanding less specialized knowledge than earlier political journals. As British press historian Alan Lee observed, "The new journalism assumed an audience with limited attention span and minimal prior knowledge, but unlimited appetite for diversion." The resulting products simultaneously democratized information access while often simplifying complex issues into entertaining narratives.

On May 15, 1911, the United States Supreme Court ordered the dissolution of Standard Oil, ruling that John D. Rockefeller's petroleum empire had illegally monopolized the industry through predatory practices. The court's decision forced the breakup of what had been the world's largest and most powerful corporation into 34 separate companies, including what would later become Exxon, Mobil, and Chevron. This landmark ruling represented the culmination of decades of struggle between industrial consolidation and attempts to maintain competitive markets. Yet even as Standard Oil fragmented, its component parts remained industrial giants, and the economic transformation it represented continued reshaping societies across the industrialized world.

The late nineteenth century witnessed unparalleled economic concentration, with individual corporations achieving scale and market dominance previously unimaginable. By 1890, Standard Oil controlled approximately 88 percent of American petroleum refining and distribution. Andrew Carnegie's steel operations, later incorporated into U.S. Steel, produced more steel than all British manufacturers combined. Similar concentration occurred across industries and nations: Germany's chemical industry consolidated into powerful cartels, while Britain's "railway interest" and banking houses exerted enormous economic influence. For the first time in human history, private corporations commanded resources rivaling those of governments, employing hundreds of thousands of workers and controlling crucial economic sectors across national boundaries.

This concentration emerged from multiple sources, beginning with technological economies of scale. Industries including steel, chemicals, petroleum refining, and electrical generation required massive capital investments in specialized equipment. Larger operations achieved lower per-unit costs that allowed them to undercut smaller competitors or survive price wars that bankrupted less-capitalized firms. As economist Alfred Chandler later described it, these industries experienced a "managerial revolution" where complex production processes required sophisticated organizational hierarchies managing specialized departments within integrated enterprises. The resulting efficiency advantages allowed larger firms to outcompete smaller rivals through legitimate productivity advantages rather than through predatory practices alone.

This economic concentration generated extraordinary personal wealth among industrialists and financiers, creating economic inequality that rivaled or exceeded any previous period. By the 1890s, the richest one percent of Americans owned more wealth than the bottom 99 percent combined, with similar patterns across industrialized nations. These disparities manifested visibly in the contrast between opulent mansions along New York's Fifth Avenue or London's Belgravia and the crowded tenements where industrial workers lived. The very landscape of industrial cities physically embodied the unequal distribution of industrialization's benefits, creating stark daily reminders of economic hierarchy.

Corporate political influence expanded alongside economic power, creating what critics viewed as a dangerous fusion of private and public authority. Campaign contributions, legislative lobbying, and outright bribery gave corporations unprecedented influence over government decisions. Railroad companies received enormous land grants and subsidies from governments while influencing regulatory decisions through strategic donations. Mining companies secured favorable access to public resources while resisting safety regulations. Tariff policies reflected manufacturing interests rather than broader public welfare.

This corporate political influence appeared most vividly in Joseph Keppler's 1889 Puck cartoon "The Bosses of the Senate," depicting enormous money bags with corporate labels looming over diminutive senators, wordlessly conveying the perception that elected officials served corporate rather than public interests.

On the morning of August 31, 1888, a London policeman made a gruesome discovery in Whitechapel's Buck's Row. The mutilated body of Mary Ann Nichols, a 43-year-old impoverished woman, marked the first confirmed victim in what would become the infamous "Jack the Ripper" murders. Over the next ten weeks, four more women would be killed with increasing brutality, creating unprecedented public fear and media sensation. The unknown killer's identity spawned endless speculation, with suspects ranging from doctors and aristocrats to butchers and tailors. Among the most persistent rumors, though lacking any substantive evidence, blamed a Jewish immigrant or foreign visitor, reflecting deeper unease about changing urban demographics in Victorian London.

The East End where these murders occurred exemplified the rapid urbanization transforming industrial societies. Between 1800 and 1900, London's population grew from approximately one million to 6.5 million, creating the world's largest urban concentration. Similar though less extreme growth occurred across industrialized regions: New York expanded from 60,000 to 3.4 million inhabitants, Berlin from 172,000 to 1.9 million, and Paris from 547,000 to 2.7 million. This unprecedented urbanization transformed not just population statistics but the fundamental character of human settlement, creating environments unlike anything in previous history.

Immigration contributed significantly to this urban transformation, with millions crossing national boundaries while millions more migrated internally from rural to urban areas. Between 1880 and 1914, approximately 25 million Europeans emigrated to the United States alone, while others settled in Canada, Australia, Argentina, and Brazil. Within Europe, industrial regions attracted migrants from rural areas and less developed regions: Poles and Italians migrated to German industrial centers, Irish moved to British cities, and rural French relocated to Paris and Lyon. This population movement created extraordinarily diverse urban environments where different languages, religions, and customs coexisted in close proximity, often for the first time.

Housing conditions in rapidly expanding cities created visible manifestations of social problems. Jacob Riis's pioneering photojournalism in "How the Other Half Lives" (1890) documented New York tenements where multiple families shared single rooms without adequate ventilation, sanitation, or light. Charles Booth's monumental "Life and Labour of the People in London" (1889-1903) mapped poverty street by street, revealing systematic patterns of deprivation in specific neighborhoods. Similar conditions existed across industrial cities, with housing construction and infrastructure development consistently lagging behind population growth. These visible conditions of urban poverty provided concrete evidence of industrialization's uneven benefits while creating environments where disease, crime, and social problems flourished.

Public health concerns became central to urban worries as medical knowledge connected disease outbreaks to specific environmental conditions. Cholera epidemics struck industrial cities repeatedly throughout the nineteenth century, with London's 1866 outbreak claiming over 5,000 lives despite previous sanitary reforms. Tuberculosis spread rapidly in overcrowded housing, becoming the leading cause of death in many urban centers. Infant mortality in poor urban districts often exceeded 200 deaths per 1,000 live births, rates comparable to the poorest countries today. These health outcomes created growing recognition that unregulated urbanization threatened not just aesthetic or moral conditions but physical survival, providing impetus for public health interventions including water purification, sewage systems, and housing regulations.

In 1859, Charles Darwin published "On the Origin of Species," introducing natural selection as the mechanism driving biological evolution through adaptation to environmental conditions. This groundbreaking scientific work transformed understanding of biological diversity while unintentionally providing a conceptual framework later applied to human societies in ways Darwin himself never advocated. By century's end, "social Darwinism" had emerged as an influential interpretive framework justifying inequality, imperialism, and hierarchy as natural outcomes of evolutionary processes rather than human-created arrangements requiring moral evaluation.

The misapplication of evolutionary concepts to human affairs emerged not from Darwin's own work but through adaptations by subsequent thinkers, most influentially Herbert Spencer. Before Darwin's publication, Spencer had already coined the phrase "survival of the fittest" to describe human social competition, later incorporating Darwinian concepts into his comprehensive philosophical system. Spencer argued that societies evolved through competition that selected superior individuals, classes, and races while eliminating inferior elements, a process producing social improvement that should proceed without interference. This framework transformed Darwin's descriptive theory of biological adaptation into a prescriptive social philosophy celebrating unrestricted competition as evolutionary necessity.

Francis Galton, Darwin's cousin, extended evolutionary thinking to human reproduction through his concept of "eugenics" (from Greek for "well-born"), first named in his 1883 "Inquiries into Human Faculty and Its Development." Galton argued that human populations could be improved through selective breeding, encouraging reproduction among those with "desirable" traits while discouraging or preventing reproduction among those deemed "unfit." This approach conceptualized human genetic variation as an engineering problem potentially manageable through scientific intervention, treating human reproductive decisions as matters for social policy rather than individual choice. Galton established eugenics as an academic discipline through research, publications, and institutional development including the Eugenics Education Society (1907), creating a scientific framework for subsequent policies including sterilization programs and marriage restrictions.

Anthropometric measurement, the precise quantification of human physical characteristics, provided empirical methodology supporting racialized evolutionary theories. Physical anthropologists including Paul Broca in France developed standardized measurement techniques for skull dimensions, facial angles, and body proportions, creating data sets purporting to demonstrate racial hierarchies through quantitative comparison. Galton's Anthropometric

Laboratory at the 1884 International Health Exhibition collected thousands of measurements from visitors, establishing statistical distributions for various physical and mental characteristics. These measurement practices created a scientific veneer for racial classifications that generally confirmed existing social hierarchies, with European measurements conveniently appearing closest to proposed ideal proportions while colonized populations appeared more distant from these standards.

On May 4, 1886, what began as a peaceful labor rally in Chicago's Haymarket Square ended in tragedy when an unidentified person threw a bomb at police officers attempting to disperse the gathering. The explosion and subsequent gunfire killed seven police officers and at least four civilians, while injuring dozens more. Though the bomb-thrower was never conclusively identified, authorities arrested eight anarchist labor organizers who had spoken at or organized the rally. Despite little evidence connecting them directly to the bombing, all eight were convicted in a highly prejudicial trial, with seven receiving death sentences. Four were executed by hanging on November 11, 1887, one committed suicide in prison, and the remaining three eventually received pardons in 1893 after significant public pressure.

The Haymarket affair exemplified growing class conflict in industrial societies and subsequent conservative reaction against worker organization. The rally itself had been organized to protest police killing of workers during a strike at the McCormick Harvesting Machine Company the previous day. These events occurred amid nationwide mobilization for an eight-hour workday, with approximately 350,000 American workers participating in strikes and demonstrations around May 1, 1886. Similar labor activism emerged across industrialized nations as workers developed increasingly sophisticated organizations addressing industrial capitalism's economic imbalances and harsh working conditions.

Trade union development accelerated during this period, creating permanent institutions representing workers within industrial economies. In Britain, union membership grew from approximately 750,000 in 1888 to over 4 million by 1914. American union membership similarly expanded, particularly after formation of the American Federation of Labor in 1886, which organized skilled workers across multiple trades. German union federations including the Free Trade Unions (socialist-affiliated) and Christian Trade Unions (Catholic-affiliated) created parallel organizational structures representing different worker constituencies. These organizations moved beyond earlier mutual aid societies and temporary protest movements to establish permanent representation structures negotiating with employers and governments over wages, working conditions, and labor policies.

On May 6, 1912, Helen Drummond glanced nervously at fellow suffragette Jennie Baines as they entered Jones & Higgins department store in South London. Each woman carried a hammer concealed within her coat. Moving purposefully toward separate display windows, they simultaneously revealed their tools and shattered the glass. As store employees rushed toward them, the women made no attempt to escape but instead distributed leaflets declaring: "Votes for Women. We break windows, they break promises."

This act of calculated property destruction represented escalation in the British women's decades-long campaign for voting rights. The Women's Social and Political Union (WSPU), founded by Emmeline Pankhurst in 1903, had adopted increasingly militant tactics after years of peaceful campaigning produced minimal progress. Window-breaking, hunger strikes, and public demonstrations generated unprecedented publicity for women's suffrage while provoking harsh government response including imprisonment, forced feeding, and police violence. These dramatic confrontations represented only the most visible aspect of broader movements expanding voting rights across gender, class, and racial boundaries, movements consistently opposed by conservative forces viewing unrestricted democracy as a threat to traditional social hierarchies and property interests.

The women's suffrage movement developed international scope while adapting to specific national contexts. New Zealand became the first self-governing country to grant women voting rights in 1893, followed by Australia (1902), Finland (1906), and Norway (1913). In the United States, western territories and states including Wyoming (1869), Utah (1870), Colorado (1893), and Idaho (1896) granted women suffrage decades before the federal Nineteenth Amendment (1920). These geographic variations reflected different political cultures and strategic decisions rather than fundamental differences in arguments for women's political participation. As Finnish feminist Alexandra Gripenberg observed at the 1888 International Council of Women, "Though our languages may differ, we speak the same words when asking for justice."

If we could observe these tumultuous changes from the celestial perspective of the stars, we might notice how scientific advancement, economic transformation, mass migration, and political movements converged to create an era of unprecedented social change. The comforting certainties of traditional society, fixed social hierarchies, homogeneous communities, stable economic relationships, and unquestioned moral codes, faced unprecedented challenges from multiple directions simultaneously. People experienced these changes not as separate developments but as interconnected aspects of a world transforming faster than at any previous period in human history.

Yet from this higher vantage point, we might also recognize patterns connecting this period to earlier cycles of human response to disruptive change. Just as the Luddites had responded to industrialization with a mixture of fear and resistance before societies gradually adapted, now a new generation faced scientific and demographic transformations with similar anxieties and eventual accommodations. The spiral of history was turning again, not in exact repetition but in recognizable patterns of challenge, resistance, adaptation, and eventual integration of changes that once seemed impossibly threatening. This perspective might remind us that societies can adapt to even the most profound transformations without abandoning what is most valuable in their traditions, though the path is rarely smooth or painless.

NO MAN'S LAND: CULTURAL PRESERVATION VS. INCLUSIVE DIVERSITY

Society requires cultural continuity and shared traditions to maintain cohesion, identity, and meaning across generations.

Pause. Notice what arises in you.

Human flourishing demands openness to different perspectives, inclusive communities, and cultural evolution through diverse influences.

Pause. Notice what arises in you.

You do not have to agree with or justify either statement. Simply hold them both in your mind and observe what comes up.

The late nineteenth century immigration debates crystallized this tension in particularly stark form. Henry Cabot Lodge, advocating immigration restriction, argued: "That the prosperity and welfare of American society must depend upon preserving its essential character seems too plain for argument." From this perspective, rapid demographic change threatened social cohesion, cultural traditions, and functional community requiring shared values and mutual understanding. Economic modernization already placed tremendous stress on social bonds; adding linguistic, religious, and cultural diversity potentially exceeded society's integrative capacity.

Yet immigration advocates like Jane Addams countered from her experience in Chicago's settlement houses: "The wonderful impressions which the immigrants received, the power to see life with fresh eyes, ought to be permanently treasured as a national asset." This viewpoint recognized diversity's generative potential, bringing new perspectives, skills, and cultural resources that could enrich rather than threaten host societies. From this stance, cultural evolution through diverse influences represented not degeneration but revitalization, preventing stagnation through continuous creative exchange.

Industrial societies navigated this tension through various approaches. American public schools simultaneously taught English and civic values to immigrant children while gradually incorporating cultural contributions from various immigrant groups into evolving national identity. European nations developed different models ranging from assimilation expectations to limited cultural pluralism within national frameworks. These approaches represented neither pure preservation of unchanging tradition nor unrestricted cultural relativism, but continuous negotiation between continuity and change.

This tension transcends specific historical contexts, representing fundamental human need for both stability and growth, belonging and exploration. Cultural preservation provides essential continuity, shared reference points, and collective identity that prevent social atomization. Cultural openness enables adaptation to changing conditions, creativity through cross-fertilization, and moral growth by engaging different perspectives. Both values contain wisdom; both contain potential pitfalls when pursued exclusively. The healthiest societies have typically found ways to maintain core cultural continuity while remaining open to diverse influences, preserving fundamental traditions while allowing their continuous reinterpretation and enrichment through engagement with difference.

Chapter Eleven

When Purity Became Policy

Under the blazing Kansas sun at the 1924 State Fair in Topeka, a curious crowd gathered around the "Eugenics Building," where large banners proclaimed: "Fitter Families for Future Firesides." Inside the white wooden structure, middle-class families sat in neat rows, awaiting their turns for examination. Children fidgeted in Sunday best while parents completed detailed questionnaires about their family histories going back three generations. Medical doctors in white coats measured head circumferences, tested reflexes, and recorded physiological data on standardized forms. A "psychometrist" administered intelligence tests in a separate booth, while staff meticulously documented physical characteristics from eye color to finger length.

"The Washburn family scores exceptionally well in all categories," announced the lead examiner, a respected physician from the University of Kansas. "Three generations free from hereditary defects, above-average intelligence scores, and excellent physical development." The Washburns, father, mother, and three fair-haired children, beamed as they received their medal inscribed with the biblical phrase: "Yea, I have a goodly heritage." The crowd applauded appreciatively as a photographer captured the moment for the Topeka Daily Capital.

Nearby, a flashing electric sign caught fairgoers' attention with its grim calculation: "Every 48 seconds a person is born in the United States who will never grow up mentally beyond the age of eight." Next to this display, colorful charts showed the supposed reproductive rates of the "fit" versus the "unfit," while carefully constructed family pedigrees purported to demonstrate how traits like "feeblemindedness," criminality, and "pauperism" passed through bloodlines. A separate exhibit displayed bottles containing preserved human brains, labeled to indicate various forms of "degeneracy."

"This is more than a competition," explained Dr. Florence Brown Sherbon to curious onlookers. "This is science applying the lessons of heredity to human betterment. Just as we've improved livestock through selective breeding, we must encourage reproduction among our finest human specimens while preventing multiplication of the unfit." Sherbon had pioneered these contests with fellow eugenicist Mary Watts at an Iowa fair in 1920, and by 1924, they had become popular attractions at state fairs across America's heartland.

The contest's respectability was underscored by its sponsors, the American Eugenics Society and the Race Betterment Foundation, and by endorsements from prominent scientists, physicians, and public officials. What made the scene remarkable was not its eccentricity but its normalcy: eugenics had entered the American mainstream, transforming ancient prejudices into modern science and traditional fears into public policy. Throughout America and beyond, ordinary citizens, respected professionals, and government officials had come to believe that controlling human reproduction, encouraging some while preventing others, represented rational, progressive action to address the supposed threats of racial "degeneration" and social disorder.

This scene captured a pivotal moment when scientific authority, public health, and deeply rooted fears converged to create extraordinary intrusions into human lives. The "Fitter Families" contests represented just the public face of a broader movement that had already achieved compulsory sterilization laws in multiple states, restrictive immigration policies targeting supposedly inferior races, and marriage prohibition laws preventing unions deemed genetically undesirable. These contests took place within a wider landscape of social purity campaigns, anti-socialist crackdowns, nationalism, and immigration restriction, all responses to perceived threats to established social orders amid rapid change.

Together, these movements demonstrated how easily scientific language could justify traditional prejudices and how readily progressive reform could transform into coercive control.

The stars that had witnessed the rise of industrial cities and mass migration now looked down upon a society seeking scientific solutions to the very changes they had created. From their celestial vantage point, these silent observers might have noticed how the pendulum of human affairs continued its perpetual motion, this time swinging toward control and categorization after a period of rapid change had disrupted established hierarchies. The spiral of history continued its turn, not returning to exactly the same position but revisiting familiar tensions between order and chaos, tradition and change, unity and diversity. Just as earlier generations had sought to manage the disruptions of industrialization, this new generation sought to manage human biology itself, applying the tools of science to reshape not just their environment but their very species.

On October 1, 1910, an explosion ripped through the Los Angeles Times building, killing twenty-one employees and devastating the newspaper's headquarters. The blast immediately became national news, with Times publisher Harrison Gray Otis declaring it "the crime of the century" and blaming "unionists, socialists, and anarchists." The bombing occurred during a bitter labor dispute between Otis, a virulent anti-union businessman, and organized labor attempting to unionize Los Angeles. Within months, authorities arrested labor organizers James and John McNamara, and the case became a flashpoint in the struggle between American labor and capital.

This incident exemplified how anti-labor and anti-socialist suppression operated during this period, combining legitimate law enforcement with exaggerated public fears and expansive targeting of political dissidents. The McNamara case revealed deeper patterns of anti-radical suppression that had been developing across industrialized nations since the 1870s, when German Chancellor Otto von Bismarck pioneered systematic anti-socialist legislation.

Bismarck's Anti-Socialist Laws, enacted in 1878 following two assassination attempts on Kaiser Wilhelm I, became the model for legal suppression of radical movements. While not criminalizing socialist beliefs themselves, these measures banned the Social Democratic Party, prohibited socialist newspapers and meetings, and authorized police to crush organizing efforts. Bismarck explicitly described this legal framework as "fighting revolution with law," creating mechanisms to suppress dissent while maintaining nominal legal legitimacy. The laws remained in force until 1890, driving socialist activity underground while simultaneously delegitimizing more moderate labor reform.

Similar legal frameworks emerged across industrialized nations. In America, anti-radical suppression initially operated primarily through state and local authorities, with federal involvement increasing during World War I. Various legal mechanisms targeted labor and socialist movements, including criminal conspiracy laws, criminal syndicalism statutes, sedition legislation, and anti-anarchist measures. The 1901 assassination of President William McKinley by Leon Czolgosz, a self-proclaimed anarchist, sparked the Immigration Act of 1903, which explicitly excluded anarchists from legal entry, one of the first ideological restrictions in American immigration law. This connection between anti-radicalism and immigration restriction would grow stronger in subsequent decades.

Legal suppression operated alongside direct force, with both public and private violence deployed against labor and socialist movements. The Haymarket incident of 1886, where an unknown person threw a bomb at police during a Chicago labor rally, leading to multiple deaths, became a pivotal moment in American anti-radical response. Though the actual bomber was never identified, authorities arrested and tried eight anarchist leaders based primarily on their political beliefs rather than direct evidence. Four were executed and one committed suicide, while the survivors were eventually pardoned in 1893 by Illinois Governor John Peter Altgeld, who concluded they had been convicted through "hysteria, packed juries and a biased judge."

On the morning of October 19, 1927, seventeen-year-old Carrie Buck was taken from the Virginia Colony for Epileptics and Feeble-minded to an operating room where she was forcibly sterilized under a Virginia law authorizing reproductive surgery on those deemed genetically "unfit." Her operation followed a legal process reaching the U.S. Supreme Court, which had ruled in Buck v. Bell that compulsory sterilization of the "unfit" was constitutional. Justice Oliver Wendell Holmes Jr., writing for the 8-1 majority, infamously declared: "Three generations of imbeciles are enough."

The facts later revealed the tragic irony: Carrie Buck was not "feebleminded" but a normal young woman institutionalized after being raped and impregnated by her foster parents' nephew. Her mother had been institutionalized primarily for poverty and supposed sexual immorality rather than intellectual disability. Carrie's infant daughter, the "third generation" in Holmes's declaration, was later evaluated by a nurse who found her "very bright." Yet all three generations were labeled "defective" to justify reproductive control, demonstrating how eugenic categories often masked social control beneath scientific language.

Buck's case exemplified the application of eugenic theory to public policy, a process that occurred across numerous nations from the 1900s through the 1930s. Eugenics transformed from abstract scientific theory to concrete policies affecting thousands of lives through sterilization laws, marriage restrictions, immigration policies, and institutionalization practices. By 1935, approximately 30 American states had enacted compulsory sterilization laws targeting those deemed "feebleminded," epileptic, criminal, or otherwise "unfit." California led implementation, ultimately sterilizing over 20,000 people, approximately one-third of all eugenic sterilizations performed in the United States. Similar policies appeared internationally, with particularly extensive programs in Canada, Sweden, Norway, Finland, and eventually Nazi Germany.

Eugenic policies extended beyond direct reproductive control to include marriage restriction laws, which prohibited unions between people with conditions deemed hereditary. Connecticut enacted the first such law in 1895, and by 1929, 29 states had similar statutes preventing marriage among persons categorized as "insane," "feebleminded," "epileptic," or having various diseases. These laws required blood tests and health certificates before marriage licenses could be issued, creating bureaucratic infrastructure to regulate reproduction. Unlike sterilization, which primarily targeted institutionalized populations, marriage laws affected the general public, extending eugenic control beyond institutional boundaries.

Immigration restriction provided another powerful implementation of eugenic principles. The Johnson-Reed Immigration Act of 1924 established nationality quotas explicitly designed to reduce immigration from southern and eastern Europe, regions whose inhabitants eugenicists classified as racially inferior to "Nordic" northwestern Europeans. Eugenicist Harry Laughlin testified before Congress that these populations showed high rates of "inborn defectiveness," presenting pseudoscientific data that significantly influenced the legislation. The law effectively reduced Italian immigration by approximately 90 percent and nearly eliminated eastern European Jewish immigration. Asian exclusion provisions prevented Japanese immigration entirely, building upon earlier Chinese exclusion policies. Together, these measures represented the largest-scale application of eugenic principles, affecting millions of lives through demographic engineering intended to preserve America's supposed racial composition.

"Destroy the traffic, root and branch. It damns our boys and girls, blasts their lives, destroys their souls, and imperils the future of our country!" The speaker, a respectable middle-aged woman in a conservative dress, addressed a crowd of several hundred people gathered before the entrance of an Ohio saloon in June 1893. Beside her stood dozens of women from the local Woman's Christian Temperance Union (WCTU), many holding Bibles and singing hymns. Several women knelt on the sidewalk in prayer while others confronted men attempting to enter the establishment. Some women carried hammers or hatchets, visible threats reflecting the movement's increasingly militant tactics. This temperance demonstration represented just one manifestation of broader social purity campaigns that sought to regulate morality, sexuality, and personal behavior during the late nineteenth and early twentieth centuries.

Social purity campaigns emerged from genuine concerns about real problems: alcoholism destroying families, workplace exploitation of women and children, unsafe urban conditions, and sexually transmitted diseases affecting public health. These movements often began with humanitarian motivations, protection of vulnerable people, improvement of family welfare, and creation of safer communities. However, they frequently evolved from voluntary reform efforts into coercive control systems imposing specific moral standards through legal prohibition, surveillance, and punishment. This transformation reflected both the limitations of voluntary reform and the appeal of scientific and state authority in addressing persistent social problems.

The temperance movement exemplified this pattern. Beginning primarily as a persuasion-based effort to encourage voluntary abstinence, it evolved into the prohibition movement demanding legal ban of alcohol production and sale. The WCTU, founded in 1874, became the largest women's organization in American history with hundreds of thousands of members by the 1890s. Under Frances Willard's leadership, it expanded from temperance advocacy to a comprehensive "Home Protection" agenda addressing prostitution, age of consent laws, labor conditions, and public health. Similar movements developed internationally, with organizations like the British Women's Temperance Association and the World's Woman's Christian Temperance Union pursuing parallel goals across borders.

Anti-vice campaigns targeted behaviors beyond alcohol, particularly prostitution, gambling, and drug use. Organizations like the New York Society for the Suppression of Vice, led by Anthony Comstock, and the American Purity Alliance created sophisticated surveillance and prosecution systems targeting "immoral" activities and publications. The Comstock Laws (1873) prohibited mailing "obscene materials," including not only pornography but also contraceptive information and devices. Comstock himself claimed responsibility for the destruction of 160 tons of literature and the arrest of over 3,000 people during his four-decade career. Similar efforts in Britain, led by the National Vigilance Association, targeted both prostitution and obscene publications through comparable methods.

As a May Day parade of socialist demonstrators marched through Berlin's working-class districts in 1912, they passed clusters of young men in patriotic organization uniforms who jeered and occasionally threw objects at the marchers. These nationalist youth belonged to organizations like the Young

German League and German Navy League, groups subsidized by industrial interests and conservative political parties to counter socialist influence among working-class Germans. The contrast between red flags on one side and imperial German flags on the other visually represented how nationalism had become a strategic conservative weapon against socialism and labor movements across industrialized nations.

This instrumental use of nationalism represented sophisticated adaptation by conservative forces facing unprecedented challenges from below. Rather than simply suppressing worker organizations through force, conservative leaders developed counter-mobilization strategies drawing working-class men away from class-based politics through appeals to patriotic sentiment and national belonging. This approach proved particularly effective because it addressed genuine psychological needs for community and identity amid industrial disruption while redirecting grievances from domestic inequalities toward external enemies or internal "others" portrayed as threatening national integrity.

Otto von Bismarck pioneered this strategic nationalism alongside his anti-socialist legislation. After passing the Anti-Socialist Laws in 1878, Bismarck implemented what historians called "state socialism," national health insurance (1883), accident insurance (1884), and old-age pensions (1889), explicitly to undercut socialist appeal. Bismarck openly acknowledged this strategy: "Whoever has a pension for his old age is far more content and far easier to handle than one who has no such prospect." This combination of repression, social welfare, and nationalist sentiment created a model for successful conservative adaptation to democratic mass politics, addressing enough material concerns to prevent revolutionary sentiment while channeling political energies toward national rather than class identification.

The passengers aboard the SS Taiyo Maru fell silent as their ship approached Angel Island in San Francisco Bay one spring morning in 1924. Unlike European immigrants processed through Ellis Island, these Japanese arrivals faced detention, intense interrogation, and likely rejection under newly enacted immigration legislation. The Johnson-Reed Act, passed earlier that year, effectively prohibited all Japanese immigration through provisions excluding "aliens ineligible for citizenship," a category created by previous court decisions specifically targeting Asian immigrants. This Japanese exclusion provision had generated formal protest from Japan's government and public demonstrations in Tokyo, but American restrictionists had prevailed, citing supposed racial incompatibility and assimilation impossibility rather than any specific actions or characteristics of actual Japanese immigrants.

The resulting policy exemplified how racial anxiety drove immigration restriction during this period, with eugenic theories providing scientific justification for policies actually motivated by complex economic, cultural, and status fears. Immigration restriction represented among the most significant policy implementations of eugenic thinking, affecting millions of lives by regulating national populations based on racial categories. While presented as rational scientific management, these restrictions actually represented reaction against changing demographics perceived as threatening traditional hierarchies and national character.

Immigration to the United States and other industrialized nations had dramatically increased during the late nineteenth century, with approximately 25 million Europeans entering America between 1880 and 1924. More significantly, the pattern shifted from northwestern European predominance (British, German, and Scandinavian) toward southern and eastern Europeans (Italians, Greeks, Poles, Russians, and other Slavic groups), who constituted over 75% of immigrants by 1896. Simultaneously, Asian immigration to Western states generated intense reaction, beginning with Chinese exclusion in 1882 and expanding to broader Asian restriction. These changing patterns triggered anxiety among established populations who perceived newer immigrants as culturally, religiously, and racially different from earlier waves.

In the elegant Manhattan brownstone of Madison Grant, the distinguished author of "The Passing of the Great Race" (1916), an exclusive gathering of wealthy New Yorkers sipped brandy while discussing the "racial crisis" facing America in 1920. Grant, a wealthy patrician, Yale and Columbia graduate, and respected naturalist, explained how "inferior" immigrant stock threatened to overwhelm superior "Nordic" bloodlines, potentially destroying American civilization. His guests included prominent physicians, professors, lawyers, and industrialists, not fringe extremists but members of America's established elite. Their conversation reflected not abstract academic interest but genuine existential anxiety about their society and, perhaps more importantly, their own position within it.

This scene captures a crucial aspect of the moral panics and restrictive movements of this period: they originated predominantly among relatively privileged groups rather than those most economically threatened by social change. The most influential eugenicists, social purity advocates, anti-socialist crusaders, and immigration restrictionists came primarily from established middle and upper classes, those with significant property, education, and social status. Their psychological motivations involved complex status anxiety that transcended simple economic self-interest, revealing deeper concerns about identity, meaning, and social position amid rapid change.

Loss aversion provides a powerful framework for understanding these reactions. Psychological research consistently demonstrates that people experience losses more intensely than equivalent gains, a pattern apparent in elite responses to democratization, economic changes, and demographic shifts. Established groups facing relative status decline (even while maintaining absolute advantages) experienced genuine psychological distress motivating defensive responses. As sociologist Arlie Russell Hochschild observed in studying modern parallels, perceived status loss creates a "deep story" of being "cut in line" by previously subordinate groups, generating emotional responses disproportionate to actual material threats.

Elite fears of revolution significantly drove reactionary politics despite limited actual revolutionary potential. The 1871 Paris Commune uprising, where working-class Parisians briefly controlled the city, created enduring trauma among European and American elites far beyond the event's actual scope. The 1917 Russian Revolution similarly generated fear disproportionate to realistic revolutionary prospects in Western democracies. These historical memories shaped elite psychology, creating pattern recognition that interpreted labor activism, socialist politics, or even moderate reform as potential revolutionary precursors. This pattern recognition often led to preemptive suppression responding more to feared possibilities than actual threats.

If we could see these events from the perspective of the stars, we might recognize how similar fears have driven similar responses throughout human history. Just as witchcraft panics had once targeted those perceived as threatening social order, now eugenicists and social purity advocates identified new categories of "dangerous" people to control. Just as religious authorities had once determined which beliefs and behaviors were acceptable, now scientific authorities claimed the power to categorize humans based on supposedly objective measurements and theories. The specific language and methods had changed, but the underlying pattern remained: the identification of certain groups as threats to social order, followed by systematic efforts to control or exclude them.

Yet these troubling developments contained seeds of their own correction. The very scientific approach that eugenicists claimed to follow would eventually undermine their theories, as more rigorous research revealed the flaws in their methods and assumptions. The democratic principles that restrictionists selectively invoked would eventually be expanded to protect the rights of those they sought to control. From a celestial perspective, we might see both the disturbing capacity of humans to justify control and exclusion through the language of their era, and their equally remarkable capacity to recognize and ultimately reject these justifications in favor of more inclusive understanding.

NO MAN'S LAND: SCIENTIFIC AUTHORITY VS. DEMOCRATIC GOVERNANCE

Complex social problems require specialized scientific expertise to develop effective evidence-based solutions.

Pause. Notice what arises in you.

Democratic societies must ultimately allow citizens, not experts, to determine policy through representative processes reflecting shared values.

Pause. Notice what arises in you.

You do not have to agree with or justify either statement. Simply hold them both in your mind and observe what comes up.

The eugenics movement exemplified this fundamental tension. When Harvard-educated zoologist Charles Davenport testified before Congress on immigration restriction, he presented complex inheritance data supposedly demonstrating racial differences in intellectual capacity. His scientific credentials and technical language proved persuasive to legislators lacking specialized training to evaluate his methodological flaws. As one congressman remarked, "Who are we to question the considered judgment of trained scientists?" This deference to expertise facilitated policies affecting millions without meaningful democratic scrutiny.

Yet scientific expertise itself contained no inherent ethical compass. Leading eugenicists included distinguished scholars from prestigious universities applying supposedly neutral methods toward value-laden social policies. Without democratic oversight reflecting broader social values, scientific authority alone provided insufficient guidance for humane policy. As Supreme Court Justice Oliver Wendell Holmes demonstrated in Buck v. Bell, scientific rationality divorced from ethical consideration could justify profound violations of human dignity through purely utilitarian calculations.

These historical examples raise essential questions that continue reverberating through contemporary societies. Scientific expertise provides essential understanding of complex problems, from public health to environmental challenges, often revealing solutions inaccessible to untrained observers. Yet democratic legitimacy requires that affected populations maintain meaningful input over decisions impacting their lives, even regarding technically complex matters. Neither pure technocracy nor uninformed majoritarianism provides satisfactory answer alone.

Successful societies have generally developed hybrid approaches: scientific advisory bodies informing democratically accountable decision-makers, transparent expert processes open to public scrutiny, and institutional constraints preventing either scientific overreach or democratic rejection of established knowledge. The eugenics era demonstrates the dangers when this balance fails, when scientific authority operates without democratic accountability or when democratic processes reject scientific integrity for ideological purposes. Each generation faces this tension anew, seeking balance between these complementary yet sometimes competing principles within specific historical contexts.

Chapter Twelve

When Evidence Cleared the Air

On June 1, 1942, Justice William O. Douglas delivered a momentous Supreme Court opinion that marked a turning point in American legal and scientific thinking. The case before the Court, Skinner v. Oklahoma, challenged a state law authorizing compulsory sterilization of "habitual criminals." Jack Skinner, imprisoned for stealing chickens and later for armed robbery, had been ordered sterilized under Oklahoma's 1935 law. But the Supreme Court unanimously struck down the statute, with Douglas noting a troubling inconsistency: the law mandated sterilization for chicken thieves but exempted embezzlers, a distinction that seemed to target the poor while sparing white-collar criminals.

"We are dealing here with legislation which involves one of the basic civil rights of man," Douglas wrote. "Marriage and procreation are fundamental to the very existence and survival of the race." These words marked a dramatic departure from the Court's position just fifteen years earlier in Buck v. Bell, when Justice Oliver Wendell Holmes had infamously declared "three generations of imbeciles are enough" while upholding Virginia's forced sterilization law. Skinner did not explicitly overturn Buck, but it effectively established limits on state power over human reproduction that would eventually lead to the dismantling of eugenic sterilization programs across the nation.

What happened between these two landmark decisions? Why did a scientific movement that once commanded support from leading universities, philanthropists, and government officials gradually lose its authority and legitimacy? The story of eugenics' rise and fall reveals how societies can correct course after periods of excess, how science itself contains mechanisms for identifying and rejecting flawed theories, and how democratic systems can, sometimes belatedly, recognize and protect fundamental human dignity.

The first half of the twentieth century witnessed not only the peak and decline of eugenic thinking but also parallel developments in several domains: the expansion of political rights despite earlier resistance, the development of regulated capitalism balancing market dynamism with social protection, the transformation of nationalist fervor into more constructive international cooperation, and the gradual acceptance of immigrant communities despite earlier fears. These interconnected trends reflected a broader pattern of societal learning and adaptation, not a straightforward march of progress, but a meandering journey with setbacks and reversals that nevertheless moved generally toward greater recognition of human complexity and dignity.

This resolution was neither complete nor perfect. Many harms had already been inflicted that could never be undone. Some prejudices persisted in new forms. Yet the rejection of simplistic biological determinism and the growing acceptance of human diversity represented genuine learning from earlier mistakes, a demonstration that societies, like individuals, can reconsider their paths and change direction when evidence and experience reveal the flaws in previous thinking. Understanding this capacity for collective correction provides valuable perspective for navigating our own periods of uncertainty and fear.

The stars that had witnessed countless human efforts to categorize, control, and exclude now looked down upon societies beginning to question these impulses. From their celestial vantage point, these silent observers might have noticed how the pendulum that had swung so far toward fear and exclusion was now moving back toward recognition of shared humanity. The spiral of history continued its turn, not returning to exactly the same position but revisiting fundamental questions about human dignity and diversity with new wisdom born of painful experience. This cycle of learning, moving from fear to understanding, from exclusion to inclusion, from pseudoscience to genuine knowledge, revealed humanity's capacity for self-correction, for recognizing mistakes and changing course even after traveling far down misguided paths.

On a crisp November morning in 1920, Carrie Chapman Catt walked purposefully into a Manhattan polling station. At 61, the veteran suffragist had spent decades fighting for this moment, the first presidential election in which American women could vote nationwide. Similar scenes unfolded across the country as millions of women exercised their newly won franchise. The Nineteenth Amendment's ratification just three months earlier had ended a struggle spanning generations, from the 1848 Seneca Falls Convention through decades of campaigns, setbacks, and incremental victories.

"I remember the look of wonder on the election officials' faces," one Connecticut woman later recalled. "They had been against us having the vote, but once it was law, they treated us with great courtesy." This matter-of-fact acceptance reflected a broader pattern: reforms that had once seemed radical or threatening to social order were eventually incorporated into the mainstream, with former opponents adapting to new realities rather than maintaining futile resistance.

Women's suffrage represented just one aspect of expanded democratic participation occurring across Western nations following World War I. Britain extended voting rights to women over 30 in 1918 and equalized the voting age at 21 in 1928. Germany's Weimar Constitution granted women's suffrage in 1919, while Austria, Czechoslovakia, Poland, and other new states included women's voting rights in their founding documents. Globally, the number of democratic systems increased dramatically after the war, with monarchies yielding to republics and aristocratic privileges giving way to citizen rights. Though many of these democratic experiments would face severe challenges in the 1930s, the principle of popular sovereignty had nonetheless gained unprecedented acceptance.

Labor rights followed a similar trajectory from radical demand to established practice. The National Labor Relations Act of 1935 (Wagner Act) in the United

States formally guaranteed workers' right to organize and bargain collectively, a remarkable reversal from earlier decades when unions faced legal prohibition and violent suppression. The law established the National Labor Relations Board to oversee union elections and prevent unfair labor practices, creating institutional infrastructure for orderly labor relations. Similar legal frameworks emerged across industrial democracies, transforming labor organizing from subversive activity to recognized component of economic systems.

This shift reflected pragmatic recognition that regulated labor relations served broader stability. As U.S. Senator Robert Wagner argued in supporting his landmark bill: "We cannot maintain a democratic society by denial to a vast number of citizens a voice in determining the conditions under which they labor." Even business leaders who had once fiercely opposed unions increasingly accepted collective bargaining as preferable to industrial warfare. The 1937 agreement between General Motors and the United Automobile Workers, following a bitter sit-down strike, established a pattern for labor relations that would endure for decades.

In January 1934, British economist John Maynard Keynes visited President Franklin Roosevelt at the White House. Their conversation symbolized a reconciliation between economic expertise and democratic governance that would shape the post-Depression world. Classical economic orthodoxy had insisted governments should maintain balanced budgets and minimal interference with markets even during crises. Keynes's revolutionary insight, that government spending could stimulate demand during downturns, provided theoretical foundation for the New Deal and similar programs internationally.

"The old classical medicine, we're all taught it, balanced budgets and so on," Roosevelt's Labor Secretary Frances Perkins later recalled him saying. "Keynes showed us another way." This "other way" represented not rejection of market economies but recognition that markets functioned within social and political contexts requiring democratic management. The resulting synthesis, variously called regulated capitalism, the mixed economy, or social market systems, balanced market dynamism with social protection, preserving capitalism's productive capacity while moderating its destabilizing tendencies.

This approach had deeper roots than the Depression emergency measures. Progressive Era reforms had established precedents for government regulation addressing market failures. The Pure Food and Drug Act (1906) protected consumers from adulterated products. The Federal Reserve System (1913) provided central banking functions stabilizing financial markets. Antitrust enforcement constrained monopolistic practices distorting competition. These measures addressed specific problems while maintaining market frameworks, demonstrating how targeted intervention could strengthen rather than undermine functioning markets.

International variations developed reflecting different national traditions. The American New Deal emphasized regulation, social insurance, and countercyclical spending while maintaining predominantly private ownership. Sweden's "Middle Way" combined strong labor unions, extensive social services, and private enterprise. Britain's more gradual evolution incorporated both Conservative and Labour contributions to welfare state development. Germany's "social market economy" integrated Catholic social teaching with market orientation. These diverse approaches shared a core recognition that industrial capitalism required social management rather than unfettered operation.

When Emperor Karl I of Austria-Hungary abdicated on November 11, 1918, the day World War I's armistice took effect, it marked the end not just of his personal reign but of a dynasty that had ruled Central Europe for over 600 years. Similar scenes unfolded across the continent: Kaiser Wilhelm II fleeing to exile in the Netherlands, ending the Hohenzollern monarchy; Tsar Nicholas II already deposed and later executed with his family; Ottoman Sultan Mehmed VI soon to lose his political authority if not yet his throne. Within months, the great continental empires that had dominated European politics for centuries had collapsed, their territories reorganized into new nation-states with predominantly republican governments.

This imperial collapse represented devastating failure for traditional conservatism, which had maintained that hereditary monarchy, aristocratic leadership, and established religion provided essential social stability. The catastrophic war had resulted directly from these regimes' policies, particularly militarism, nationalism, and diplomatic brinkmanship, yet proved beyond their capacity to manage once unleashed. The conflict they started ultimately destroyed them, discrediting not just specific rulers but the entire political framework they represented. As British Conservative Leo Amery acknowledged: "The old world has been blown to pieces by the explosion of the last five years. Neither the old landmarks nor the old signposts exist."

Conservative thinking required dramatic recalibration to remain relevant in this transformed landscape. The most successful adaptation came in Britain, where Stanley Baldwin's Conservative Party accepted democratic legitimacy, women's suffrage, and basic labor rights while maintaining traditional values in other domains. Baldwin's approach, sometimes called "New Conservatism," acknowledged irreversible social changes while preserving core conservative commitments to gradual development, social cohesion, and practical rather than theoretical governance. This pragmatic adaptation enabled Conservatives to win democratic elections and govern effectively despite dramatically expanded suffrage.

Continental European conservatives faced greater challenges given monarchy's collapse in many countries. German conservatives initially struggled to accept the Weimar Republic, with many supporting monarchist restoration or authoritarian alternatives. However, Gustav Stresemann and others gradually developed democratic conservative approaches working within republican frameworks. The Democratic People's Party (DVP) and German People's Party (DNVP) represented conservative constituencies while accepting, initially reluctantly, democratic governance. Similar evolution occurred across new Central European republics, with conservative parties gradually accommodating themselves to democratic systems despite preferences for traditional authority.

In 1936, geneticist Theodosius Dobzhansky published "Genetics and the Origin of Species," a groundbreaking work synthesizing laboratory genetics with natural population studies. Among its many scientific contributions, Dobzhansky's work directly contradicted fundamental eugenic assumptions by demonstrating that genetic diversity rather than "purity" promoted population health and adaptability. His research showed how recessive genes persisted in populations through natural processes, making eugenic efforts to eliminate them through selective breeding not just ethically problematic but scientifically misguided.

Dobzhansky's work represented part of a broader scientific rejection of eugenic theories emerging through normal scientific processes of evidence gathering, hypothesis testing, and theory refinement. This scientific correction occurred alongside ethical and political reconsiderations but maintained a distinct character as empirical rather than merely moral rejection. The rising field of population genetics systematically dismantled eugenic claims while developing more accurate understanding of heredity's complex mechanisms, demonstrating science's capacity for self-correction through methodological rigor rather than external pressure.

Early challenges to eugenic thinking had emerged even during the movement's ascendance. William Castle's experiments with hooded rats between 1914-1930 demonstrated that supposedly fixed "degenerate" traits could be modified through selection, contradicting eugenic claims about trait permanence. Raymond Pearl, initially supporting eugenics, published "The Biology of Superiority" (1927) questioning basic eugenic assumptions after examining actual inheritance data. Statistician Karl Pearson, despite supporting eugenics politically, developed mathematical approaches revealing the statistical impossibility of eliminating recessive genes through sterilization programs.

Anthropologist Franz Boas provided crucial evidence against racial determinism through empirical research rather than philosophical objection. His landmark study "Changes in Bodily Form of Descendants of Immigrants" (1911) demonstrated that skull shapes, previously considered fixed racial characteristics, changed within a single generation in new environments. This research directly contradicted claims that physical characteristics reflected innate racial qualities rather than environmental influences. Boas and his students, including Margaret Mead and Ruth Benedict, accumulated extensive evidence showing how behavior patterns attributed to racial inheritance actually reflected cultural learning, research with profound implications for eugenic racial theories.

The Holocaust's revelation dramatically accelerated scientific rejection of racial theories and eugenic practices. The Nuremberg Doctors' Trial (1946-1947) exposed how the German medical establishment had implemented increasingly extreme eugenic measures culminating in genocide. This shocking demonstration of where eugenic logic could lead prompted scientific organizations worldwide to explicitly reject racial theories and eugenic practices. The United Nations Educational, Scientific and Cultural Organization (UNESCO) issued a landmark "Statement on Race" (1950) definitively rejecting scientific racism and declaring "race is less a biological fact than a social myth."

In 1945, Frank Sinatra released "The House I Live In," a short film and song promoting religious and racial tolerance. Against a backdrop of children bullying a Jewish boy, Sinatra intervened with a message that America comprises people "of every color, religion, and race." The film won an Academy Award and reached millions at a crucial moment when American society reassessed attitudes about ethnic and religious differences. This mainstream cultural production advocating inclusion represented a dramatic shift from earlier periods when popular media typically reinforced rather than challenged prejudices.

This attitudinal evolution did not occur suddenly nor without resistance, but the general direction toward greater acceptance of diversity marked significant social learning. The Second World War played a crucial role in this transformation through multiple mechanisms: exposure of Nazi racism's horrific consequences, patriotic service by previously marginalized groups, wartime labor shortages creating opportunities for excluded populations, and international context requiring clearer distinction between American pluralism and fascist racial ideology. These factors accelerated pre-existing trends toward greater inclusion while creating new mandates for addressing persistent discrimination.

Jewish American experience exemplified broader integration patterns. Despite continuing antisemitism through the 1930s, when prestigious universities maintained Jewish quotas, restrictive covenants blocked housing access, and social clubs excluded Jewish members, gradual acceptance proceeded through multiple avenues. Military service during World War II demonstrated patriotic commitment. Professional achievement established value to broader society.

Cultural contributions from Broadway to Hollywood integrated Jewish perspectives into American mainstream. Religious institutions developed distinctively American forms balancing tradition with adaptation. These multifaceted integration processes occurred despite rather than because of official policies, demonstrating society's capacity for informal adaptation alongside formal policy changes.

Italian Americans followed a similar though distinct trajectory from "undesirable" immigrants facing significant discrimination to accepted community contributing to broader culture. Early stereotypes associating Italians with criminality gradually yielded to recognition of diverse contributions across domains from business to politics to culture. Food perhaps most visibly demonstrated this transformation, as Italian cuisine evolved from exotic foreign fare to American dietary staple. This culinary integration reflected broader cultural evolution blending distinctive heritage with American context, maintaining cultural elements while participating fully in broader society. Similar patterns occurred across European immigrant groups, with distinctive cultural contributions gradually recognized as enriching rather than threatening American identity.

In 1949, Gunnar Myrdal published "An American Dilemma," his landmark study of American race relations. The Swedish economist concluded that the tension between America's egalitarian ideals and discriminatory practices created inherent instability destined to resolve toward greater equality. "America is continuously struggling for its soul," he wrote. This observation captured a broader truth about societies' capacity for moral learning, not through revolutionary transformation but through gradual reconciliation of practices with professed values. The incremental yet meaningful progress from earlier periods of fear and exclusion toward greater recognition of human dignity and diversity demonstrated this adaptive capacity in action.

Several recurrent patterns emerged across domains from scientific rejection of pseudoscience to political democratization to cultural integration. Understanding these patterns provides a valuable framework for navigating periods of social anxiety and change, not a prescriptive formula guaranteeing specific outcomes but insight into processes through which societies learn from experience rather than remaining trapped by fear or ideology. These insights transcend particular historical circumstances, offering perspective applicable to diverse contexts despite their specific manifestations.

Fear-based responses typically prove counterproductive when implemented as policy. Eugenic measures based on fear of "racial degeneration" created genuine harm while failing to address actual social problems they purported to solve. Immigration restrictions motivated by cultural anxiety prevented valuable contributions that later became universally recognized. These patterns suggest skepticism toward policies justified primarily through fear narratives rather than evidence, not because fears lack emotional legitimacy but because fear-driven policies typically address symptoms rather than causes while creating unintended consequences worse than the feared outcomes.

Duration matters significantly in social adaptation, with time enabling learning impossible during immediate crisis. Fifteen years separated the Supreme Court's Buck and Skinner decisions, allowing scientific evidence to accumulate contradicting earlier assumptions. Decades passed between anti-immigrant panics and recognition of immigrant contributions. This temporal dimension suggests both patience regarding complex social processes and skepticism toward permanent solutions to temporary conditions. Crisis responses addressing immediate concerns may prove counterproductive when extended into permanent policies without adjustment based on experience.

Looking upward from these troubled yet ultimately hopeful developments, we might imagine how the stars perceived humanity's journey through this difficult period. From their distant perspective, they would have witnessed not just the particular events of this era but the recurring pattern of fear giving way to understanding, of exclusion gradually yielding to inclusion. The celestial observers might have noted how societies that had implemented the harshest restrictions based on eugenics and xenophobia eventually came to recognize their error, though often too late for those who had already suffered irreparable harm. This capacity for collective learning, for acknowledging mistakes and changing course, represents one of humanity's most precious qualities, though one that operates far more slowly than we might wish.

The spiral of history had completed another turn. Just as religious persecution had eventually given way to greater tolerance, and industrial disruption had led to more balanced economic arrangements, now the scientific categorization and control of human populations was yielding to more nuanced understanding of human diversity and dignity. This perspective reminds us that our current fears and anxieties, however overwhelming they may feel in the moment, exist within larger patterns of human experience, patterns that typically move, however gradually and imperfectly, toward greater wisdom and compassion over time.

NO MAN'S LAND: PRESERVING HISTORY VS. ACKNOWLEDGING HARM

We must preserve accurate historical understanding of past scientific movements like eugenics without censoring their complexity or context.

Pause. Notice what arises in you.

We must clearly acknowledge the profound harm caused by these movements and resist normalizing pseudoscientific theories that dehumanized vulnerable populations.

Pause. Notice what arises in you.

You do not have to agree with or justify either statement. Simply hold them both in your mind and observe what comes up.

How we remember eugenics matters nearly as much as how we rejected it. The Harvard biologist Richard Lewontin recounted attending a genetics conference where a senior colleague nostalgically recalled early eugenics research without mentioning the suffering it caused, citing only flawed methodology. "His scientific criticism was correct," Lewontin noted, "but science disconnected from humanity becomes its own kind of error."

Yet simplistic dismissal of this history as merely "bad science done by bad people" misses crucial insights. Many eugenicists were not moral monsters but respected professionals working within prevailing assumptions of their time. Leading universities, philanthropic foundations, and government agencies all supported eugenic research. Understanding how thoughtful people embraced theories later recognized as profoundly flawed helps us recognize our own vulnerability to similar errors.

Some institutions address this dilemma by removing names of prominent eugenicists from buildings while creating educational materials explaining the history. Others maintain names but add contextual information acknowledging problematic aspects alongside genuine contributions. Museums develop exhibits exploring eugenics' complex history without either whitewashing or oversimplifying. These approaches acknowledge rather than erase difficult history while ensuring harmful aspects receive proper recognition.

Historical understanding requires holding complexity without seeking false comfort in either selective memory or righteous condemnation. We need both comprehensive knowledge of how respected institutions participated in harmful movements and clear moral recognition of the suffering these movements caused. Neither historical accuracy nor moral clarity alone provides sufficient guidance; we need both together to learn fully from past mistakes.

Cycle 5: When Neighbors Became Strangers

Chapter Thirteen

When Shadows Wore Suits

On August 29, 1949, a flash of light brighter than the desert sun briefly illuminated the Kazakhstan steppe as the Soviet Union detonated its first atomic bomb. Code-named "First Lightning" by the Soviets and "Joe-1" by Americans monitoring from afar, the explosion shattered America's nuclear monopoly years earlier than Western experts had predicted. When President Harry Truman announced the news to a shocked American public on September 23, his carefully measured words belied the seismic shift in global security: "We have evidence that within recent weeks an atomic explosion occurred in the USSR."

That simple sentence transformed how millions of Americans understood their place in the world. Suddenly, the awesome force that had leveled Hiroshima and Nagasaki might be directed at American cities. Children practicing "duck and cover" drills in schools across the country crawled under desks at the sound of air raid sirens, following cartoon turtle Bert's advice in case of atomic attack. Families built backyard fallout shelters stocked with canned goods and board games to pass the time during a nuclear apocalypse. A new existential dread permeated American consciousness, the possibility that civilization itself might end not over centuries or millennia, but in minutes.

This nuclear anxiety emerged at a moment of dramatic transition. World War II had ended the Great Depression through massive government spending and full employment, but peacetime brought fresh uncertainties. Would the economy collapse again without war production? How would returning veterans reintegrate into civilian life? What would become of women who had entered the workforce during the war? These economic and social questions intertwined with geopolitical tensions as former allies became adversaries in what would soon be called the Cold War.

The speed of this transformation astonished even seasoned observers. In 1945, American and Soviet soldiers had embraced at the Elbe River, celebrating their joint victory over Nazi Germany. Just four years later, they faced each other across an Iron Curtain dividing Europe, backed by competing nuclear arsenals and ideological systems. This rapid shift from allies to enemies created cognitive dissonance for ordinary citizens struggling to reconcile wartime Soviet heroism with postwar Soviet threat narratives.

This disorienting transition reopened fundamental questions about American identity and values. What balance between national security and civil liberties would protect both the nation's physical safety and its democratic character? How could legitimate concerns about espionage be addressed without descending into paranoia? What role should government play in managing the economy and ensuring prosperity? These complex questions defied simple answers, creating space for competing visions of America's future and heated debates about the proper means of securing it.

The resulting tensions produced both constructive adaptations and destructive excesses over the following decade. At their best, Cold War challenges spurred creative solutions strengthening democratic institutions and expanding prosperity. At their worst, they generated fear-driven reactions undermining the very values they claimed to protect. Understanding this period's complexity helps us recognize how societies navigate existential fears, sometimes manufacturing needless panic, sometimes addressing genuine threats, often doing both simultaneously through imperfect but gradually improving responses that reflect our human capacity for both error and correction.

Perhaps the stars, witnessing this new chapter in human history, observed with cosmic detachment as the pendulum swung from wartime alliance to Cold War hostility. From their eternal perspective, they had seen civilizations rise and fall, but never before had humanity possessed the means to potentially extinguish itself in a single afternoon. The same ingenuity that unlocked the atom's energy now threatened existence itself. This paradox, that our greatest scientific achievement could lead to our greatest catastrophe, created an unprecedented anxiety that would shape a generation.

When Edward R. Murrow invited viewers into his CBS television studio on March 9, 1954, for a special edition of "See It Now," fewer than half of American households owned television sets. Yet this broadcast marked a pivotal moment in media history, demonstrating both television's unprecedented power to shape public opinion and journalism's capacity to challenge fear-driven narratives rather than amplify them.

"This is no time for men who oppose Senator McCarthy's methods to keep silent," Murrow declared, his deep voice steady as cigarette smoke curled around his face. For thirty minutes, the respected journalist methodically dissected Senator Joseph McCarthy's accusations and tactics, using the senator's own words and footage to demonstrate inconsistencies and excesses. Murrow closed with words that would become famous: "We must not confuse dissent with disloyalty... We will not be driven by fear into an age of unreason."

The Murrow broadcast illustrated the complex role media played in the early Cold War period. The same medium that had amplified McCarthy's accusations now provided a platform for their critique. This duality reflected broader patterns in postwar media development, where expanding communication technologies simultaneously spread fear and offered tools for countering it.

The media landscape Americans inhabited in the late 1940s and early 1950s differed dramatically from earlier periods. Radio had reached near-universal penetration, with sets in over 95% of American homes by 1950. Newspaper circulation peaked at approximately 70 million daily copies. Television, though still in its infancy, grew exponentially, from about 6,000 sets in 1946 to over 12 million by 1951. This media saturation created unparalleled capacity for rapid information dissemination to a national audience.

Commercial imperatives shaped how this expanding media system functioned. Competition for audience attention rewarded sensational coverage, with fear-inducing stories about communist threats reliably attracting readers and viewers. The Chicago Tribune exemplifies this pattern with headlines like "RED CANCER SPREADS IN U.S. GOVERNMENT" and "REDS BORING FROM WITHIN U.S. COLLEGES." Such alarming framing wasn't limited to conservative publications; mainstream outlets regularly employed similar language when covering alleged communist infiltration.

"One third of the world was living in a new and terrible slavery," declared Republican Senator Arthur Vandenberg in a 1947 speech supporting the Truman Doctrine providing military aid to Greece and Turkey against communist insurgents. His dramatic framing reflected growing conviction among American leaders that the Soviet Union represented not just a competing power but an existential threat to Western civilization. This perception, that ideological conflict with the Soviet Union constituted a zero-sum struggle between irreconcilable systems, would define American foreign policy for decades and shape domestic politics at their core.

The psychological impact of this framing cannot be overstated. For most Americans, World War II had represented a clear moral crusade against fascist aggression, with victory promising expected peace dividends. Instead, barely two years after celebrations in Times Square, they heard that another totalitarian threat demanded continued vigilance and sacrifice. This rapid pivot from celebrating allied victory to fearing former allies created cognitive dissonance requiring explanation. The emerging Cold War narrative provided that explanation while generating new anxieties about ideological contamination and nuclear threat.

Soviet actions certainly contributed to these concerns. Stalin's imposition of communist governments across Eastern Europe violated wartime agreements regarding self-determination. The Soviet blockade of Berlin in 1948-49 demonstrated willingness to use coercive measures against Western positions. Communist victory in China in 1949 suggested revolutionary momentum threatening vital American interests in Asia. Soviet nuclear testing confirmed technological capacity matching stated ideological hostility. These developments lent credibility to threat perceptions that might otherwise have seemed exaggerated.

The resulting fear manifested in various forms. Nuclear anxiety emerged as the most visible expression, especially after Soviet acquisition of atomic weapons. A 1951 Gallup poll found 51 percent of Americans believed a world war would erupt within five years, with similar percentages expecting their communities might be bombed. Civil defense preparations became part of daily life, with air raid drills in schools and workplaces creating regular reminders of vulnerability. Popular magazines published detailed fallout shelter specifications, while government pamphlets advised citizens on post-attack survival techniques. This constant emergency footing sustained psychological stress regardless of actual attack probability.

As World War II ended in August 1945, economic forecasters painted bleak prospects for the American economy. The memory of the Great Depression's massive unemployment lingered, while wartime government spending, which had finally ended that depression, rapidly wound down. Labor Secretary Lewis Schwellenbach warned that 8 million war workers would lose their jobs within months. The financial publication Kiplinger's cautioned ominously: "There is real danger of a prompt and serious business setback."

Yet what followed instead was one of history's most remarkable economic expansions. Between 1945 and 1960, the American economy grew by over 50% in real terms. Median family income rose approximately 30% during the 1950s alone. Homeownership soared from 43.6% in 1940 to 61.9% by 1960. By mid-decade, America with just 6% of world population generated nearly half of global manufacturing output. This prosperity transformed daily life through automobile ownership, suburban housing developments, household appliances, and previously unimaginable consumer abundance.

This extraordinary transition proceeded neither smoothly nor equitably. Immediate post-war inflation reached 14.4% in 1947, eroding purchasing power for many families. The adjustment from wartime production created economic dislocations in defense-dependent communities. Though unemployment never reached Depression levels, economic anxieties persisted through postwar recessions in 1949 and 1953. The prosperity decade featured genuine advances alongside continued insecurities, with remarkable progress coexisting with lingering fears of potential reversal.

On July 26, 1948, President Harry Truman signed Executive Order 9981, declaring "there shall be equality of treatment and opportunity for all persons in the armed services without regard to race, color, religion, or national origin." This directive marked a decisive break with longstanding military segregation, initiated fundamental changes in one of America's largest institutions, and foreshadowed broader civil rights struggles that would define the coming decades. Though implemented gradually and sometimes reluctantly, the order established the principle that public institutions should not enforce racial distinctions, a revolutionary concept in a nation still operating separate water fountains.

The timing reflected both domestic political calculation and international reality. Truman faced a difficult 1948 election with his Democratic coalition fracturing over civil rights issues. African American voters concentrated in key Northern states represented a crucial voting bloc that Truman could not afford to lose, particularly with Progressive Party candidate Henry Wallace appealing to liberal constituencies. Simultaneously, America's global leadership claims against Soviet communism faced embarrassing contradiction in segregation practices undermining human rights rhetoric. These pragmatic factors joined moral considerations in producing unprecedented federal action against racial discrimination.

More transformative legal change arrived on May 17, 1954, when Chief Justice Earl Warren delivered the unanimous Supreme Court opinion in Brown v. Board of Education declaring "separate educational facilities are inherently unequal." This decision directly overturned the 1896 Plessy v. Ferguson "separate but equal" doctrine that had constitutionally sanctioned segregation for nearly sixty years. Though focused specifically on education, Brown's reasoning undermined legal foundations for all forms of segregation, establishing a principle that would guide subsequent challenges to discriminatory practices across domains.

The response revealed competing visions of American identity and values. NAACP leader Roy Wilkins called the decision "the greatest constitutional victory for negroes since the Emancipation Proclamation." Southern resistance quickly mobilized, with Virginia Senator Harry Byrd calling for "massive resistance" strategies to prevent integration. Alabama Governor George Wallace vowed to stand "against intrusion by the federal government" through defying integration orders. These divergent reactions represented not merely policy disagreements but fundamental conflicts about national character and constitutional interpretation.

On July 5, 1954, a young truck driver named Elvis Presley stepped into Sun Records studio in Memphis and recorded "That's All Right," a blues song by Arthur "Big Boy" Crudup delivered with electrifying energy and vocal style blending country, gospel, and rhythm and blues traditions. When radio DJ Dewey Phillips played the record on his "Red, Hot and Blue" program days later, the station's switchboard lit up with callers demanding to hear it again. Many asked whether the singer was white or black, a question with revolutionary implications in the segregated South where musical traditions remained as divided as drinking fountains.

This seemingly small cultural moment signaled tectonic shifts in American society. A distinctive teenage culture was emerging with its own music, fashion, language, and values increasingly divergent from parent generations. This development stemmed from multiple converging factors: extended adolescence through increased high school attendance, greater disposable income from part-time jobs, expanded mass media targeting youth demographics, and demographic bulge as baby boom children reached adolescence. Together these created unprecedented conditions for youth culture formation less constrained by traditional authority structures.

Economic prosperity fueled this development through material resources supporting youth autonomy. Teenagers in middle-class families often controlled disposable income without adult financial responsibilities, creating consumer power attracting commercial attention. Record companies, clothing manufac-turers, and entertainment venues increasingly targeted this demographic with products designed specifically for youth tastes. This commercial relationship created feedback loops where youth preferences shaped market offerings which further reinforced distinctive youth identity, a self-reinforcing cycle generating ever-greater cultural differentiation.

Music provided the most visible expression of emerging youth identity. Rock and roll fused previously separated traditions, bringing together musical ele-ments from African American rhythm and blues, country and western, and gospel traditions. This integration at the cultural level paralleled and sometimes preceded legal integration efforts, creating shared experiences across racial lines among young listeners. Artists including Chuck Berry, Little Richard, Bud-dy Holly, and Elvis Presley became cultural icons representing new sensibili-ties emphasizing emotional expression, physical energy, and implied rebellion against establishment constraints.

In March 1953, Russell Kirk published "The Conservative Mind," a scholarly work tracing conservative intellectual tradition from Edmund Burke through the present. Its unexpected commercial success, selling over a million copies and spending months on bestseller lists, signaled renewed interest in conserv-ative philosophy during a period often characterized as a liberal consensus era. Kirk's emphasis on tradition, hierarchy, and religious values provided intellec-tual framework distinguishing conservatism from mere opposition to change or defense of wealth. His work helped transform conservatism from a reactive stance into a positive vision appealing to those concerned about social disorder amid material prosperity.

This conservative intellectual revival responded to specific postwar con-ditions rather than representing simple continuation of earlier conservative thought. Traditional conservatism had emphasized limited government, but new conservative thinkers confronted the reality of permanently expanded fed-eral presence following New Deal and war mobilization. Rather than futilely opposing this expansion, sophisticated conservatives increasingly focused on how government power should be directed, advocating a vigorous national security state while opposing welfare programs and regulation. This selective approach to government activity distinguished the emerging conservative movement from both traditional small-government conservatives and contemporary liberals.

Religious revival provided essential foundation for the conservative resurgence. Church membership reached historic highs during the 1950s, with approximately 65% of Americans holding formal religious affiliations. Popular movements including Billy Graham crusades attracted massive crowds, while religious publications and broadcasts reached unprecedented audiences. Religious institutions offered organizational infrastructure supporting conservative values, while theological frameworks gave cosmic significance to cultural and political positions. The resulting religious-political fusion imbued policy disagreements with moral dimensions, transforming debates from pragmatic differences into fundamental value conflicts.

If we were to gaze at the stars during this turbulent period, we might imagine how they witnessed this particular spiral of history unfolding, a society simultaneously experiencing unprecedented prosperity and existential dread, expanding rights and restricting freedoms, embracing tradition while being transformed by new technologies and cultural forms. The pendulum swung between security and liberty, between conformity and rebellion, between optimism about material progress and anxiety about nuclear annihilation. The spiral continued its turn, not returning to exactly the same position as previous cycles of fear and reaction, but revisiting similar human tendencies with new contexts and consequences.

From the stars' perspective, this particular moment in human history represented something genuinely new, the first time a species had developed the capacity to destroy itself entirely. Yet they had also witnessed humanity's remarkable resilience and capacity for self-correction, for recognizing excesses and pulling back from the brink. This pattern of fear, reaction, and eventual recalibration reflected deeper rhythms of human experience playing out across generations. The Cold War's particular manifestations were unique, but the underlying dynamics of how societies respond to perceived threats echoed earlier cycles we have explored.

NO MAN'S LAND: SECURITY VS. LIBERTY

A society must vigorously protect itself against legitimate threats to its citizens' safety and its government's integrity through robust security measures.

Pause. Notice what arises in you.

A democratic society must zealously safeguard civil liberties and due process rights that form its essential character, resisting the impulse to sacrifice freedoms for security.

Pause. Notice what arises in you.

You do not have to agree with or justify either statement. Simply hold them both in your mind and observe what comes up.

The 1950 Internal Security Act passed over President Truman's veto, requiring Communist organizations to register with the government and establishing detention camps for suspected subversives during national emergencies. Senator Pat McCarran defended these measures as "protecting this Nation from those who would destroy it." Truman's veto message countered that the law "would make a mockery of our Bill of Rights" and ultimately undermine the security it sought to protect.

Neither perspective lacked legitimacy. Soviet espionage represented genuine threat documented through decoded Venona cables and Soviet archives opened decades later. Meanwhile, loyalty investigations ruined innocent lives, chilled free expression, and contradicted fundamental constitutional principles through guilt by association and limited due process.

Justice Robert Jackson articulated this tension in a 1949 dissenting opinion: "The choice is not between order and liberty. It is between liberty with order and anarchy without either." His words acknowledged the complementary relationship often obscured during security debates, that liberty requires security to flourish, while security without liberty protects a society no longer worth defending.

American history reveals repeated cycles of security overreach during perceived crises, followed by corrective measures once immediate fears subside. Courts eventually check executive excesses; legislative reforms establish new protections; public opinion shifts from fear toward concern about rights violations. This pattern suggests neither absolute position fully addresses the genuine tension between security imperatives and liberty principles.

Perhaps the wisest approach lies not in resolving this tension but in mindfully holding it, recognizing legitimate concerns on both sides while resisting the human tendency to simplify complex realities through exclusive commitment to either security or liberty. The difficult balance requires ongoing adjustment rather than permanent resolution, demanding continuous democratic deliberation rather than fixed formulas. This approach acknowledges both values as essential rather than opposing, creating space for thoughtful navigation between legitimate imperatives that remain in creative tension.

Chapter Fourteen

When Lists Held Lives

On February 9, 1950, in the Grand Ballroom of the McClure Hotel in Wheeling, West Virginia, Republican Senator Joseph McCarthy addressed the local Women's Republican Club. As the evening proceeded, McCarthy pulled a sheet of paper from his pocket. "I have here in my hand," he declared, "a list of 205 that were made known to the Secretary of State as being members of the Communist Party and who nevertheless are still working and shaping policy in the State Department." Those improvised words, delivered to a modest audience in a small city, would give name to an era and dramatically alter American life for the next half-decade.

No reporter present asked to see the list, which McCarthy would later variously describe as containing 205, 57, or 81 names. When a Salt Lake City reporter finally requested to examine it days later, McCarthy refused, claiming it contained "very secret" information. The alleged list remained elusive, but fear proved more tangible. McCarthy's accusations tapped into existing anxieties about communist infiltration, providing specific targets for amorphous dread. His genius, or perhaps his tragedy, lay in recognizing how willing many Americans were to believe the worst about their institutions and fellow citizens when viewed through the lens of ideological terror.

The moment crystallized a peculiar paradox of the early Cold War period. America had emerged from World War II as the world's most powerful nation, economically prosperous and militarily dominant. Yet this objective security coexisted with deep subjective insecurity about invisible threats from within. How could a country simultaneously feel so powerful and so vulnerable? The answer lies partly in the nature of ideological conflict itself. Unlike conventional warfare with visible enemies and defined battlefields, the struggle against communism occurred largely in the realm of ideas, loyalties, and beliefs, intangible territories where traditional defenses seemed inadequate.

McCarthy's meteoric rise from obscure senator to household name demonstrated how this ideological insecurity transformed American institutions and daily life. His accusations targeted not just government agencies but also Hollywood, universities, labor unions, and eventually even the United States Army. The resulting investigations, loyalty oaths, blacklists, and firings affected thousands directly and millions indirectly through the culture of suspicion they generated. American democracy had weathered previous periods of fear-driven excess, from the Alien and Sedition Acts of 1798 to the Palmer Raids of 1919-1920, but the Cold War's ideological dimensions created unprecedented challenges to traditional liberties.

If the stars above could witness this latest turn in the human spiral, they might have recognized familiar patterns playing out in new forms. Throughout history, societies facing perceived existential threats have often turned inward, seeking invisible enemies to explain complex challenges. The celestial observers would have seen how the pendulum of human response swung from reasonable vigilance toward excessive suspicion, as it had in previous cycles of fear. Yet even from their distant vantage point, the stars might have noted something genuinely new in this cycle, the shadow of nuclear weapons creating an existential anxiety that humanity had never before encountered.

Senator Joseph McCarthy did not create the Red Scare; he amplified and personified dynamics already in motion. By the time he delivered his Wheeling speech in February 1950, the House Un-American Activities Committee (HUAC) had been investigating alleged communist infiltration for over a decade. Alger Hiss, a former State Department official, had been convicted of perjury related to espionage charges just weeks earlier. The Soviet Union had detonated its first atomic bomb the previous August, while communist forces advanced toward victory in China. These developments created fertile ground for McCarthy's accusations, which offered simple explanation for complex geopolitical setbacks: treason from within.

What distinguished McCarthy's approach was his intuitive grasp of media dynamics. Rather than following established investigative procedures, McCarthy fed newspapers a steady stream of accusations timed to coincide with press deadlines, ensuring publication before fact-checking could occur. As journalist Richard Rovere observed: "He knew that few publishers would risk seeming soft on Communism by refusing to print charges against supposed Communists." McCarthy's method created a no-win situation for the accused: denials received less coverage than accusations, while invoking constitutional rights against self-incrimination was portrayed as evidence of guilt.

The effectiveness of these tactics catapulted McCarthy from backbench senator to national phenomenon. From 1950 to 1954, polls consistently showed between 35 and 50 percent of Americans holding favorable opinions of McCarthy, with strongest support coming from Republicans, Catholics, and those with high school rather than college education. His supporters viewed him as a courageous truth-teller challenging a complacent establishment. Wisconsin voter Ruth Murray expressed this sentiment in a letter to her local newspaper: "Thank God for McCarthy. At last someone has the courage to expose the traitors who have been selling our country out."

In October 1947, screenwriter Ring Lardner Jr. faced a pivotal choice before the House Un-American Activities Committee. Asked whether he was or had ever been a member of the Communist Party, Lardner responded: "I could answer the question exactly the way you want, but I don't think this is pertinent to the inquiry, and I don't think this committee has the right to ask any American citizen such questions." For this response, neither confirming nor denying membership, but challenging the committee's authority, Lardner was cited for contempt of Congress, sentenced to prison, and blacklisted from working in Hollywood for over a decade.

Lardner belonged to the "Hollywood Ten," a group of writers and directors who refused to answer questions about political affiliations on First Amendment grounds. Their legal strategy proved unsuccessful, as the Supreme Court declined to review their contempt convictions, but established an important precedent of resistance. Following their imprisonment, subsequent witnesses faced starker choices: answer all questions including naming colleagues with communist associations, or refuse and face professional destruction. This dilemma fractured friendships, marriages, and creative partnerships as individuals made different choices under impossible circumstances.

The entertainment industry blacklist operated through unofficial but highly effective mechanisms. No law prohibited hiring those with communist affiliations, but studio executives issued the "Waldorf Statement" following the Hollywood Ten hearings, announcing they would not "knowingly employ a Communist." This voluntary industry action stemmed from multiple motivations: genuine anticommunism among some executives, economic concerns about potential boycotts, and desire to prevent government regulation by demonstrating private sector responsibility. The resulting system required performers to obtain "clearance" before being hired, effectively proving negative evidence of non-association with suspect organizations or individuals.

The human toll proved devastating. Accomplished directors like Edward Dmytryk initially refused to cooperate but later named colleagues after prison time and professional isolation. Talented performers including Zero Mostel found themselves unemployable in television and film, surviving through less visible work in theater or other fields. Writer Dalton Trumbo, one of Hollywood's highest-paid screenwriters before blacklisting, continued working under pseudonyms at greatly reduced rates. The blacklist affected not just those directly named but also anyone who defended them or questioned the process, creating expanding circles of silence and complicity.

On March 12, 1956, ninety-nine Southern congressmen and senators signed the "Southern Manifesto," formally titled "Declaration of Constitutional Principles." This extraordinary document denounced the Supreme Court's *Brown v. Board of Education* decision as "a clear abuse of judicial power" that had "destroyed the amicable relations between the white and Negro races." The signatories pledged to use "all lawful means" to reverse the desegregation ruling. Though carefully avoiding explicit calls for unlawful resistance, the manifesto provided political legitimacy to defiance of federal authority and established "massive resistance" as a coordinated regional strategy against integration.

This fusion of civil rights opposition with Cold War anti-communism created a politically potent combination. Southern politicians increasingly framed desegregation efforts as communist plots to create social disorder. Georgia Governor Herman Talmadge told supporters: "The meddlers, demagogues, race-baiters and Communists are determined to destroy every vestige of states' rights." This framing transformed civil rights activists from advocates for constitutional rights into suspected subversives, allowing segregationists to portray themselves as defenders of American values rather than opponents of equality. The resulting ideological framework justified surveillance, harassment, and suppression of civil rights work as national security measures.

The most dramatic manifestation of massive resistance emerged through school closures rather than integration compliance. When federal courts ordered integration of schools in Little Rock, Arkansas, Governor Orval Faubus deployed National Guard troops to block Black students from entering Central High School in September 1957. After President Eisenhower federalized the Arkansas National Guard and sent Army paratroopers to enforce court orders, Faubus responded by closing all Little Rock high schools for the 1958-59 academic year. Similar closures spread across the South, most extensively in Prince Edward County, Virginia, which shuttered its entire public school system from 1959 to 1964 rather than integrate.

In March 1955, Portland, Oregon radio station KEX announced a new policy: it would no longer play songs by Elvis Presley. Station manager Herb Hollister explained: "If I had a daughter, I wouldn't want her listening to Presley. His rhythm and blues appeals to all the base instincts." Similar bans soon appeared at stations nationwide, often accompanied by ceremonial destruction of Presley records. These reactions to emerging rock and roll music reflected broader cultural anxieties about changing social norms, particularly regarding youth behavior, racial integration, and sexuality. The resulting conflicts revealed how Cold War tensions extended beyond geopolitics into daily cultural practices and personal identities.

Rock and roll sparked particular concern because it embodied multiple perceived threats simultaneously. Its musical roots in African American rhythm and blues raised racial anxieties at the moment integration battles intensified. Its appeal to teenagers created generational divisions when family cohesion seemed essential to national security. Its dance styles and suggestive lyrics implied sexual liberation contrary to traditional moral codes. Concert scenes showing teenage girls screaming with apparent abandon for performers like Presley seemed to confirm parents' worst fears about rock's effect on youth self-control. These overlapping concerns made rock music a perfect symbolic target for those worried about rapid social changes.

Religious leadership often spearheaded opposition to cultural changes. Baptist pastor Jimmy Snow organized anti-rock crusades where teenagers surrendered records for destruction, symbolically rejecting musical "temptation." Catholic universities canceled rock performances as morally inappropriate. Billy Graham warned that juvenile delinquency stemmed from cultural degeneracy requiring spiritual renewal. These religious framings elevated cultural conflicts from matters of taste to moral imperatives, transforming preferences about music or entertainment into statements of spiritual allegiance or rebellion. The moral weight assigned to cultural choices intensified conflicts by raising perceived stakes on all sides.

On June 14, 1954, President Dwight Eisenhower signed legislation adding the words "under God" to the Pledge of Allegiance, declaring the change would "strengthen those spiritual weapons which forever will be our country's most powerful resource." Two years later, Congress established "In God We Trust" as the national motto, mandating its appearance on all currency. These symbolic measures received overwhelming bipartisan support and minimal public opposition. They demonstrated how Cold War ideological struggle transformed

American institutions, inserting religious references into daily civic rituals specifically to distinguish American identity from "godless communism." This religious framing of national identity reflected a broader pattern of institutional changes responding to perceived ideological threats.

The legal architecture supporting these measures had begun developing years earlier. The Internal Security Act of 1950 (McCarran Act) represented the most comprehensive legislative response to perceived communist threat, requiring communist organizations to register with the government, establishing detention facilities for potential use during national emergencies, and expanding grounds for denying entry or deporting immigrants with suspect political backgrounds. President Truman vetoed the legislation, warning it would "make a mockery of our Bill of Rights" and put the government "in the business of thought control," but Congress overrode his veto with substantial bipartisan majorities. This extraordinary support revealed how security concerns had temporarily overcome traditional civil liberties protections across the political spectrum.

In Connecticut, a third-grade girl regularly awoke screaming from the same nightmare: Soviet bombs falling as she desperately searched for her parents. In California, a nine-year-old boy insisted on wearing a Superman cape to school, believing it would protect him during nuclear attack. In New York, a high school student developed elaborate plans for surviving in the woods after atomic devastation. According to psychiatrist Sibylle Escalona, who documented these cases in 1962, such reactions represented normal psychological responses to the abnormal reality of potential nuclear annihilation. Children's fears reflected broader societal anxiety that distinguished the Cold War era from previous conflicts, the unprecedented possibility that civilization itself might end nearly instantaneously through human decision.

The psychology of nuclear fear differed fundamentally from traditional war anxiety because it involved threats without historical precedent or clear defensive possibilities. Earlier generations feared invasion, occupation, or conventional bombing based on historical experiences providing conceptual frameworks for understanding potential dangers. Nuclear weapons introduced entirely new possibilities, immediate destruction of entire cities, deadly radiation persisting long after initial blast, potential climate effects threatening global survival. These novel threats exceeded existing psychological coping mechanisms, requiring new responses at both individual and societal levels.

Civil defense programs attempted to create an illusion of control amid these unprecedented dangers. The famous "duck and cover" drills, introduced to schools nationwide through films featuring Bert the Turtle, instructed children to hide under desks during nuclear attack. Fallout shelter programs encouraged families to construct home shelters or identify public shelter locations. Government publications provided detailed instructions for post-attack survival, including recommendations for removing radioactive particles from food. These programs served psychological functions beyond their limited practical value, creating a sense of agency amid overwhelming threat while demonstrating government acknowledgment of dangers citizens already perceived.

If we could look at these events from the stars' eternal perspective, we might see the profound irony in the situation. At the very moment humans had achieved unprecedented technological mastery, splitting the atom and harnessing nuclear energy, they had also created the means for their own extinction. The same brilliance that allowed humanity to reach toward the stars now threatened to extinguish human civilization in an afternoon. The pendulum of human progress had swung to an extreme where advancement itself created existential danger. Yet even in this darkest moment, when children practiced hiding from atomic bombs under school desks, the spiral of history continued its turn. The excesses of fear would eventually prompt correction, as they had in earlier cycles of panic and persecution.

From the celestial vantage point of the stars, this particular moment in the human journey represented something genuinely new, the first time in Earth's long history that a single species had developed the capacity to alter the planet irreversibly or even render it uninhabitable. The Cold War's nuclear standoff created an unprecedented existential question that no previous generation had faced. Yet the underlying human tendencies, the fear of invisible enemies, the search for security through conformity, the tension between liberty and safety, echoed patterns seen throughout history.

The spiral had turned again, not bringing humanity back to exactly the same position, but revisiting fundamental questions about how societies balance security and freedom, conformity and individuality, in new contexts with higher stakes than ever before. The stargazers might have observed how this time, the consequences of failing to find that balance could be final in a way previous cycles of fear had never been. Yet they might also have noted humanity's remarkable resilience, the capacity to live with unprecedented danger while still continuing the essential tasks of building, creating, loving, and eventually finding paths back from the brink.

NO MAN'S LAND: CONFORMITY VS. INDIVIDUALITY

In uncertain times, society has legitimate need for cohesion around core values, with individuals accepting certain constraints for collective stability and security.

Pause. Notice what arises in you.

In uncertain times, society has essential need for independent thinkers willing to challenge consensus, raise uncomfortable questions, and defend individual conscience against group pressure.

Pause. Notice what arises in you.

You do not have to agree with or justify either statement. Simply hold them both in your mind and observe what comes up.

When journalist Edward R. Murrow prepared his famous 1954 broadcast challenging McCarthy, CBS executive William Paley worried about potential sponsor backlash but ultimately approved the program. After it aired, Murrow received both praise for moral courage and condemnation for undermining national security. The broadcast itself acknowledged this tension, with Murrow concluding: "We proclaim ourselves defenders of freedom, but we cannot defend freedom abroad by deserting it at home."

Similar tensions confronted countless Americans during the McCarthy era. Connecticut schoolteacher Margaret Schofield, refusing to sign a loyalty oath she considered violation of academic freedom, lost her position of twenty years. Her superintendent, while implementing the requirement, privately acknowledged the contradiction between teaching democratic values while requiring conformity pledges. Both perspectives contained legitimate concerns, the community's interest in teacher trustworthiness and the teacher's commitment to modeling independent citizenship.

The fundamental tension between conformity and individuality cannot be permanently resolved because both serve essential functions in healthy societies. Shared values provide necessary social cohesion, while independent thinking prevents stagnation and corrects collective errors. What historian Richard Hofstadter called "the paranoid style in American politics" emerges when this balance tilts too far toward enforced conformity, yet complete individualism without common values would create dysfunctional fragmentation.

Perhaps wisdom lies in recognizing both values simultaneously rather than choosing between them. Democratic societies function best when they maintain space for individual conscience while fostering voluntary commitment to core shared principles. This dynamic balance requires continuous adjustment rather than permanent resolution, with different historical moments sometimes requiring greater emphasis on cohesion or dissent depending on specific challenges faced. The McCarthy era eventually demonstrated how American institutions could correct course after temporarily privileging conformity over individual rights, suggesting inherent corrective capacity when either value becomes excessively dominant.

Chapter Fifteen

When Courage Found Its Voice

On the afternoon of June 9, 1954, millions of Americans watched their television screens as Joseph Welch, a 63-year-old Boston attorney representing the U.S. Army, finally lost his patience. Senator Joseph McCarthy had just attacked one of Welch's young associates, Frederick Fisher, for having once belonged to the National Lawyers Guild, which McCarthy characterized as "the legal bulwark of the Communist Party." Welch, who had maintained his courtly demeanor through weeks of hearings despite McCarthy's provocations, responded with quiet intensity that would forever alter American political life.

"Until this moment, Senator, I think I never really gauged your cruelty or your recklessness," Welch said, his voice steady but emotion evident. "Little did I dream you could be so reckless and so cruel as to do an injury to that lad." When McCarthy attempted to continue, Welch interrupted: "Let us not assassinate this lad further, Senator. You have done enough. Have you no sense of decency, sir, at long last? Have you left no sense of decency?"

The hearing room erupted in spontaneous applause, the first public demonstration against McCarthy in an official setting. Television cameras captured McCarthy's face, suddenly uncertain, as he fumbled with papers before calling for the next witness. The hearings continued, but something fundamental had changed. In that moment, the bubble of fear that had sustained McCarthy's influence began to deflate. Within months, the Senate would censure him; within three years, he would die, largely forgotten. The four-year period of accusation, suspicion, and career destruction that bore his name was ending not with revolutionary upheaval or dramatic revelation, but through the quiet reassertion of fundamental decency.

This resolution exemplifies how democratic systems typically recover from periods of fear-driven excess. Not through single dramatic moments, though Welch's confrontation came close, but through accumulating small corrections that gradually restore balance. Supreme Court decisions reestablished First Amendment protections. Media organizations learned to scrutinize accusations rather than simply amplify them. Politicians discovered that opposing demagogic tactics served their interests better than enabling them. None of these corrections happened immediately or completely, but their cumulative effect restored norms of fairness, due process, and proportionality that fear had temporarily overwhelmed.

Similar patterns emerged in other domains affected by Cold War anxieties. Civil rights advocates successfully challenged "massive resistance" to integration, not through revolutionary transformation but through persistent legal action, strategic nonviolent protest, and gradual shifts in public opinion. Nuclear fears channeled into arms control agreements and crisis prevention mechanisms rather than either resignation or panic. The American political system eventually incorporated legitimate security concerns while rejecting extraordinary measures that undermined core constitutional principles.

This recovery process was neither quick nor complete. Some careers remained permanently derailed; some civil liberties protections took decades to restore; some nuclear anxieties persisted throughout the Cold War. Yet the overall direction, toward more balanced approaches to genuine security concerns, demonstrated democratic systems' capacity for self-correction. Understanding how this restoration occurred provides valuable insight into society's resilience when facing intense fears, not through immunity to fear itself, but through gradually reactivating institutional and cultural antibodies against its most destructive manifestations.

From their distant perspective among the stars, the silent celestial observers might have witnessed this process of recovery with a certain detached fascination. They had seen the pendulum swing toward fear and suspicion, and now they watched as it gradually returned toward balance. The stars, in their eternal patience, understood what humans often struggle to comprehend: that cycles of fear and panic eventually exhaust themselves, that societies possess inherent capacity for self-correction, and that the spiral of history continues its turn, not returning to exactly the same position, but revisiting similar challenges with the hard-won wisdom of experience.

Three days after Joseph Welch's famous confrontation with McCarthy, Vermont Republican Senator Ralph Flanders rose in the Senate chamber to introduce a resolution expressing concern about McCarthy's conduct. Flanders, a 73-year-old industrial machinery manufacturer with a traditional Republican commitment to institutional propriety, had watched with growing alarm as McCarthy's reckless accusations damaged both individuals and the Senate itself. "He dons war paint," Flanders observed of his colleague. "He goes into his war dance. He emits his war whoops. He goes forth to battle and proudly returns with the scalp of a pink Army dentist."

Flanders' colorful rhetoric masked serious purpose. His resolution, which initially attracted little support, initiated a process that would eventually lead to McCarthy's formal censure by his colleagues. This patient, institutionally-oriented response typified how democratic systems ultimately address fear-driven excesses, not through dramatic confrontation but through applying established procedures that gradually restore institutional norms and balance. The Senate, after exhaustive debate and investigation, would eventually condemn McCarthy's conduct by a vote of 67-22 in December 1954, a judgment that dramatically diminished his influence while preserving the Senate's own institutional integrity.

McCarthy's downfall stemmed not from single causes but from a confluence of factors gradually undermining his effectiveness. His tendency to attack increasingly powerful targets eventually generated organized opposition that earlier victims had been unable to mount. His methods, initially shocking enough to command attention, became predictable and less newsworthy over time. Public opinion shifted as the consequences of unchecked accusation became more visible. Most importantly, alternative voices, from Edward R. Murrow's methodical television exposé to Judge Welch's courtroom confrontation, provided counternarratives that challenged McCarthy's monopoly on patriotic imagery and language.

The press played crucial if belated role in this rebalancing. While many publications had initially amplified McCarthy's accusations without adequate scrutiny, journalistic standards evolved in response to McCarthy's manipulation of deadline pressure. Major newspapers including The Washington Post and The New York Times developed more rigorous fact-checking procedures for evaluating McCarthy's claims. Television, still establishing its journalistic practices, recognized how its visual immediacy could expose demagogic tactics through unfiltered presentation rather than interpretive analysis. As CBS producer Fred Friendly later reflected regarding Murrow's McCarthy broadcast: "We decided to use McCarthy to defeat McCarthy, his own words and pictures."

On September 4, 1957, fifteen-year-old Elizabeth Eckford put on the new dress she had made for her first day at Central High School in Little Rock, Arkansas. Unaware that the other eight Black students chosen to integrate the school had arranged to arrive together, Eckford approached the campus alone. She encountered a hostile crowd of white adults shouting "Lynch her! Lynch her!" while Arkansas National Guard troops, deployed by Governor Orval Faubus to prevent integration, blocked her entry. As Eckford sought safety, a white woman named Grace Lorch helped her reach a bus stop and board a public bus to escape the mob. Photographs of Eckford's dignified suffering amid hatred became iconic images that fundamentally shifted how many Americans understood the integration struggle.

The Little Rock crisis exemplified how "massive resistance" to integration ultimately failed despite its temporary effectiveness. Governor Faubus's defiance of federal court orders initially prevented integration and boosted his political standing among segregationists. Yet his actions forced President Eisenhower, personally cautious about integration pace, to demonstrate federal authority by sending 1,200 paratroopers from the 101st Airborne Division to enforce court-ordered desegregation. This decisive federal action established that state officials could not nullify federal authority on racial questions, resolving constitutional questions dating back to the Civil War while creating precedent for subsequent federal civil rights enforcement.

This pattern, segregationist resistance generating stronger federal response, repeated across the South throughout the late 1950s and early 1960s. Each crisis temporarily blocked progress while ultimately strengthening legal and political momentum toward equality. The Montgomery bus boycott (1955-56) began as local protest against segregated public transportation but culminated in Supreme Court ruling against bus segregation nationwide. Sit-ins starting in Greensboro, North Carolina (1960) originated as spontaneous student actions but evolved into coordinated movement accelerating public accommodation desegregation. Mississippi officials' imprisonment of Freedom Riders (1961) intended to halt integration efforts instead generated national attention leading to Interstate Commerce Commission desegregation orders. Each apparent segregationist victory proved Pyrrhic, advancing rather than preventing the very changes resistance sought to block.

In 1960, director Otto Preminger publicly announced that blacklisted screenwriter Dalton Trumbo would receive screen credit for writing "Exodus." Shortly afterward, Kirk Douglas revealed Trumbo had written "Spartacus," bringing the blacklisted writer out of the shadows where he had worked for years under pseudonyms at drastically reduced rates. These public acknowledgments by powerful industry figures effectively ended Hollywood's formal blacklist after more than a decade. The blacklisting system, which had once seemed a permanent fixture of American cultural landscape, collapsed not through dramatic government intervention or industrial revolution but through accumulating individual decisions that its maintenance no longer served even its original supporters' interests.

This pattern, gradual normalization rather than dramatic vindication, characterized how most McCarthy-era cultural restrictions eventually dissolved. Former blacklistees rarely received formal apologies or compensation for lost income and opportunities. Many never regained professional momentum interrupted during prime career years. The entertainment industry never officially acknowledged the blacklist's injustice while it operated, and only decades later did organizations like the Academy of Motion Picture Arts and Sciences correct credits and recognize blacklisted artists' contributions. Yet despite this incomplete justice, the practical effect, resumption of creative careers and dissolution of political screening systems, represented significant restoration of cultural freedom previously constrained by ideological fear.

President John F. Kennedy's 1961 inaugural address, asking Americans to "ask not what your country can do for you, ask what you can do for your country," established a notably different tone from the fearful anticommunism dominating the previous decade's political discourse. While maintaining firm anticommunist foreign policy, Kennedy framed ideological struggle positively rather than defensively, emphasizing American capacity to demonstrate democratic system's superiority through accomplishment rather than merely preventing subversion through suspicion. This reframing didn't reject security concerns but integrated them into broader conception of national purpose transcending defensive posture. The resulting political vision maintained anticommunist commitment while creating space for domestic policy innovation addressing previously neglected social and economic challenges.

This tonal shift reflected broader political recalibration following McCarthy-era excesses. The 1960 election, with both Kennedy and Nixon distancing themselves from McCarthy's methods while maintaining strong anticommunist positions, demonstrated how mainstream politics had incorporated legitimate security concerns while rejecting unconstrained fear-mongering. Congressional leadership in both parties similarly distinguished between robust security measures and constitutional violations, developing oversight mechanisms preventing executive branch overreach while maintaining necessary security functions. This bipartisan evolution created political foundation supporting both anticommunist foreign policy and domestic civil liberties protections rather than presenting them as irreconcilable alternatives requiring absolute choice.

As William F. Buckley Jr. prepared to launch National Review magazine in 1955, he sought to develop intellectually coherent conservatism transcending both McCarthy's conspiratorial anticommunism and Eastern establishment Republicanism. Buckley's statement of principles declared the magazine "stands athwart history, yelling Stop" while acknowledging "Big Government" could only be gradually reduced rather than immediately dismantled. This sophisticated approach, accepting practical constraints while maintaining principled opposition to liberal consensus, established foundation for conservative movement capable of eventual electoral success rather than merely expressing oppositional frustration. Through patient institution-building rather than apocalyptic warnings, Buckley and colleagues transformed conservatism from marginal protest to governing philosophy.

This conservative revival required careful distinctions from McCarthy-era excesses while maintaining anticommunist commitment. Conservative intellectuals including Frank Meyer developed "fusionist" philosophy integrating traditional values, limited government economics, and robust foreign policy into coherent worldview. Organizations like Intercollegiate Studies Institute built campus conservative presence through philosophical and historical education rather than loyalty investigations or radical accusations. Publications including Russell Kirk's "The Conservative Mind" (1953) established intellectual lineage connecting contemporary conservatives to historical figures including Edmund Burke, creating respectable philosophical tradition rather than reactive movement. These scholarly activities occurred alongside continued anticommunist activism but established conservatism as comprehensive worldview addressing full range of political questions rather than single-issue security movement vulnerable to excesses born from narrow focus.

Looking upward at the night sky, we might imagine how the stars perceived this gradual restoration of balance in American society. From their cosmic perspective, they had witnessed the same human patterns repeat throughout history: the surge of fear in response to genuine threats, the temporary abandonment of principles in the name of security, and then the gradual recalibration as societies remembered what truly defined them. The celestial observers might have noted how this particular spiral of history brought unique challenges, nuclear weapons that could end civilization in an afternoon, ideological conflicts that divided the world into hostile camps, yet still followed recognizable patterns of human response and adaptation.

The stars would have witnessed how democratic systems bend under fear but rarely break entirely, how they contain within themselves the capacity for self-correction when they stray too far from their foundational principles. This resilience doesn't emerge from dramatic revolutions or heroic individual acts alone, though these sometimes play important roles. Rather, it develops through countless small readjustments across institutions: a journalist who decides to verify before publishing, a judge who insists on due process despite public pressure, a senator who places institutional integrity above partisan advantage, ordinary citizens who eventually tire of suspicion and demand a return to decency.

When faced with genuine security threats, democratic societies often experience tension between security measures and civil liberties protections. The McCarthy era represented a particularly extreme manifestation of this tension, as legitimate concerns about Soviet espionage and influence expanded into comprehensive ideological scrutiny affecting ordinary citizens far removed from sensitive positions. The period's eventual resolution, through institutional correction rather than either permanent securitization or complete abandonment of legitimate protections, demonstrated democratic systems' capacity for self-correction following temporary imbalance. This resilience emerged not from single dramatic interventions but through multiple adjustments across institutions gradually restoring balance between competing values without sacrificing either entirely.

Several crucial lessons emerged from this experience. First, democratic institutions contain inherent correction mechanisms that function imperfectly but persistently when temporarily overwhelmed by fear. The judicial branch, though initially deferential to security claims, gradually reasserted constitutional principles through cases establishing proper boundaries for investigations and sanctions. Legislative bodies eventually provided oversight preventing executive branch overreach, while developing internal rules preventing abuses like McCarthy's committee manipulation. Media organizations developed professional practices balancing newsworthiness against verification requirements. These overlapping corrections demonstrated how democratic resilience resides not in single institutions but distributed responsibility across multiple entities, creating redundant protection against systemic failure.

Second, democratic resilience requires mobilizing positive values rather than merely opposing negative developments. Civil rights movement success derived not from simply condemning discrimination but articulating positive vision connecting American ideals with practical reform. Conservative movement transcended McCarthy-era anticommunism by developing comprehensive philosophical framework extending beyond security concerns. Great Society programs addressed genuine social problems that security preoccupation had temporarily overshadowed. In each case, positive articulation of democratic values proved more sustainable than reactive opposition to perceived threats, creating foundation for constructive action rather than merely preventing destructive excesses.

The spiral of history had completed another turn. Just as religious persecution had eventually yielded to greater tolerance, and industrial disruption had led to more balanced economic arrangements, now the excesses of ideological fear were gradually being corrected through democratic processes. The pendulum that had swung so far toward suspicion and conformity was moving back toward a more balanced position that could accommodate both legitimate security concerns and essential liberties. This pattern, fear followed by excess followed by correction, revealed once again humanity's capacity to learn from experience, to recognize when fear has driven us too far from our core values, and to find our way back to a more balanced path.

NO MAN'S LAND: Progress vs. Tradition

Societies must embrace necessary change, discard outdated practices, and actively pursue justice even when disrupting comfortable arrangements for some citizens.

Pause. Notice what arises in you.

Societies must preserve valuable traditions, respect historical continuity, and approach change with humility recognizing that even flawed arrangements may contain underappreciated wisdom.

Pause. Notice what arises in you.

You do not have to agree with or justify either statement. Simply hold them both in your mind and observe what comes up.

The Cold War's resolution phase demonstrated how societies navigate this tension between necessary change and valuable continuity. Chief Justice Earl Warren, who led the Supreme Court through landmark civil rights decisions, had previously overseen Japanese American internment as California governor during World War II. He maintained institutional respect for precedent while gradually extending constitutional protections to previously excluded groups. His approach represented neither wholesale rejection of tradition nor rigid adherence to past practice, but thoughtful evolution guided by enduring principles.

Similarly, President Eisenhower combined military tradition as former Supreme Allied Commander with willingness to enforce desegregation through federal troops when necessary. Despite personal reservations about integration's pace, he recognized constitutional principles required defending Black students' rights against mob violence. His decision balanced respect for states' traditional authority with recognition that fundamental national values sometimes required federal intervention.

The most sustainable social changes typically incorporate valuable elements from existing arrangements while reforming their injustices. The civil rights movement succeeded partly through framing demands within American constitutional tradition rather than rejecting it entirely. Conservative movement gained influence by articulating philosophical roots extending to founding principles while addressing contemporary challenges. Both movements integrated change and continuity rather than treating them as mutually exclusive alternatives.

This balanced approach recognizes that human societies require both stability and adaptation to thrive. Purely revolutionary approaches creating comprehensive breaks with tradition often produce unintended consequences through discarding accumulated wisdom alongside genuine injustices. Conversely, rigid traditionalism refusing any adaptation eventually collapses under pressure from unaddressed problems that tradition cannot solve. The wisest path typically involves discerning which traditional elements contain enduring value while recognizing where change, even disruptive change, has become necessary despite transition costs.

Cycle 6: When the Center Couldn't Hold

Chapter Sixteen

When Youth Refused the Script

On the evening of February 25, 1964, millions of Americans gathered around their television sets to witness a pivotal moment in boxing history. The charismatic 22-year-old Cassius Clay, a 7-1 underdog, danced, jabbed, and taunted his way to victory over the seemingly invincible heavyweight champion Sonny Liston. But what captivated viewers transcended athletic spectacle, it was what happened afterward. In a moment broadcast live across the nation, Clay shouted to reporters, "I shook up the world!" The next morning, he announced his conversion to Islam and his adoption of a new name: Muhammad Ali.

This televised transformation, athletic, religious, personal, and political, embodied the cultural revolution beginning to sweep across America. Like Ali himself, the nation was shedding old identities and embracing new possibilities, often in ways that shocked the established order. The intimate immediacy of television meant Americans didn't just read about these transformations; they witnessed them in their living rooms, creating an unprecedented sense of participation in historical events unfolding in real time.

The period from roughly 1960 to the late 1970s marked one of the most dramatic cultural shifts in American history. Civil rights activists challenged centuries of racial segregation. Anti-war protesters questioned America's military interventions abroad. Women demanded equal treatment in workplaces and re-lationships. Environmental advocates raised alarms about industrial pollution. Young people rejected conventional lifestyles in favor of experimentation and self-expression. Each movement generated social unease as established norms, many dating back generations, suddenly appeared vulnerable to rapid change.

What distinguished this period was not simply the presence of social move-ments, which had emerged periodically throughout American history, but their convergence, visibility, and interconnection. Civil rights activists inspired anti-war protesters, who influenced women's rights advocates, who informed environmental activists, each movement learning tactics and borrowing moral authority from the others. Television broadcast these movements directly into American homes, making previously invisible struggles impossible to ignore. The resulting cultural transformation generated both extraordinary progress and deep disquiet, as Americans struggled to adapt to a social landscape chang-ing with unprecedented speed.

This cycle of cultural revolution and backlash echoed familiar patterns we've seen in previous historical periods. Like the religious upheavals of the 1600s, it involved fundamental questions about societal values. Like the revolution-ary era of the late 1700s, it challenged established authority structures. Like the industrial revolution of the early 1800s, it confronted rapid technological and economic change. Like the social purity movements of the late 1800s, it grappled with evolving definitions of morality and propriety. The specific issues differed, but the underlying dynamics, rapid change generating both progress and fear, followed recurring historical patterns.

Understanding this cycle illuminates our present moment in two crucial ways. First, it reminds us that periods of cultural transformation inevitably pro-duce both positive advances and legitimate concerns, with neither representing the complete story. Second, it demonstrates how societies eventually integrate necessary changes while preserving valuable traditions, finding workable bal-ances rather than swinging perpetually between extremes. By examining how Americans navigated this tumultuous period, with all its achievements, excesses, and eventual accommodations, we gain perspective on navigating our own era of cultural transformation and the apprehensions it inevitably produces.

From the timeless vantage point of the stars, this period might have appeared as yet another turn in humanity's spiraling journey. The celestial observers had witnessed similar patterns of cultural transformation and reaction throughout human history, moments when societies faced fundamental questions about identity, authority, and values. They had seen how each generation must navigate the tension between preserving what is valuable from the past and embracing necessary changes for the future. Yet even these eternal watchers might have noted something distinctive about this particular historical moment: the unprecedented speed and visibility of change, accelerated by new technologies that connected humans across vast distances and made previously invisible struggles impossible to ignore.

When John F. Kennedy and Richard Nixon faced each other in the first televised presidential debate on September 26, 1960, they unwittingly demonstrated television's transformative power. Radio listeners generally thought Nixon had won the debate with his substantive arguments. Television viewers, however, overwhelmingly favored Kennedy, who appeared young, relaxed, and vibrant against the pale, sweating Nixon. The medium hadn't just transmitted the candidates' words, it had fundamentally altered how those words were received, prioritizing visual impression over verbal content.

This debate marked a crucial inflection point in American media history. By 1960, television had penetrated approximately 90% of American households, creating the first truly national audience witnessing events simultaneously. Where newspapers had once framed events through editorial decisions and radio had added the intimacy of human voices, television added the visceral impact of visual images that seemingly bypassed critical thought to create immediate emotional connections. Political communication, entertainment, news, advertising, and social movements all had to adapt to this new visual landscape or risk irrelevance.

The transformation affected every aspect of American society. Television's national reach accelerated the homogenization of American culture, with regionally distinct lifestyles gradually yielding to nationally shared experiences. Television networks concentrated unprecedented cultural influence, with just three companies, CBS, NBC, and ABC, controlling what most Americans saw. Programming schedules reorganized family routines, with dinner times adjusted to accommodate favorite shows and living room furniture arranged around the television set rather than conversation areas. Most significantly, television shifted the balance between public and private experience, bringing formerly distant events directly into intimate domestic spaces.

Television's impact proved particularly powerful during the Vietnam War, the first major conflict broadcast directly into American living rooms. Where previous wars had been presented through carefully controlled government information, sanitized photographs, and patriotic newsreels, Vietnam appeared on television with stark immediacy. Scenes of wounded soldiers, burning villages, and body bags contradicted official optimism about the war's progress, creating what became known as the "credibility gap" between government statements and visible reality. This gap altered the relationship between citizens and authorities, making Americans more skeptical of official narratives contradicted by visual evidence.

On December 1, 1955, Rosa Parks boarded a Montgomery city bus after a long day working as a seamstress. When the driver ordered her to give up her seat to a white passenger, Parks quietly refused. Her subsequent arrest sparked a 381-day bus boycott that transformed both Montgomery's transit system and the national civil rights movement. What made Parks' defiance particularly powerful wasn't just the action itself but its transmission through increasingly sophisticated media networks, first local newspapers, then radio, then television, and eventually international news services. A local incident became a national symbol precisely because media technologies could now transmit both the factual details and the emotional resonance of Parks' dignified resistance.

This interplay between grassroots activism and media coverage defined the civil rights movement's most effective period. Organizations like the Southern Christian Leadership Conference (SCLC) and Student Nonviolent Coordinating Committee (SNCC) developed sophisticated strategies leveraging television's visual impact to advance their cause. When Birmingham Public Safety Commissioner Bull Connor directed fire hoses and police dogs against peaceful protesters in 1963, television cameras captured images that shocked the nation and generated unprecedented pressure for federal action. This strategic use of media represented not manipulation but recognition that centuries of injustice had persisted partly because most Americans had never directly witnessed their brutal implementation.

The movement's strategic brilliance lay in its nonviolent approach, which created stark visual contrasts between peaceful protesters and violent authorities. By deliberately staging confrontations in which disciplined activists faced escalating repression, civil rights leaders forced television viewers to choose sides between visibly gentle demonstrators and visibly violent defenders of segregation. Dr. Martin Luther King Jr. articulated this strategy explicitly, noting, "We will not obey unjust laws or submit to unjust practices. We will do this peacefully, openly, cheerfully because our aim is to persuade." This emphasis on moral persuasion rather than physical confrontation perfectly suited television's visual dynamics, creating compelling narratives with clear heroes and villains.

The movement's victories accumulated through persistent application of these strategies. The Montgomery bus boycott succeeded in December 1956 when the Supreme Court declared bus segregation unconstitutional. The 1960 Greensboro lunch counter sit-ins spread to dozens of cities, generating economic pressure that desegregated many businesses. The 1961 Freedom Rides forced federal action ensuring desegregated interstate transportation. The 1963 Birmingham campaign created pressure resulting in the desegregation of that city's businesses. The 1965 Selma voting rights campaign directly inspired passage of the Voting Rights Act. Each victory built momentum for the next, creating a sense of inevitable progress despite continuing resistance.

On February 27, 1968, Walter Cronkite, the trusted anchor viewed by millions of Americans as the embodiment of journalistic objectivity, concluded his CBS Evening News broadcast with an unprecedented editorial. After reporting from Vietnam following the Tet Offensive, Cronkite told viewers: "To say that we are mired in stalemate seems the only realistic, yet unsatisfactory, concl usion... It is increasingly clear to this reporter that the only rational way out then will be to negotiate, not as victors but as an honorable people who lived up to their pledge to defend democracy, and did the best they could." When President Johnson watched this broadcast, he reportedly told an aide, "If I've lost Cronkite, I've lost Middle America." Johnson's recognition of television's power to shape public opinion reflected how thoroughly the medium had transformed political communication.

The Vietnam War represented the first major American conflict experienced primarily through television rather than print, radio, or carefully controlled government information. Between 1965 and 1972, evening news programs devoted between 20% and 40% of their coverage to the war, bringing unprecedented visibility to combat operations and their consequences. This coverage initially supported administration policy but gradually adopted a more skeptical tone as the gap widened between official optimism and visible reality. Images of wounded American soldiers, Vietnamese civilian casualties, and burned villages contradicted government assertions about military progress, creating a "credibility gap" that fundamentally shifted the relationship between citizens and authorities.

The draft system created personal stakes for millions of families, transforming abstract policy debates into immediate life-or-death concerns. Young men faced difficult choices: comply with conscription that might send them to a war they opposed, seek deferments available primarily to privileged students, pursue conscientious objector status through complex bureaucratic processes, or resist the draft through non-compliance carrying legal penalties including imprisonment. These dilemmas forced families across America to confront moral questions about individual conscience versus governmental authority, creating dinner-table debates that transcended traditional political boundaries and contributed to the war's growing divisiveness.

On August 26, 1970, fifty years after women won the right to vote, the National Organization for Women (NOW) organized the Women's Strike for Equality. Tens of thousands of women marched down Fifth Avenue in New York City, carrying signs with slogans like "Don't Cook Dinner – Starve a

Rat Today" and "Don't Iron While the Strike is Hot." Similar demonstrations occurred in cities across the country, drawing unprecedented media attention to women's demands for equal rights. The strike exemplified the second-wave feminist movement's strategic sophistication, combining serious policy demands with humor and visual spectacle designed to capture media coverage while making equality claims accessible to mainstream audiences.

This renaissance of women's activism emerged from multiple sources. Betty Friedan's 1963 book "The Feminine Mystique" had articulated the "problem that has no name," the dissatisfaction many educated women felt despite achieving the supposed suburban housewife ideal. Women working in civil rights and anti-war movements had experienced marginalization even within these progressive causes, with male leaders often relegating them to clerical roles despite their educational and organizational abilities. The 1960 introduction of oral contraceptives had created unprecedented reproductive autonomy, allowing women to plan pregnancies and careers with greater certainty. These converging factors created conditions for a movement addressing women's specific concerns rather than subsuming them within broader social justice causes.

The movement pursued multiple strategies simultaneously. Legislative efforts secured laws prohibiting sex discrimination in employment, credit, education, and other domains. Legal challenges through organizations like the ACLU Women's Rights Project, led by future Supreme Court Justice Ruth Bader Ginsburg, systematically challenged sex-based legal distinctions. Consciousness-raising groups helped women recognize shared experiences rather than individual problems, creating collective identity necessary for political mobilization. Public protests generated media attention highlighting specific inequalities. Educational initiatives established women's studies programs examining historical and contemporary gender dynamics. This multifaceted approach addressed both institutional policies and cultural attitudes, recognizing that formal equality required changing both laws and mindsets.

On April 22, 1970, twenty million Americans, roughly 10% of the U.S. population at that time, participated in the first Earth Day, attending rallies, cleanup events, and educational programs focused on environmental protection. This massive demonstration emerged from growing concerns about industrial pollution, wilderness preservation, and long-term sustainability. While environmental activism had existed for decades, primarily through conservation organizations like the Sierra Club, Earth Day represented unprecedented mainstream engagement with ecological issues. The event's extraordinary scale demonstrated how environmental concerns had transcended niche interests to become broad public priorities, creating political momentum that would produce landmark environmental legislation throughout the 1970s.

This environmental awakening resulted from multiple converging factors. Rachel Carson's 1962 book "Silent Spring" had documented pesticides' ecological impacts in accessible prose, creating widespread awareness of industrial chemicals' unintended consequences. The 1969 Santa Barbara oil spill released three million gallons of crude oil into coastal waters, creating dramatic images of oil-soaked beaches and wildlife that received extensive television coverage. The 1969 Cuyahoga River fire in Cleveland, where industrial pollution made the waterway so contaminated it literally ignited, symbolized industrial excess threatening basic natural systems. Photographs of Earth from space missions provided new planetary perspective, showing a beautiful but finite world without visible political boundaries. These catalyzing events created public consciousness necessary for environmental movement's rapid growth.

"Don't trust anyone over thirty."

This slogan, popularized during Berkeley's Free Speech Movement in 1964, captured the unprecedented generational divide emerging across American society. The Baby Boom generation, raised in unprecedented prosperity, educated in expanding university systems, and coming of age amid rapid social change, developed perspectives dramatically different from their parents' generation. Where their parents had experienced economic depression and world war, leading to emphasis on security and conformity, Baby Boomers grew up with relative affluence and peace, allowing greater focus on self-expression and social criticism. This generational divide created not merely different political opinions but fundamentally different worldviews, with divergent assumptions about authority, identity, tradition, and success that transformed American culture across multiple domains.

These generational differences became most visible through youth counterculture emerging in the mid-1960s. Long hair, colorful clothing, communal living experiments, sexual openness, recreational drug use, and rock music became external markers of internal value shifts. Where mainstream culture emphasized career advancement, material acquisition, and social conformity, countercultural youth prioritized authenticity, experience, and self-discovery. While only a minority of young people fully embraced countercultural lifestyle, its visibility through media coverage created an impression of fundamental generational rupture that influenced even those maintaining more conventional appearances and behaviors. The resulting cultural anxiety reflected genuine uncertainty about social continuity when the younger generation seemed to reject foundational values their parents had assumed universal.

If the stars could observe humanity across the vast expanses of time, they might have recognized in this cultural revolution both something new and something ancient. The specific manifestations, television bringing distant realities into intimate spaces, technologies separating sexuality from reproduction, movements challenging centuries-old hierarchies, were unprecedented. Yet the underlying pattern, of generations renegotiating inherited values and institutions in light of changed circumstances, represented a recurring feature of human societies. The stars had witnessed this cycle play out countless times before, as each generation struggled to balance preserving what was valuable from the past with adapting to new realities that their ancestors could never have imagined.

Perhaps the stars would have noticed how this particular turn in humanity's spiral journey contained both remarkable progress and legitimate anxieties. Civil rights movements advanced human dignity while disrupting established social orders. Anti-war protests questioned unjustified violence while challenging traditional authority. Women's liberation expanded opportunities while transforming family structures. Environmental consciousness protected natural systems while confronting industrial practices. Each advance brought both genuine benefits and real costs, with societies struggling to integrate necessary changes while preserving valuable traditions.

From their eternal perspective, the stars might have observed that societies ultimately find their way not through perfection but through workable balances, not by eliminating tensions but by creating frameworks for their productive expression. The most sustainable social changes incorporate elements of continuity alongside necessary transformations, respecting the wisdom embedded in traditions while acknowledging when those traditions require adaptation to changed circumstances. The spiral continues its turn, not returning to exactly the same position, but revisiting similar questions at higher levels of integration as humanity learns, however imperfectly, from its ongoing experience.

NO MAN'S LAND: Protest vs. Order

Societies must protect the right to protest, challenge authority, and disrupt normal operations to draw attention to injustice, even when this creates temporary disorder or discomfort for uninvolved citizens.

Pause. Notice what arises in you.

Societies must maintain public order, respect established decision-making processes, and protect citizens from disruption and intimidation, even when protesters believe their cause justifies extraordinary measures.

Pause. Notice what arises in you.

You do not have to agree with or justify either statement. Simply hold them both in your mind and observe what comes up.

The 1960s and 1970s repeatedly confronted Americans with this fundamental tension. When civil rights activists staged lunch counter sit-ins, they deliberately disrupted normal business operations to highlight segregation's injustice. When anti-war protesters blocked draft board entrances, they interfered with government functions to oppose policies they considered immoral. When law enforcement removed these protesters, they upheld existing legal frameworks while sometimes limiting expression of dissenting views. Both protesters and authorities could claim legitimate purposes, one advancing necessary change, the other maintaining necessary order.

The wisest responses recognized valid elements in both positions. Courts generally protected peaceful protest while prohibiting direct interference with essential functions or public safety. Effective social movements developed disciplined nonviolent tactics that highlighted injustice without alienating potential supporters through excessive disruption. Law enforcement agencies that distinguished between peaceful demonstrators and genuine threats maintained legitimate authority more effectively than those treating all protesters as dangerous subversives. These balanced approaches recognized that democratic societies must simultaneously protect both dissent and functionality rather than sacrificing either entirely to preserve the other.

Democratic systems ultimately derive strength from navigating rather than eliminating this tension. The right to protest creates accountability mechanisms ensuring authorities remain responsive to citizens rather than becoming self-perpetuating power structures. Simultaneously, maintaining functional processes allows implementation of policies benefiting majority without constant disruption by energized minorities with intense preferences. Neither unlimited protest nor absolute order serves democratic functioning; the perpetual balance between these competing imperatives creates space for both necessary stability and necessary change, allowing societies to adapt without disintegrating.

Chapter Seventeen

When Order Pushed Back

O n November 3, 1969, President Richard Nixon addressed the nation from the Oval Office. American troops were fighting in Vietnam, anti-war protests had swept across college campuses, and the nation still reeled from the assassinations of Martin Luther King Jr. and Robert Kennedy the previous year. Rather than attempting to bridge this divide, Nixon deliberately appealed to those Americans who felt alienated by the counterculture's visibility and influence. "To you, the great silent majority of my fellow Americans," he declared, "I ask for your support."

With this carefully crafted phrase, Nixon transformed a heated public debate into a contest between a vocal minority and a supposedly larger, quieter group of "real" Americans who supported traditional values and government policies. In that moment, he codified a political strategy that would reshape American politics for decades, one that reframed cultural conflicts not as complex debates about values and priorities, but as struggles between an authentic majority and disruptive minorities who commanded disproportionate attention.

The speech ignited starkly different reactions across American society. In living rooms throughout the heartland, many viewers nodded in agreement, relieved that someone had finally acknowledged their discomfort with youth rebellion and cultural transformation. Meanwhile, in college dormitories and urban apartments, young activists and their allies heard an explicit attempt to delegitimize their concerns about war, inequality, and environmental degradation. Both groups felt validated in their respective worldviews, one believing they represented the silent but "real" America, the other increasingly convinced that power structures would exploit majoritarian appeals to block necessary social change.

This division reflected an intense cultural anxiety that had developed in response to the rapid social changes of the 1960s. The highly visible youth counterculture, civil rights advances, anti-war movement, feminism, and environmentalism collectively created an impression of American society in transformation, even revolution. For those who had found security, meaning, and status in traditional arrangements, these changes appeared not as progress but as potential collapse. Their anxiety manifested as genuine fear that civilization's foundations, family structures, work ethic, respect for authority, patriotism, religious values, were eroding beyond repair.

The resulting cultural collision produced a backlash that transformed American politics and society. Traditional authority structures developed new strategies to reassert control. Political movements mobilized voters around cultural anxieties rather than purely economic interests. Media outlets increasingly segregated by audience ideology. Law enforcement expanded powers to address perceived threats to social order. This reaction, while sometimes excessive, reflected legitimate concerns about rapid change that deserved understanding rather than mere dismissal. Similarly, the movements prompting this reaction, while sometimes naively utopian, identified genuine issues requiring address rather than simple suppression.

Understanding this period of backlash helps illuminate recurring patterns in how societies respond to rapid cultural change. When traditional norms appear threatened, those invested in existing arrangements typically respond first with dismissal, then with moral panic, and finally with organized resistance. This pattern appeared in earlier cycles we've examined, from reactions against religious diversity in the 1600s to responses to industrialization in the 1800s. Each time, societies eventually found balanced accommodations rather than embracing either revolutionary transformation or complete rejection of change. The same pattern would eventually emerge from the cultural conflicts of the 1960s and 1970s, though not before a period of genuine social struggle and anxiety.

From their eternal vantage point among the stars, cosmic observers might have recognized in this human drama a familiar pattern. Throughout history, societies have oscillated between periods of stability and upheaval, with each generation negotiating the delicate balance between preserving valuable traditions and embracing necessary changes. The pendulum of human affairs swings from innovation to tradition, from disruption to order, from challenging questions to reassuring answers. The stars, witnesses to countless such oscillations across millennia, might have noted how the specific manifestations change, from religious conflicts to industrial disruptions to cultural revolutions, while the underlying human dynamics remain remarkably consistent.

Time magazine's July 7, 1967 cover story, "The Hippies: Philosophy of a Subculture," marked a pivotal moment in America's relationship with its emerging counterculture. The article described a community that "reject[s] the organized society, in America and elsewhere," substituting instead "a colorful, mystical world of love, drugs, tranquility and quite often anything goes communal property and communal sex." This seemingly anthropological examination of hippies, treating them as an exotic tribe rather than fellow citizens, reveals how thoroughly mainstream culture viewed the counterculture as alien and potentially threatening despite sharing the same cities, media landscape, and often even family homes.

This perception gap fueled a moral panic that transcended ordinary political disagreement. When young people grew their hair long, experimented with drugs, embraced sexual freedom, rejected traditional career paths, or explored Eastern spirituality, many older Americans experienced these choices not as different preferences but as existential threats to civilization itself. A 1968 Gallup poll found that 56% of Americans believed the country was experiencing "a breakdown in moral standards," with a majority specifically identifying long hair on men, revealing clothing, lack of respect for parents, and changing sexual norms as evidence. These concerns reflected genuine fear that counterculture values would corrode the foundations of social order if left unchecked.

Local communities responded with measures that now appear extreme but reflected authentic anxiety. School boards across America implemented strict dress codes prohibiting long hair on boys and revealing clothing on girls. Town councils passed ordinances against public gathering or sleeping in parks to prevent hippie congregations. Law enforcement agencies conducted dramatic drug raids on communes and youth centers. Local newspapers published alarmist stories about drug use, communal living, and sexual experimentation. Parents sent teenagers to psychiatrists or controversial "rehabilitation" programs when they displayed countercultural leanings. These responses demonstrated not just disagreement with youth culture but genuine fear of its perceived consequences.

Charles Manson's crimes in August 1969 provided the most potent symbol for those predisposed to see counterculture as inherently dangerous. Though Manson represented a deeply pathological extreme disconnected from mainstream hippie philosophy, his superficial adoption of counterculture aesthetics, communal living arrangements, and fragmentary spiritual ideas created associations that many critics eagerly amplified. Prosecutor Vincent Bugliosi later described how the case "represented the death knell of hippies and all they symbolically represented...They could never again be viewed as harmless, happy children holding flowers." This conflation of peaceful counterculture participants with violent criminals reinforced mainstream anxiety about cultural boundaries dissolving in dangerous ways.

On October 21, 1967, approximately 100,000 anti-war demonstrators marched on the Pentagon in a dramatic escalation of protest against the Vietnam War. As the crowd approached the building, they encountered military police and federal marshals who formed defensive lines to prevent entry into the facility. Some protesters attempted symbolic "levitation" of the building through group meditation, while others placed flowers in the rifle barrels of nervous young soldiers. By nightfall, more confrontational elements began challenging the perimeter, leading to nearly 700 arrests. This event crystallized the growing divide in how Americans understood both the war itself and domestic opposition to it: protesters viewed themselves as patriotic citizens exercising democratic rights to prevent immoral policy, while many observers saw dangerous radicals undermining American security and disrespecting those serving in uniform.

This interpretive divide reflected deeper tensions about citizenship's meaning in a democratic society. For anti-war activists, true patriotism meant holding government accountable when it violated foundational values like human rights, democratic consent, and proportional use of force. For their critics, patriotism required supporting official policies during international conflicts regardless of personal opinions, particularly when fellow citizens risked their lives implementing those policies. These competing frameworks created fundamentally different understandings of the same events: what protesters experienced as moral witness against injustice, critics perceived as demoralizing to troops and encouraging to enemies. This gap in perception, more than specific policy disagreements, made the Vietnam era's divisions so difficult to bridge.

Military families often felt particularly betrayed by anti-war activism. Many had sent sons, husbands, and fathers to Vietnam believing in their mission's necessity and morality, only to see protesters portray that service as participation in immoral aggression or even war crimes. Gold Star mothers who had lost children in combat found protest slogans like "Hey, hey, LBJ, how many kids did you kill today?" not just politically disagreeable but personally devastating. Veterans returning from combat often encountered not gratitude but suspicion or outright hostility, creating psychological wounds beyond those already sustained in war. These personal dimensions transformed abstract policy debates into deeply emotional conflicts where reconciliation seemed impossible because the stakes felt existential rather than merely political.

Richard Nixon's presidential victory in 1968 emerged directly from America's cultural divisions. Having lost narrowly to John F. Kennedy in 1960, Nixon recognized that the intervening years had transformed the nation's political landscape. Urban riots, campus protests, counterculture visibility, and crime rate increases had created pervasive anxiety among many middle-class and working-class Americans about social stability. Rather than attempting to bridge these divisions, Nixon's campaign deliberately appealed to those who felt threatened by rapid change, positioning himself as defender of "forgotten Americans" against intellectual elites, protest movements, and cultural revolutionaries. This strategy produced narrow victory over Hubert Humphrey despite George Wallace's third-party candidacy drawing many similarly inclined voters in southern states.

Nixon's November 1969 "Silent Majority" speech represented masterful political framing. Speaking directly to television viewers, he contrasted anti-war protesters' visibility with a supposedly larger group of Americans who supported the war but remained quiet. "The more divided we are at home," he argued, "the less likely the enemy is to negotiate." This formulation brilliantly transformed political disagreement into potential disloyalty while elevating policy support into patriotic duty. The phrase "silent majority" itself contained powerful implications: that protesters represented a mere minority despite their media prominence; that "real" Americans maintained traditional values despite cultural turbulence; that quiet dignity trumped vocal activism. The resulting framework provided psychological comfort to those uncomfortable with social change while delegitimizing critics as unrepresentative despite their articulate arguments.

On July 23, 1967, Detroit erupted in one of the most destructive urban riots in American history. Five days of violence left 43 people dead, 1,189 injured, over 7,200 arrested, and more than 2,000 buildings destroyed. Similar though less severe disturbances occurred in dozens of American cities between 1965 and 1968, creating a pervasive sense of social breakdown among many citizens. Official investigations, including the Kerner Commission report, identified structural causes including police brutality, housing discrimination, unemployment, and inadequate public services in predominantly Black neighborhoods. Public perception, however, increasingly focused on immediate symptoms rather than underlying causes, creating political opportunity for candidates emphasizing "law and order" rather than social reform as the appropriate response to urban unrest.

This focus on order maintenance rather than justice advancement reflected genuine anxiety about changing social conditions. FBI statistics showed violent crime rates doubling between 1960 and 1970, with homicides increasing 55% and robberies rising 120%. Property crime similarly surged, with burglaries up 161% and auto theft increasing 152%. These trends affected communities across demographic lines, though urban neighborhoods experienced particularly sharp increases. Media coverage amplified these statistics through sensationalist reporting emphasizing random violence against innocent victims, creating the impression that traditional public spaces had become dangerous territories requiring heightened enforcement rather than community spaces needing investment. The resulting fear, based on both genuine trends and their media amplification, created a receptive audience for political messaging prioritizing security over other considerations.

In 1972, the Equal Rights Amendment (ERA) appeared destined for ratification after passing Congress with bipartisan support and quickly securing approval from 28 of the required 38 states. The amendment's text was straightforward: "Equality of rights under the law shall not be denied or abridged by the United States or by any State on account of sex." This seemingly uncontroversial principle, however, generated organized opposition that permanently altered American political dynamics. Led by conservative activist Phyllis Schlafly, the "STOP ERA" campaign mobilized traditionalist women concerned that formal equality would eliminate protections they valued, including exemption from military draft, husband's financial obligations, and gender-specific workplace accommodations. By framing formal equality as potential loss rather than empowerment, opponents transformed an abstract constitutional principle into concrete threat to established gender roles many women found meaningful and protective.

This resistance reflected genuine anxiety about social change rather than mere opposition to women's advancement. Many ERA opponents sincerely believed traditional family structures, with complementary rather than identical male and female roles, provided the optimal environment for child development, social stability, and female security. They viewed differentiated gender roles not as oppressive restrictions but as pragmatic arrangements recognizing biological realities and protecting women from exploitation. The language of "women's liberation" struck them not as empowering but threatening, suggesting freedom from family obligations rather than freedom to pursue additional opportunities. Their concerns, while often dismissed by progressives as reactionary or manipulated, represented an authentic perspective deserving engagement rather than dismissal, particularly since many opponents were women themselves rather than men seeking to maintain patriarchal control.

On March 8, 1971, a group calling themselves the Citizens' Commission to Investigate the FBI broke into a small FBI office in Media, Pennsylvania, stealing over 1,000 classified documents which they anonymously mailed to several newspapers. These materials revealed COINTELPRO (Counter Intelligence Program), a secret FBI initiative targeting domestic political organizations through infiltration, psychological warfare, harassment, and sometimes illegal surveillance. The documents showed operations against civil rights leaders, anti-war activists, feminist organizations, and environmental groups, many engaged in constitutionally protected activities with no connection to violence or foreign influence. This revelation fundamentally challenged prevailing assumptions about government agencies, suggesting that institutions supposedly protecting democracy were actively undermining it through programs hidden from public accountability and congressional oversight.

The scope of revealed operations shocked even those skeptical of government authority. FBI agents had infiltrated Black student organizations, attempting to prevent coalition-building between racial justice advocates and other progressive movements. They had sent anonymous letters to civil rights leader Martin Luther King Jr. threatening to expose extramarital affairs unless he committed suicide. They had distributed fabricated materials designed to create conflicts between different activist organizations. They had conducted "black bag jobs," illegal break-ins to gather information or plant listening devices, against citizens engaged in lawful political advocacy. Most disturbing, these activities targeted Americans based on their political beliefs rather than specific illegal actions, effectively criminalizing dissent itself rather than actual law violations potentially emerging from particular movements.

If we could look up at the stars during this turbulent period of cultural collision, we might imagine how these eternal witnesses perceived humanity's struggles. From their cosmic perspective, they had seen this pattern unfold countless times before, the spiral of history turning through another cycle of challenge and response, progress and resistance. The stars had observed how societies throughout time have navigated the delicate balance between necessary innovation and essential stability, between challenging outworn traditions and preserving valuable social foundations.

From their vantage point, the specific conflicts of the 1960s and 1970s, over hair length and music styles, gender roles and military service, political dissent and social order, would appear as the latest manifestations of an ancient human negotiation: how to incorporate necessary changes while maintaining social cohesion. They might have noted how, despite the heated rhetoric from both counterculture advocates and traditional defenders, most Americans actually occupied middle positions, accepting certain changes while resisting others, embracing some new freedoms while worrying about potential consequences, hoping for both greater justice and continued stability.

The stars, having witnessed the entire spiral of human history, might observe that these cultural collisions, though painful and divisive in the moment, ultimately serve an essential function. They force societies to consciously examine assumptions and practices that have become automatic, to distinguish between traditions worth preserving and habits ready for evolution. The pendulum swing between change and tradition, between challenge and reassurance, creates a dynamic balance that allows human societies to adapt without disintegrating, to transform gradually rather than through either rigid stagnation or chaotic revolution.

NO MAN'S LAND: MAJORITY RIGHTS VS. MINORITY PROTECTION

Democratic societies must respect majority preferences and empower elected officials to implement policies reflecting the will of the people, even when those policies contradict some citizens' deeply held values or beliefs.

Pause. Notice what arises in you.

Democratic societies must protect minority rights and perspectives against majority overreach, even when doing so frustrates the immediate desires of electoral majorities or appears to privilege certain groups' concerns.

Pause. Notice what arises in you.

You do not have to agree with or justify either statement. Simply hold them both in your mind and observe what comes up.

This fundamental tension, between majority rule and minority protection, defined America's cultural conflicts during the 1960s and 1970s. When Richard Nixon invoked the "Silent Majority," he implicitly suggested that majority preferences should prevail over vocal minority concerns. Yet the Constitution itself contains numerous counter-majoritarian provisions specifically designed to prevent majority domination, including Bill of Rights protections, judicial review, and structural features protecting smaller states against larger ones.

The period's conflicts often centered on which framework should apply to specific issues. Should local majorities determine racial integration policies, or did minority rights to equal protection supersede majority preferences? Should majority cultural standards govern obscenity regulations, or did free expression rights protect controversial content regardless of popularity? Should majority religious views influence laws governing personal behavior, or did individual liberty rights create protected zones beyond majority control? These questions involved not simply policy disagreements but fundamental conflicts about democracy's proper functioning.

The most productive resolutions typically involved neither absolute majority dominance nor unlimited minority rights, but thoughtful accommodation recognizing both principles' legitimacy. Courts protected essential minority rights while allowing democratic majorities significant policy discretion within constitutional boundaries. Legislatures incorporated minority perspective protections within majority-approved frameworks. Executive agencies implemented majority-supported policies while establishing procedural safeguards against arbitrary enforcement disproportionately affecting vulnerable populations. This balanced approach, respecting majority governance while protecting minority rights, represents democracy's distinctive strength compared to both pure majoritarianism lacking minority protections and minority rule lacking majority consent.

Chapter Eighteen

When Change Made Its Bargains

For eight consecutive nights in January 1977, America came to a virtual standstill. Stores emptied, restaurants sat vacant, and streets quieted as an estimated 130 million Americans, more than half the country's population, gathered around their television sets to watch the miniseries "Roots." Based on Alex Haley's novel tracing his family's history from African capture into slavery and eventually to freedom, the program forced the nation to confront its painful racial history through the intimate lens of one family's experience. White and Black viewers alike witnessed the brutality of the slave trade, the crushing weight of human bondage, and the enduring resilience of people fighting to maintain their dignity and cultural identity against overwhelming oppression.

The unprecedented popularity of "Roots" represented something remarkable: a cultural phenomenon unimaginable just a decade earlier. A searingly honest portrayal of American slavery, showing white Americans as perpetrators of cruelty while celebrating Black resistance, family bonds, and cultural heritage, had become not controversial protest art but mainstream entertainment embraced across demographic lines. The series won nine Emmy Awards, a Peabody Award, and a Golden Globe, while generating nationwide discussion about race, history, and identity in America.

This cultural moment perfectly illustrated the complex integration of once-radical perspectives into American mainstream institutions during the mid-to-late 1970s. The social movements that had emerged as disruptive challenges to established norms in the 1960s, civil rights activism, feminism, environmentalism, gay rights, anti-war protest, were undergoing a significant transformation. Their most basic demands, once considered revolutionary, were increasingly accepted as reasonable reforms. Their language and symbols, formerly shocking, became familiar elements of popular culture. Their underlying values, previously framed as threats to tradition, gradually reshaped institutional practices across American society.

This integration process was neither complete victory nor co-optation defeat for the movements that had driven such dramatic change. Rather, it represented the characteristic way democratic societies ultimately process substantial challenges to established norms, by incorporating elements that prove adaptable while maintaining core stabilizing structures. The most extreme demands from both progressive and reactionary voices typically fall away, with workable compromises emerging through institutional adaptation rather than revolutionary replacement or rigid preservation. This pattern had appeared in each historical cycle we've examined, from religious tolerance emerging after witch hunts to labor protections developing after industrial disruption.

If we were to gaze up at the stars during this period of transition, these ancient witnesses to humanity's recurring patterns, they might observe with cosmic patience how societies move through cycles of challenge and integration. From their celestial perspective, they would have seen this pattern repeated throughout human history: the passionate energy of social movements gradually channeling into institutional structures, their revolutionary impulses finding expression within reformed systems rather than destroying them entirely. The stars, in their eternal presence, remind us that transformative change rarely happens through sudden revolution or complete rejection, but through this spiral process of challenging, absorbing, and evolving.

On November 16, 1977, a frail 63-year-old African American woman stepped to the podium in the East Room of the White House. President Jimmy

Carter had just signed legislation strengthening the 1965 Voting Rights Act, extending protections to language minorities and eliminating barriers facing Native Americans, Asian Americans, Alaskan Natives, and Hispanic Americans. Fannie Lou Hamer, who had been beaten nearly to death for attempting to register to vote in Mississippi just fourteen years earlier, witnessed this expansion of a law that had fundamentally changed American democracy. Though still suffering from the health effects of that brutal 1963 jail beating, Hamer observed a transformed political landscape where voting rights protections enjoyed broad bipartisan support and where Black elected officials had increased from fewer than 1,000 nationwide in 1965 to over 4,300 by 1977.

This moment exemplified how the legal system gradually institutionalized many civil rights movement demands that had once seemed radical. The mid-to-late 1970s saw remarkable legislative achievements that expanded and solidified earlier breakthrough laws. The Equal Credit Opportunity Act (1974) prohibited discrimination based on race, color, religion, national origin, sex, marital status, or age in credit transactions. The Fair Housing Act gained substantial enforcement tools through the 1974 Housing and Community Development Act. The U.S. Commission on Civil Rights expanded its jurisdiction to include sex discrimination in 1972, bridging civil rights and women's movements. These incremental legal advances lacked the dramatic quality of earlier landmark legislation but cumulatively strengthened the institutional framework supporting equal rights.

Women's rights similarly advanced through legislative and regulatory action, though with significant limitations. Title IX's 1975 implementation regulations dramatically expanded educational and athletic opportunities, with women's college sports participation increasing sixfold between 1972 and 1980. The Pregnancy Discrimination Act (1978) amended Title VII of the Civil Rights Act to prohibit sex discrimination on the basis of pregnancy, childbirth, or related medical conditions. Credit laws changed to allow women to obtain credit in their own names regardless of marital status. These achievements fell short of the Equal Rights Amendment's comprehensive constitutional protection, which stalled after gaining 35 of the needed 38 state ratifications, but nonetheless represented substantial institutional integration of feminist principles.

Environmental protection achieved perhaps the most complete legislative transformation. Building on the foundational National Environmental Policy Act, Clean Air Act, and Clean Water Act of the early 1970s, subsequent legislation created comprehensive regulatory frameworks. The Endangered Species Act (1973) protected threatened wildlife and habitats. The Safe Drinking Water Act (1974) established national standards for water quality. The Resource Conservation and Recovery Act (1976) regulated hazardous waste management. These laws institutionalized environmental values that had recently seemed radical, creating lasting regulatory structures that survive today despite periodic political challenges.

In 1967, over 100,000 people gathered for the "Human Be-In" at Golden Gate Park, where Timothy Leary famously urged young people to "turn on, tune in, drop out" while advocating rejection of mainstream society. Just eight years later, in 1975, Leary appeared in advertisements for Anderson-Jacobson, a computer terminal manufacturer, and began lecturing about space migration and intelligence increase rather than consciousness expansion through drugs. This transformation, from countercultural guru urging youth to abandon conventional society to technological enthusiast working within commercial structures, symbolized broader shifts occurring across movement cultures during the mid-1970s. The raw energy, confrontational tactics, and utopian aspirations that had characterized 1960s activism increasingly gave way to more institutional approaches, pragmatic goals, and professional organizations.

Civil rights organizations exemplified this evolution from protest to institution-building. The Congressional Black Caucus expanded from 13 members in 1971 to 16 by 1979, creating a formal voice for Black concerns within Congress itself. By 1977, over 4,300 Black elected officials nationwide, including mayors of major cities like Los Angeles, Detroit, and Atlanta, represented institutional power rather than outsider protest. The NAACP moved from direct action toward legal challenges, economic opportunities, and educational equality initiatives, with membership rebounding from 300,000 in 1970 to nearly 500,000 by 1977. These changes represented not abandonment of movement goals but strategic adaptation to changing circumstances, translating protest energy into sustainable institutional influence.

Women's movement organizations underwent similar professionalization. The National Organization for Women grew from 7,000 members in 1970 to over 200,000 by 1980, developing state and local chapters with professional staff and lobbying operations. The National Women's Political Caucus, founded in 1971, focused on increasing women's political representation through candidate recruitment and electoral support. Women's studies programs increased from 17 in 1970 to over 300 by 1980, creating academic institutionalization of feminist perspectives. Women's health clinics, bookstores, credit unions, and publishing houses established parallel feminist infrastructure. These organizational developments created sustainable structures that could survive beyond initial enthusiasm, maintaining movement influence through institutional presence rather than street demonstrations or consciousness-raising groups alone.

In 1968, a Gallup poll found that only 20% of Americans approved of marriage between Blacks and whites. By 1978, that figure had nearly doubled to 36%, still a minority position, but representing remarkable attitudinal shift within a single decade. This pattern of dramatic though incomplete attitude change appeared across numerous social issues during the 1970s. Support for equal job opportunities regardless of gender reached 83% by 1978, up from 69% in 1970. Environmental concerns became mainstream, with 81% of Americans self-identifying as "environmentalists" by 1980 compared to 58% in 1970. Acceptance of premarital sex increased from 33% in 1969 to 43% by 1977. Opposition to employment discrimination against homosexuals grew from 56% in 1973 to 68% by 1980. These shifts, while varying in magnitude, collectively represented significant transformation in American social attitudes occurring simultaneously with institutional changes.

These attitude changes varied significantly across demographic groups, creating complex patterns of acceptance and resistance. Educational attainment consistently predicted greater acceptance of social change, with college-educated Americans showing 20-30% higher support for gender equality and racial integration than those with high school education or less. Regional variations remained significant, though southern states showed more dramatic attitude shifts than other regions, partially closing historical gaps. Rural residents remained 15-20% less supportive of cultural changes than urban dwellers across most measures, with suburbs occupying middle position. Age consistently predicted attitudes, with each successive generation showing more progressive views than predecessors, creating demographic momentum for continuing change.

Media representations both reflected and accelerated these attitude shifts. Television shows like "All in the Family" (1971-1979) directly addressed previously taboo social issues including racism, homosexuality, and women's liberation, using humor to make controversial topics accessible to mainstream audiences. "Roots" (1977) made slavery and racial injustice central to national conversation through shared viewing experience. "The Mary Tyler Moore Show" (1970-1977) portrayed an independent working woman focused on career rather than marriage, with 67% of adult Americans viewing at least one episode. Children's programming including "Free to Be You and Me" (1974) and "Schoolhouse Rock" (1973-1985) incorporated progressive messages for younger viewers. These media portrayals both responded to changing attitudes and further normalized previously controversial perspectives through sympathetic representation.

On November 6, 1978, California voters approved Proposition 13 with 65% support, placing strict limits on property tax increases and launching what became known as the "tax revolt." The overwhelming popularity of this anti-tax, small-government initiative in America's most populous state signaled profound political realignment occurring even as progressive social movements were achieving significant institutional integration. This paradoxical development, simultaneous progressive policy advances and conservative political ascendance, characterized the mid-to-late 1970s. While social movements successfully institutionalized many of their core demands through legislation, court decisions, and corporate policy, American electoral politics and governance philosophy underwent significant rightward shift that would ultimately constrain further advances.

The conservative movement had been steadily building organizational infrastructure since Barry Goldwater's 1964 presidential campaign defeat. By the mid-1970s, this infrastructure reached critical mass through organizations including the Heritage Foundation (founded 1973), the Conservative Caucus (1974), the Committee for the Survival of a Free Congress (1974), and the American Legislative Exchange Council (1973). Conservative media expanded through both traditional print publications and innovative direct mail techniques pioneered by Richard Viguerie, which raised $25 million annually by 1977. The College Republicans tripled membership between 1973-1980, building a youth leadership pipeline. These developments created sustainable movement capacity beyond individual candidates or campaigns, establishing parallel structures to those progressive movements had earlier developed.

Religious conservatives, previously largely apolitical, became an increasingly organized political force. Jerry Falwell's Moral Majority (1979) mobilized evangelical Christians around social issues including abortion, homosexuality, and the Equal Rights Amendment. Phyllis Schlafly's STOP ERA campaign effectively employed grassroots organizing techniques to defeat a previously popular constitutional amendment. The Christian Broadcasting Network increased viewership from 700,000 households in 1970 to over 4.5 million by 1978. Private religious schools increased from 2,500 in 1972 to over 15,000 by 1980 in response to secular public education concerns. These developments represented not only political mobilization but a comprehensive worldview challenging progressive social changes at philosophical rather than merely tactical levels.

During the 1977 Academy Awards, actress and activist Jane Fonda appeared on stage wearing a modest pantsuit, an unexceptional fashion choice that would have been unthinkable just a decade earlier, when women were expected to wear dresses for formal occasions. This quiet fashion revolution symbolized broader transformation occurring across American society, as previously radical cultural innovations became unremarkable elements of everyday life. From clothing to language, entertainment to consumer products, workplace norms to family structures, American culture incorporated elements of 1960s counterculture and social movements while discarding their more extreme manifestations. The resulting cultural landscape combined genuine transformation with substantial continuity, creating evolutionary rather than revolutionary change that proved more sustainable precisely because it maintained connection with enduring values while adapting to new realities.

Family structures underwent particularly significant evolution. Divorce rates nearly doubled between 1970-1980, reaching 5.3 per 1,000 population by 1981. Average marriage age increased from 20.8 for women in 1970 to 22.0 by 1980, reflecting expanded educational and career opportunities. Single-person households increased from 17% of all households in 1970 to 23% by 1980. The percentage of married mothers in the workforce grew from 40% in 1970 to 54% by 1980. Formal childcare usage increased 400% between 1970-1980. These statistical shifts represented profound lived experience changes for millions of Americans, as family arrangements diversified beyond the nuclear household model that had dominated post-war culture. The resulting diversity created both new freedoms and new challenges, requiring social adaptation across institutions from schools to workplaces, religious organizations to government programs.

From the perspective of the stars, these transformations would appear as part of humanity's eternal dance between stability and change. These celestial observers, who had witnessed countless civilizations rise and fall, would recognize in this moment not just specific policy changes or cultural shifts, but a recurring pattern in how societies evolve. They would see how the passionate energy of revolutionary movements gradually finds sustainable expression within existing institutions, how radical ideas become mainstream through a process of adaptation rather than replacement. The stars, unchanging in their cosmic positions yet witnessing constant change below, remind us that human progress moves not in straight lines but in spirals, returning to similar points but always at a different level.

When Martin Luther King Jr. delivered his famous "I Have a Dream" speech at the 1963 March on Washington, few observers would have predicted that within a decade, his birthday would be celebrated as a state holiday in multiple states, with federal holiday designation following in 1983. This transformation, from controversial activist to nationally honored figure, illustrates how social movements can achieve lasting cultural impact even when their immediate policy demands remain partially unfulfilled. The social movements of the 1960s and their subsequent evolution through the 1970s provide valuable insights into effective strategies for achieving sustainable change within democratic systems, lessons that remain relevant for addressing contemporary challenges across the political spectrum.

Successful movements consistently demonstrated capacity to operate simultaneously inside and outside established institutions. When civil rights organizations combined litigation through courts with direct action in streets, they created complementary pressure that neither approach alone could generate. When women's movement organizations developed both professional lobbying operations and grassroots consciousness-raising groups, they addressed both policy specifics and cultural frameworks. When environmental advocates simultaneously pursued regulatory changes, consumer awareness, and corporate engagement, they created multidimensional influence affecting diverse decision-makers. This inside-outside approach recognizes that democratic systems require both institutional engagement and external pressure, with social movements serving as crucial bridging mechanisms between grassroots constituencies and formal governance structures.

The most enduring lesson may be the importance of balancing transformational vision with incremental pragmatism. Movements maintaining inspiring long-term goals while securing concrete short-term wins sustained momentum more effectively than those demanding immediate total victory or accepting minimal symbolic changes. Civil rights leaders articulated fundamental equality vision while securing specific legal protections incrementally. Environmental advocates maintained ecological sustainability vision while negotiating particular regulatory improvements. Women's organizations pursued comprehensive gender equality while securing specific policy reforms step by step. This balanced approach recognizes democratic change processes' inherently incremental nature while maintaining moral clarity and directional purpose that purely pragmatic politics often lacks.

If we look again to the night sky, we might imagine these ancient stars watching over the human drama with patient understanding. They have seen how societies throughout history have navigated these tensions between vision and pragmatism, between revolution and evolution. The stars remind us that transformative change rarely happens in a single moment of dramatic rupture, but through this continuous process of challenging, adapting, and integrating. They have witnessed how human progress moves not through perfect victories or complete defeats, but through this messy, imperfect process of democratic negotiation, a pattern that has characterized our species' development throughout time.

NO MAN'S LAND: PRESERVING VS. TRANSCENDING IDENTITY

Democratic societies must protect and celebrate distinct cultural, racial, gender, and other identities that provide meaning, community, and historical continuity for their members, even when emphasizing these differences creates boundaries between groups.

Pause. Notice what arises in you.

Democratic societies must move beyond rigid identity categories toward recognition of our common humanity and shared values, even when this transcendence seems to diminish the significance of genuine historical experiences and community bonds

Pause. Notice what arises in you.

You do not have to agree with or justify either statement. Simply hold them both in your mind and observe what comes up.

The mid-to-late 1970s perfectly illustrated this fundamental tension. The "Roots" phenomenon simultaneously celebrated specific African American historical experience while creating shared national understanding transcending racial boundaries. Civil rights advances secured specific protections for racial minorities while establishing universal principles applicable to all Americans. Women's movement organizations advocated gender-specific policies while articulating universal human values. Gay rights activists emphasized their distinctive community while appealing to common human dignity transcending sexual orientation.

This dual movement, both preserving distinct identities and transcending their limitations, characterizes healthy democratic evolution. Identity provides essential meaning, community, and historical continuity giving individuals sense of place within larger story. Simultaneously, rigid identity categories can create boundaries preventing full human connection and recognition across differences. Neither complete separation into isolated identity groups nor forced assimilation into artificial uniformity serves human flourishing; instead, genuine community develops through holding both distinct identity and transcendent connection simultaneously.

The most productive resolutions emerged not through abstract philosophical resolution but through practical engagement creating space for both particularity and universality. Multicultural education acknowledged distinct historical experiences while identifying common human patterns. Religious dialogue respected theological differences while discovering shared ethical commitments. Political coalitions maintained separate organizational identities while coordinating around common objectives. These approaches didn't perfectly resolve philosophical tensions but created workable frameworks allowing both identity affirmation and boundary transcendence within complex democratic society.

Cycle 7: When Everything Was Dangerous

Chapter Nineteen

When Daycare Hid Devils

On the evening of November 21, 1980, an estimated 83 million Americans, a staggering 76 percent of all television viewers in the United States, tuned in to the same program simultaneously. They weren't watching breaking news about a national emergency or a presidential address. Instead, they were collectively captivated by a single question that had dominated water cooler conversations and newspaper headlines for eight agonizing months: "Who shot J.R.?"

The resolution of this fictional cliffhanger from the television drama "Dallas" became, at that time, the highest-rated single television episode in American history. The phenomenon transcended entertainment, evolving into a shared cultural touchstone that crossed political, geographic, and demographic lines. Betting pools formed in workplaces across the country. "Who Shot J.R.?" t-shirts sold by the millions. Even the incoming Reagan administration, preparing for its January inauguration after a decisive electoral victory, found itself competing with J.R. Ewing for media attention.

This cultural moment revealed the transformation of the American media landscape as the 1970s gave way to the 1980s. Television had evolved from a novel technology delivering mostly shared cultural experiences into an all-encompassing force capable of focusing national attention with unprecedented power. The "Dallas" phenomenon demonstrated how effectively mass media could now create collective emotional experiences, in this case, harmless entertainment suspense that united viewers across dividing lines.

Yet this same media infrastructure, with its expanding reach and emotional impact, would soon demonstrate an equal capacity to amplify fears, spread moral panics, and heighten societal anxieties throughout the 1980s and 1990s. The technologies that allowed millions to share in the frivolous mystery of a fictional oil tycoon's shooting would soon transmit more consequential narratives, about satanic cults allegedly infiltrating daycare centers, deadly new diseases interpreted as divine punishment, environmental catastrophes threatening civilization, and technological systems potentially triggering millennium-ending collapses.

As the curtain rose on the 1980s, American society stood at a crossroads. The progressive social movements of the previous two decades had achieved significant institutional integration, but a powerful conservative backlash gained momentum. Economic uncertainty loomed as stagflation persisted. New technologies transformed daily life at an accelerating pace. The Cold War entered a newly tense phase after the relative détente of the 1970s. Family structures evolved rapidly, creating both new freedoms and new insecurities.

If we step back and view this moment through the perspective of the stars, those ancient, patient observers of human history, we might recognize familiar patterns unfolding. Throughout time, periods of rapid change have triggered compensatory reactions as societies struggle to maintain balance. The stars have witnessed this pendulum swing countless times: the euphoria of revolutionary moments followed by the yearning for stability, the excitement of technological advancement coupled with anxiety about its consequences, the liberation from old constraints accompanied by uncertainty about new boundaries. From their cosmic vantage point, these recurring cycles appear not as chaotic disruptions but as the natural rhythm of human societies seeking equilibrium amid continuous change.

In January 1983, NBC aired a primetime television special titled "The Devil Worship: Exposing Satan's Underground" hosted by Geraldo Rivera. Watched by 20 million Americans, the program made sensational claims about a vast underground network of satanic cults allegedly responsible for ritual child abuse, animal mutilation, and human sacrifice. "The odds are your town is a center of satanic cult activity," Rivera warned the nationwide audience, claiming without evidence that "more than one million Satanists" were secretly operating across America. The special featured dramatic reenactments, tearful testimony from supposed former cult members, and self-proclaimed occult experts connecting disparate criminal cases into an apparent vast conspiracy.

This broadcast marked a watershed moment in the evolution of television journalism, not for its accuracy, which was virtually nonexistent, but for its demonstration of how effectively the medium could now spread moral panic through a potent combination of visual dramatization, emotional testimonials, and authoritative framing. The Rivera special generated the highest ratings of any documentary in NBC's history, creating immediate financial incentives for similar content across networks. Within months, talk shows, local news programs, and other documentaries amplified these unsubstantiated claims, creating the impression of independent confirmation when they were merely echoing the same unfounded allegations.

This transformation in media's role reflected larger structural changes in the American information landscape. By the early 1980s, cable television had expanded from reaching just 16 million homes in 1975 to over 34 million, dramatically increasing available programming hours that needed filling. CNN launched in 1980 as the first 24-hour news network, creating unprecedented demand for constant content and intensifying competition for viewer attention. Deregulation under the Reagan administration reduced public interest obligations for broadcasters, while media ownership consolidated into fewer corporate hands with greater emphasis on profitability over journalistic standards.

These structural changes fostered a media environment primed to amplify fear. The introduction of overnight Nielsen ratings increased pressure to grab viewer attention immediately. Local television news, facing intense competition, increasingly adopted the mantra "if it bleeds, it leads," prioritizing crime coverage even when actual crime rates remained stable or declined. The success of prime-time programs like "20/20" and "60 Minutes" demonstrated the ratings potential of investigative formats, spawning numerous imitators that often sacrificed rigorous reporting for emotional impact. "We used to worry about getting it right," lamented veteran CBS producer Don Hewitt in 1985. "Now everyone worries about getting it first and getting it watched."

On a warm August morning in 1980, Ronald Reagan stood before a crowd of 15,000 evangelical Christians at the Religious Roundtable's National Affairs Briefing in Dallas, Texas. Though not himself a regular churchgoer, Reagan understood the political moment. "I know you can't endorse me," he told the assembled pastors and religious leaders, "but I want you to know that I endorse you and what you are doing." The enthusiastic response from this previously apolitical constituency signaled a dramatic shift in American cultural and political alignment, one that would shape responses to moral and systemic anxieties throughout the coming decades.

This emerging religious-conservative alliance transcended mere electoral strategy. It expressed genuine cultural anxiety about rapid social changes that had transformed American life during the previous two decades. Between 1960 and 1980, divorce rates had more than doubled. Premarital sex had become increasingly accepted, with the percentage of women who had engaged in sex before marriage rising from 33% in 1965 to 64% by 1979. The Supreme Court had removed prayer from public schools, legalized abortion, and expanded protections for obscenity under the First Amendment. Gay rights movements had gained visibility and early legal protections in some municipalities. These changes, while representing liberation and progress to some Americans, signaled moral decay and social breakdown to others.

Religious institutions responded to these changes with growing political engagement. The Moral Majority, founded in 1979 by televangelist Jerry Falwell, explicitly sought to mobilize evangelical Christians as a voting bloc focused on "pro-family, pro-life, pro-morality, and pro-American" positions. Membership grew from 400,000 at its founding to over 4 million by 1981. Similar organizations including the Religious Roundtable, Christian Voice, and Concerned

Women for America collectively built a new infrastructure connecting thousands of previously independent evangelical churches into coordinated political action networks with sophisticated media operations, mailing lists, and lobbying capabilities.

In October 1984, a young mother named Judy Johnson made a disturbing phone call to police in Manhattan Beach, California. She claimed that her two-year-old son had been sexually abused by Raymond Buckey, a teacher at the prestigious McMartin Preschool. This single allegation eventually spiraled into what became the longest and costliest criminal trial in American history, featuring allegations of animal sacrifice, underground tunnels, and ritualistic abuse that prosecutors claimed had occurred at the daycare center. The case captured national attention not because it was unusual for the time, but because it perfectly crystallized a widespread anxiety about the safety of children in a rapidly changing social landscape.

The McMartin case erupted against a backdrop of profound transformation in American family structures. Between 1970 and 1985, the percentage of mothers with young children working outside the home jumped from 30% to over 60%. By 1985, approximately 11 million American children under age six spent at least part of their day in the care of someone other than their parents. This shift, driven by both economic necessity as stagflation strained family budgets and by changing gender roles following the women's movement, created what sociologists called a "care gap" that various childcare arrangements rushed to fill.

This massive transition generated deep ambivalence in American society. While many celebrated women's increased workplace opportunities, others worried about the impact on children and family structures. Conservatives often portrayed these changes as abandonment of traditional motherhood, while even some progressives expressed concern about institutional care for very young children. A 1981 ABC News poll found that 73% of Americans believed "children are more likely to be properly raised when their mothers do not work outside the home," revealing the cultural tensions underlying this social transformation.

On June 5, 1981, the Centers for Disease Control's Morbidity and Mortality Weekly Report published a brief notice documenting five cases of Pneumocystis carinii pneumonia, an extremely rare lung infection, among previously healthy young men in Los Angeles. This modest scientific communication, barely noticed at the time, announced the arrival of what would become known as AIDS (Acquired Immune Deficiency Syndrome). The ensuing health crisis quickly transcended medicine to become a profound social and moral battleground that brought longstanding tensions about sexuality, morality, and marginalized communities violently to the surface.

The timing of AIDS' emergence proved tragically significant. The disease appeared just as conservative reaction against the sexual liberalization of the 1960s and 1970s gained momentum. Throughout those decades, dramatic changes had occurred in American sexual attitudes and behaviors. The Stonewall uprising of 1969 had launched a more visible gay rights movement, with homosexuality removed from the American Psychiatric Association's list of mental disorders in 1973. Birth control access had expanded, separating sexuality from reproduction. Pornography had become more widely available following court decisions limiting obscenity restrictions. Premarital sex had become increasingly accepted, with the percentage of women who had engaged in sex before marriage rising from 33% in 1965 to 64% by 1979.

These changes sparked significant counterpressure from religious and social conservatives, who viewed sexual liberalization as undermining family stability and traditional moral values. Organizations like the Moral Majority specifically included opposition to homosexuality and pornography among their founding principles. Phyllis Schlafly's successful campaign against the Equal Rights Amendment emphasized fears that the amendment would promote homosexuality and undermine traditional gender roles. Anti-gay rights initiatives had appeared on ballots in multiple states and municipalities. When AIDS emerged within this context, it became immediately entangled with these pre-existing moral and political conflicts.

The stars, in their eternal watching of human affairs, might observe how deeply recurring these patterns are, how societies throughout history have re-

sponded to disease with a mixture of scientific investigation and moral interpretation. They have witnessed how, across cultures and eras, illness that affects
marginalized groups initially receives less attention and more judgment, how
the first response to new threats is often to find someone to blame, and how
scientific understanding gradually but inevitably overcomes superstition and
stigma. The stars might recognize in AIDS not just a specific disease, but another
iteration of humanity's complex relationship with vulnerability, difference, and
the unknown, a relationship that has shaped responses to plagues and pandemics throughout recorded time.

In March 1985, three British scientists from the Antarctic Survey published
a paper in the journal Nature that would transform how humans viewed their
relationship with the planet. Joseph Farman, Brian Gardiner, and Jonathan
Shanklin reported discovering a massive thinning in the protective ozone layer
over Antarctica, a phenomenon soon dubbed the "ozone hole." Within months,
this scientific finding had sparked international concern and by 1987 had generated unprecedented global environmental action through the Montreal Protocol treaty. This response to ozone depletion demonstrated both humanity's
capacity to address planetary-scale threats and the distinctive mix of scientific
understanding, media amplification, and cultural anxiety that characterized
environmental concerns in the 1980s.

The ozone discovery emerged within a broader context of growing environmental consciousness. The first Earth Day in 1970 had demonstrated mass
public interest in environmental issues, with an estimated 20 million Americans participating. Congress had passed landmark environmental legislation
including the Clean Air Act (1970), Clean Water Act (1972), and Endangered Species Act (1973). Environmental concerns about nuclear power had
gained prominence following the Three Mile Island accident in 1979. Books
like Rachel Carson's Silent Spring (1962) had introduced ecological concepts to
mainstream audiences, while films like The China Syndrome (1979) dramatized
environmental threats through popular entertainment. By the early 1980s, approximately 65% of Americans self-identified as "environmentalists," reflecting
widespread adoption of at least nominal environmental awareness.

What distinguished environmental concerns of the 1980s from earlier environmental issues was their increasingly global and existential character. Earlier problems had typically involved local or regional pollution with direct human health impacts. The new environmental threats operated at planetary scale with potential civilization-ending consequences. Ozone depletion threatened to increase skin cancer rates worldwide and potentially disrupt entire ecosystems. Climate change (then more commonly called the "greenhouse effect") raised the possibility of agricultural disruption, coastal flooding, and other widespread impacts. Tropical deforestation, proceeding at record rates, threatened what media reports often called "the lungs of the planet." These concerns shared a common structure: human technological and economic activities unknowingly destabilizing natural systems upon which civilization itself depended.

In October 1989, USA Today ran the headline "Growing Computer Date Problem Has Experts Worried," introducing mainstream America to what would become known as the "Y2K bug." The article explained how early computer programming had saved storage space by using only two digits to represent years. When the calendar turned to 2000, these systems would interpret "00" as 1900 rather than 2000, potentially causing critical failures. This seemingly mundane technical issue eventually spawned extraordinary anxiety, generating doomsday predictions, massive remediation efforts, and a cultural moment that perfectly captured America's ambivalent relationship with technology at the century's end.

The Y2K issue arose within a broader context of rapidly accelerating technological dependence. Between 1980 and 1995, computers transformed from specialized tools for technical professionals into everyday necessities. Personal computer ownership increased from under 2% of American households in 1980 to over 35% by 1995. Automated teller machines proliferated, with installations growing from approximately 18,500 in 1980 to over 139,000 by 1995. Computerized inventory management, reservation systems, and transaction processing became standard across industries. Digital control systems increasingly operated critical infrastructure including power grids, water treatment facilities, telecommunications networks, and transportation systems. Society's fundamental operations now depended on technologies that most citizens didn't understand and couldn't control.

This technological transformation generated profound ambivalence. Americans enthusiastically adopted devices and services that increased convenience, productivity, and entertainment options. Yet surveys consistently revealed underlying anxiety about dependency and vulnerability. A 1993 Times Mirror poll found that 65% of Americans believed technology made life "more complicated," while 73% worried about privacy implications of computerized information systems. The introduction of the World Wide Web in 1991 and its rapid commercialization after 1994 intensified these concerns, adding new worries about online predators, information overload, and social isolation. Each innovation simultaneously promised enhancement and threatened disruption, creating a psychological tension that needed resolution.

Looking upward to the stars once more, we might imagine how these celestial observers would perceive our technological anxieties. They have witnessed humanity's relationship with technology evolve from the first stone tools, through the mastery of fire, the development of agriculture, the industrial revolution, and now the digital age. From their cosmic perspective, each technological leap has followed similar patterns: initial enthusiasm followed by recognition of unintended consequences, worries about dependence coupled with excitement about new possibilities, fears about lost traditions alongside hopes for better futures. The Y2K phenomenon might appear to them as just the latest iteration of this ancient dance, where humans simultaneously embrace and fear their own creations, always seeking to harness power while struggling to maintain control.

These varied anxieties, about media manipulation, conservative backlash, family structure, AIDS, environmental threats, and technological vulnerability, shared common patterns despite their different specific contexts. Each arose from a genuine societal transition that created both real challenges and exaggerated fears. Each combined legitimate concern with moral panic elements that distorted rational response. Each reflected deeper uncertainties about changing social structures and values amid rapid transformation. And each eventually resolved through some combination of practical adaptation, institutional response, and the simple passage of time revealing which fears were warranted and which were not.

Understanding these recurring patterns helps provide perspective on our own era's anxieties. As we face concerns from pandemics to climate change, artificial intelligence to political polarization, we can recognize both the legitimacy of genuine threats and the human tendency to amplify them through psychological and social processes that have characterized every historical period of rapid change. By studying these previous cycles, we learn not to dismiss real challenges but to approach them with balanced perspective that avoids both complacency and panic, the same perspective that will likely help future generations navigate the inevitable uncertainties of their own time.

NO MAN'S LAND: EXPERT AUTHORITY VS. PERSONAL EXPERIENCE

In times of uncertainty, we should defer to experts who have dedicated their lives to studying complex problems.

Pause. Notice what arises in you.

Personal experience and intuition can reveal truths that expert consensus misses or dismisses.

Pause. Notice what arises in you.

You do not have to agree with or justify either statement. Simply hold them both in your mind and observe what comes up.

The moral panics and systemic anxieties of the 1980s and 1990s repeatedly raised this fundamental tension. During the Satanic Panic, self-proclaimed "occult crime experts" with minimal credentials gained remarkable authority in courtrooms and media coverage, sometimes overriding common sense observations that questioned fantastic allegations. In the AIDS crisis, the opposite pattern appeared: medical experts initially dismissed the experiences and insights of affected communities, while activists with lived experience but no formal training eventually helped transform research priorities and treatment protocols. Environmental threats demonstrated both the essential value of expert scientific consensus and the limitations of specialist perspectives that sometimes missed human dimensions of environmental problems.

This tension between expert authority and personal experience reflects deeper questions about how we determine what is true and who gets to decide. Experts offer depth of knowledge, methodological rigor, and systematic analysis that individuals rarely achieve alone. Their specialized training helps identify patterns, evaluate evidence, and distinguish correlation from causation. Yet expertise can also create blind spots: disciplinary silos, confirmation bias, groupthink, and reluctance to consider information from outside established frameworks. Personal experience provides immediate, contextual knowledge often invisible to distant analysis. It offers moral clarity and motivation that abstract expertise may lack. Yet personal experience remains limited by individual perspective, vulnerable to cognitive biases, and difficult to generalize beyond specific circumstances.

Neither approach alone provides complete understanding. The most effective responses to complex challenges typically integrate both expert analysis and experiential knowledge. When AIDS activists gained "a seat at the table" in research planning, they brought crucial perspectives that improved study designs. When environmental scientists collaborated with local communities, they developed more effective and equitable solutions. When claims about ritual abuse were eventually subjected to rigorous investigative methods rather than accepted based on authority or anecdote, the truth gradually emerged. These examples suggest that holding both perspectives simultaneously, respecting expertise while valuing experience, creates more robust understanding than either perspective alone can provide.

Chapter Twenty

When Panic Found Its Stage

On the morning of March 22, 1984, seven teachers at the prestigious McMartin Preschool in Manhattan Beach, California arrived to find television news crews and police officers surrounding their workplace. They watched in disbelief as cameras captured the startling scene of several colleagues being escorted from the building in handcuffs. The staff members, all women except for one man, Raymond Buckey, faced what would become one of the most extraordinary criminal prosecutions in American history. They stood accused of 208 counts of child abuse involving allegations that grew to include ritualistic animal sacrifice, underground tunnels, hidden rooms, and occult ceremonies.

Despite the fantastical nature of these claims and the complete absence of physical evidence, the case consumed seven years, cost taxpayers $15 million, and resulted in the longest criminal trial in American history. Parents throughout the country suddenly viewed daycare centers with suspicion. Communities across America launched similar investigations based on increasingly implausible allegations. Police departments established special "occult crime" units. Therapists developed specialties in detecting "ritual abuse." A wave of panic about satanic influence swept across the nation, emerging from a potent combination of genuine child protection concerns and deeper cultural anxieties that found expression through sensational claims and media amplification.

The McMartin case exemplified how moral panics manifest in society, not as simple mass delusions or cynical manipulations, but as complex social phenomena where genuine concerns transform into something far more expansive and distorted. This manifestation process typically follows a recognizable pattern: an initial triggering event taps into existing anxieties; authorities and media amplify concerns; self-proclaimed experts emerge to provide explanatory frameworks; anecdotal evidence accumulates through suggestion and social contagion; institutional responses validate fears; and a feedback loop develops where each new claim reinforces and expands earlier ones.

The 1980s and early 1990s witnessed several distinct yet interconnected moral panics and systemic collapse anxieties that followed this general pattern. The Satanic Panic, AIDS crisis, ozone layer depletion, Y2K bug, video game violence fears, and welfare anxieties each represented different manifestations of the same underlying process: legitimate concerns transforming into disproportionate fears through predictable social and psychological mechanisms.

If we could look to the stars for perspective on these human episodes, these ancient celestial witnesses might recognize patterns all too familiar across the sweep of human history. From medieval witch hunts to Victorian anxieties about moral degradation, from ancient fears of comets as harbingers of doom to recurring end-times prophecies, the stars have observed how human societies repeatedly transform legitimate concerns into exaggerated fears that temporarily overwhelm rational assessment. The eternal cosmos, unmoved by our momentary panics, might remind us that such episodes are neither unique to our era nor signs of particular modern weakness, but rather recurring manifestations of how human minds and social systems process uncertainty and change.

The allegations against the McMartin Preschool began in August 1983, when Judy Johnson, mother of a 2½-year-old student, reported to police that her son had been sodomized by Raymond Buckey, the only male teacher at the school. Johnson, who was later diagnosed with acute paranoid schizophrenia and died of alcohol-related liver disease before the trial concluded, subsequently expanded her allegations to include claims that her son had witnessed animal mutilations and had been forced to watch church ceremonies where babies were sacrificed.

Rather than proceeding with traditional investigative techniques, the Manhattan Beach Police Department took the unusual step of sending a form letter to approximately 200 McMartin Preschool families. The letter informed parents that their children might have been victims of abuse and instructed them to ask specific questions about "oral sex," "fondling of genitals," "sodomy," and "photographs being taken of children without their clothing." This approach virtually guaranteed parental anxiety and introduced suggestive concepts to both parents and children before any forensic interviews took place.

Children were then referred to the Children's Institute International (CII), where therapists used now-discredited interview techniques that were highly suggestive and coercive. Interviewers asked leading questions, refused to accept denials, rewarded children who provided allegations with praise, and told children that other students had already disclosed abuse. Recorded interviews revealed questions like, "What kind of games did you play with Mr. Ray?" followed by "He played the touching game with you, didn't he?" When children denied abuse, interviewers would respond with statements such as, "You're just scared to tell, but all the other children already told."

Through this process, allegations expanded dramatically in scope and implausibility. Children eventually claimed they had witnessed baby sacrifices, been forced to drink blood, seen teachers fly, watched mutilations of animals including a horse, traveled in hot air balloons, been flushed down toilets to secret rooms, and been transported through underground tunnels. Despite these increasingly fantastic claims, prosecutors charged seven teachers with 208 counts of child abuse in March 1984.

Media coverage played a crucial role in fueling public fear and spreading the panic beyond the original case. The Los Angeles Times alone published over 100 articles about McMartin in 1984-85, often presenting allegations as potential facts rather than unverified claims. Television coverage featured dramatic music, shadowy imagery, and experts affirming the plausibility of even the most fantastic accusations. When a mother in Jordan, Minnesota reported similar concerns shortly after McMartin made national news, the pattern repeated: allegations expanded, dozens were charged, and media coverage intensified. The pattern would replicate in numerous communities including Kern County, California; Wenatchee, Washington; and Edenton, North Carolina.

On July 3, 1981, just one month after the CDC's first report on an unusual cluster of pneumonia cases among gay men, the New York Times published a small article on page A20 titled "Rare Cancer Seen in 41 Homosexuals." This modest placement, buried deep in the paper, belied the significance of what would become one of the most devastating public health crises of the modern era. The article's framing, explicitly linking the condition to a specific demographic group, foreshadowed how the disease would become immediately entangled with existing social prejudices and moral judgments rather than being approached primarily as a medical challenge.

The early months of the AIDS epidemic demonstrated how scientific uncertainty creates space for fearful projections. With no known cause or transmission mechanism, the mysterious condition originally called Gay-Related Immune Deficiency (GRID) generated widespread speculation. Medical professionals observed that the syndrome appeared concentrated among gay men, particularly those with multiple sexual partners, and later among intravenous drug users, Haitian immigrants, and hemophiliacs receiving blood products. This epidemiological pattern reinforced existing stereotypes about "promiscuity" and "deviance" among affected groups, leading many to interpret the disease through a moral rather than medical framework.

Media coverage amplified these moral interpretations while simultaneously conveying genuine medical uncertainty. Headlines like "Gay Plague" (New York Post, 1982) and "The Gay Plague: Why Is A Deadly New Disease Striking Only Homosexuals?" (Newsweek, 1982) reinforced the connection between sexuality and disease. Television news often filmed AIDS patients in shadows, reinforcing associations with shame and stigma. Religious interpretations gained significant public attention, with televangelist Jerry Falwell declaring in 1983 that "AIDS is the wrath of God upon homosexuals," a sentiment echoed by numerous religious leaders. Opinion polls revealed the prevalence of moral framing, with a 1985 Los Angeles Times survey finding that 51% of Americans agreed that "AIDS is a punishment for the decline in moral standards."

On March 24, 1987, approximately 250 people gathered at the Lesbian and Gay Community Services Center in New York City to form the AIDS Coalition to Unleash Power, or ACT UP. Their founding statement declared a simple but urgent message: "We are in a crisis, and our response to it must be equal to the task." Two days later, these activists staged their first demonstration on Wall Street, holding signs with slogans like "SILENCE = DEATH" and demanding greater access to experimental AIDS drugs. Seventeen demonstrators were arrested. This protest launched a remarkable movement that would fundamentally transform how American society responded to the AIDS epidemic and, in the process, revolutionize patient advocacy more broadly.

ACT UP emerged directly from frustration with inadequate institutional responses to AIDS. By 1987, the death toll had risen dramatically, yet FDA approval for potentially life-saving treatments remained sluggish, with only one drug (AZT) approved and priced at $10,000 per year, beyond reach for many patients. Insurance companies routinely denied coverage to people with AIDS. Research funding remained insufficient, and clinical trials excluded many patients most in need of experimental treatments. Government public health campaigns either avoided explicit discussion of transmission prevention or emphasized abstinence rather than practical risk reduction. Media coverage had diminished despite increasing cases. Against this backdrop of institutional failure, those most affected by the disease recognized that waiting for traditional channels to respond adequately meant accepting unnecessary deaths.

What distinguished ACT UP from traditional advocacy organizations was its confrontational direct action tactics paired with sophisticated understanding of medical science, media dynamics, and visual communication. The group specialized in disruptive, theatrical protests designed for maximum media impact. In October 1988, more than 1,000 activists surrounded the FDA headquarters, effectively shutting it down for a day while demanding accelerated drug approval processes. ACT UP members infiltrated the New York Stock Exchange to protest pharmaceutical pricing, chaining themselves to balconies while unfurling banners. The organization staged "die-ins" where protesters lay motion-less representing AIDS deaths at locations including St. Patrick's Cathedral, the National Institutes of Health, and pharmaceutical company offices. These dramatic actions guaranteed media coverage that more conventional advocacy approaches had failed to generate.

From the cosmic perspective of the stars, this human drama might appear as another iteration of a recurring pattern: how those facing existential threats must sometimes disrupt established orders to secure their survival. Throughout history, the stars have watched marginalized groups transform desperation into powerful collective action, slaves organizing rebellions, workers forming unions, women demanding suffrage. They have observed how societies often resist acknowledging suffering until forced to see it through disruptive action, and how those closest to a problem frequently develop the most effective solutions when empowered to apply their knowledge. The stars might recognize in ACT UP not just a specific movement addressing a specific disease, but an example of humanity's capacity to transform grief and rage into focused action that ultimately saves lives.

In March 1985, British Antarctic Survey scientists Joseph Farman, Brian Gardiner, and Jonathan Shanklin published a paper in the journal Nature that would fundamentally alter human understanding of our relationship with the planet. Their research documented a dramatic thinning of the ozone layer over Antarctica, what would soon be dubbed the "ozone hole." Unlike other moral panics of the era, the ozone crisis represented a genuine global threat substan-tiated by rigorous scientific evidence. Yet it still demonstrated characteristic patterns of fear amplification, competing interpretations, and the challenge of translating scientific findings into public understanding and policy action.

The ozone discovery immediately generated intense media coverage and public concern. Television news programs aired dramatic graphics showing the expanding hole, with colors shifting ominously from reassuring blues to alarming reds and purples. Magazine covers featured Earth with its protective atmosphere peeling away. Newspapers published headlines like "Shield Against Cancer-Causing Rays Is Depleting Rapidly" (Chicago Tribune, 1985) and

"Ozone Hole: Earthly Ticking Time Bomb" (USA Today, 1987). These vivid visual and verbal representations effectively communicated the gravity of the situation while sometimes sacrificing scientific nuance for immediate emotional impact.

Unlike other panics where experts emerged primarily from non-scientific backgrounds, the ozone crisis featured established atmospheric scientists as primary authorities. NASA quickly confirmed the British findings using satellite data, and subsequent research determined that chlorofluorocarbons (CFCs), chemicals used in aerosol sprays, refrigeration, and foam production, were causing the depletion by releasing chlorine into the stratosphere. Scientists explained that without the ozone layer's protection, increased ultraviolet radiation reaching Earth's surface would cause higher rates of skin cancer, cataracts, and immune system suppression while potentially disrupting ecosystems and agriculture. This expert consensus based on empirical evidence differentiated the ozone concern from panics driven primarily by anecdote or moral interpretation.

In January 1999, Time magazine's cover featured an ominous headline in bold red letters, "The Y2K Bug," superimposed over a menacing image of a computer bug. The subtitle read: "How to Protect Your Family, Your Money, and Your Life." This apocalyptic framing of what was essentially a technical issue involving date formatting in computer systems perfectly captured how a limited, albeit genuine, problem had transformed into a full-blown panic about technological collapse and societal breakdown. The Y2K episode illustrated society's profound ambivalence about technological dependence at the millennium's end while demonstrating how uncertainty creates fertile ground for extreme scenarios ranging from wild speculation to reasoned preparation.

The technical issue underlying Y2K concerns was straightforward but real. Early computer programmers had conserved then-precious memory space by using two digits rather than four to represent years. Without correction, these systems would incorrectly interpret "00" as 1900 rather than 2000, potentially causing calculation errors, data corruption, or system failures. This "millennium bug" could affect everything from banking transactions to power grids, air traffic control to manufacturing processes. Unlike some panics based on purely speculative threats, Y2K involved a genuine technical problem requiring correction, though the potential consequences remained uncertain.

Media coverage dramatically amplified these uncertainties into catastrophic scenarios. Television specials with titles like "Y2K: The Day the World Shuts Down" and "Millennium Meltdown" portrayed worst-case outcomes involving simultaneous failures across critical infrastructure systems. Magazines published detailed survival guides. Books with apocalyptic titles like Time Bomb 2000 and The Millennium Meltdown topped bestseller lists. Radio host Art Bell dedicated hundreds of broadcast hours to Y2K predictions, including scenarios where nuclear plants would melt down and satellites would fall from the sky. Even technology publications contributed to alarm, with Computerworld describing Y2K as "a disaster just waiting to happen." This coverage created self-reinforcing cycles where increased public concern generated demand for more stories, which further intensified anxiety regardless of the underlying risk level.

On April 20, 1999, two teenage students entered Columbine High School in Littleton, Colorado and murdered twelve fellow students and one teacher before taking their own lives. This horrific event triggered immediate efforts to explain the seemingly inexplicable: why would teenagers commit such an atrocity against their peers? Among the explanations that quickly emerged, violent video games received particular attention when investigators discovered the perpetrators had been avid players of the first-person shooter game Doom. This connection sparked renewed concerns about media violence that would intensify throughout the following year, representing yet another form of moral panic where legitimate questions about cultural influences transformed into oversimplified narratives about causation and exaggerated threats to youth.

The video game panic built upon longstanding concerns about media influences on children. Since the 1950s, successive waves of anxiety had targeted comic books, television violence, heavy metal music, and role-playing games as potential threats to youth development. Each wave featured similar narratives about vulnerable children corrupted by new media forms, with scientific evidence interpreted selectively to support predetermined concerns. Video games represented the latest iteration of this pattern, with interactive digital violence raising distinctive questions about potential behavioral effects. The timing of Columbine, coinciding with rapidly advancing game technology that rendered violence more realistically, created perfect conditions for renewed focus on these underlying anxieties.

The stars, in their ancient wisdom, might observe how these varied moral panics and collapse anxieties, seemingly distinct in their specific manifestations, share fundamental patterns that have characterized human societies across millennia. They would recognize how genuine threats and exaggerated fears intertwine in ways that make separating them difficult even for the most rational minds. They would see how societies struggling with uncertainty often project specific anxieties onto symbolic targets rather than addressing more complex underlying issues. They would note how these psychological and social processes transcend particular historical moments, appearing in different forms but following similar patterns whether in ancient Rome, medieval Europe, or modern America.

Yet the stars might also recognize something hopeful in this recurring pattern, how societies eventually find their way back to balance, distinguishing between warranted concern and unnecessary fear, developing measured responses to real threats while gradually discarding the most extreme manifestations of panic. They would observe that while these cycles of anxiety and adjustment often involve painful learning processes with genuine casualties along the way, they ultimately demonstrate humanity's capacity to navigate uncertainty through an imperfect but effective combination of initial emotional response, subsequent critical reflection, and eventual practical adaptation. The stars, having witnessed this pattern countless times, might view our modern moral panics not as evidence of unique contemporary failings, but as familiar manifestations of an ongoing human struggle to make sense of an inherently uncertain world.

NO MAN'S LAND: Protection vs. Paranoia

Societies must actively protect their members, especially the most vulnerable, from genuine threats, even when protective measures restrict some freedoms or appear excessive to those not directly at risk.

Pause. Notice what arises in you.

Fears about potential threats can spiral into paranoia that causes more harm than the original danger, creating unnecessary restrictions and diverting attention from more significant risks that lack emotional resonance.

Pause. Notice what arises in you.

You do not have to agree with or justify either statement. Simply hold them both in your mind and observe what comes up.

This tension between protection and paranoia emerged repeatedly throughout the moral panics of the 1980s and 1990s. The Satanic Panic originated in genuine concern for child welfare but spiraled into fantastical allegations that damaged innocent lives while diverting attention from more common abuse contexts. AIDS response required legitimate public health measures yet generated stigma and counterproductive policies based on exaggerated transmission fears. Environmental concerns like ozone depletion justified protective regulation while sometimes inspiring apocalyptic scenarios exceeding scientific evidence. Y2K preparation ranged from reasonable technical corrections to extreme survivalist responses disconnected from likely outcomes. Video game restrictions reflected authentic interest in child psychological health yet often presumed causal relationships unsupported by research evidence.

The challenge remains discerning where reasonable caution ends and excessive fear begins, a boundary rarely clear in real time. Protection requires anticipating potential harms before they manifest fully, inherently involving some speculation about uncertain futures. Yet this same anticipatory thinking creates vulnerability to confirmation bias, where ambiguous information gets interpreted as confirming pre-existing fears. Protective decision-making operates under asymmetric risk, as the consequences of inadequate protection often seem more severe than those of excessive caution. Yet precautionary approaches can themselves generate substantial costs through restriction of liberty, economic disruption, or resource misallocation away from less emotionally salient but more statistically significant threats.

This balance becomes particularly challenging in contexts involving children, where protective instincts naturally intensify. Parents reasonably monitor media consumption, supervise social activities, and advocate for safety measures in schools and communities. Yet excessive protection can restrict healthy development, create unwarranted fear, or teach children to perceive normal risks as overwhelming threats. Similar dynamics apply to public health, environmental policy, and technological security, where legitimate protective measures can sometimes evolve beyond evidence-based proportionality into performative security theater or moral enforcement disconnected from actual risk profiles.

Chapter Twenty-One

When Truth Took Back the Microphone

As the digital clocks ticked over from 11:59 PM on December 31, 1999, to 12:00 AM on January 1, 2000, millions of people around the world held their breath. For years, experts had warned that this precise moment could trigger widespread computer failures, potentially disrupting everything from banking systems to power grids, air traffic control to nuclear facilities. Billions of dollars had been spent on remediation. Government agencies had established emergency operations centers. Individuals had stockpiled supplies. Some had even retreated to remote locations to await potential societal collapse.

And then... almost nothing happened.

A few credit card machines malfunctioned in Britain, a weather service in Australia showed incorrect dates, a nuclear power plant in Japan had a monitoring equipment error that was quickly resolved. But the apocalyptic scenarios of darkened cities, crashed planes, and financial chaos simply did not materialize. In the days that followed, headlines shifted from breathless anticipation to puzzled reflection: "Y2K Bug Turns Out to Be Mostly a No-Show" (Washington

Post), "Much Ado About Nothing?" (Time Magazine), "Y2K Fizzle: Massive Preparations Pay Off, Or Overkill?" (USA Today).

This anticlimactic resolution to one of the most extensively anticipated potential disasters in modern history raised vital questions about how societies anticipate, prepare for, and ultimately resolve perceived threats. Was Y2K a wasteful panic based on exaggerated fears, or a triumph of foresight and preparation that averted genuine catastrophe? The answer, as with most complex issues, contained elements of both interpretations, revealing patterns that would repeat across the various moral panics and systemic anxieties of this era.

Looking up at the night sky, with its ancient, patient stars that have witnessed countless human fears come and go, we might find perspective on these cycles of anxiety and resolution. The stars have observed how societies throughout time have confronted threats both real and imagined, how fear can distort perception but also motivate necessary action, how collective efforts to address dangers often produce unexpected benefits, how each cycle of concern and response leaves communities changed in ways both subtle and profound. From their timeless vantage point, these celestial witnesses might remind us that our struggles to discern genuine threats from exaggerated fears, to balance protection with proportion, are not unique to our era but represent recurring human challenges across the spiral of history.

On January 18, 1990, a jury in Los Angeles County Superior Court delivered not guilty verdicts on 52 counts against Peggy McMartin Buckey, while deadlocking on 13 additional charges. This outcome marked the final collapse of the most notorious prosecution in the "Satanic Panic" that had consumed American public attention for nearly seven years. Ray Buckey, Peggy's son, faced a retrial on the 13 deadlocked counts, which also ended without conviction. The McMartin Preschool case, the longest and most expensive criminal trial in American history at that time, had finally concluded, having produced zero convictions despite seven years of proceedings, approximately $15 million in costs, and the disruption of dozens of lives.

This judicial outcome constituted just one element in the broader collapse of what had become a nationwide moral panic. The disintegration occurred through multiple interlocking processes: accumulating case failures in court, scientific research undermining foundational claims, official investigations finding no evidence, reformed interview procedures yielding different results, and gradual media reassessment. Together, these developments illustrated how evidence-based approaches can eventually overcome even deeply entrenched societal fears, though often at considerable cost to those caught in the crossfire.

The legal system's confrontation with satanic ritual abuse claims proved particularly revealing. Beyond McMartin, other high-profile cases similarly collapsed under evidentiary scrutiny. In Kern County, California, 36 convictions were eventually overturned after appellate courts found egregious prosecutorial misconduct and coercive interviewing techniques. The Fells Acres Day Care case in Massachusetts was eventually ordered for retrial due to improper interview procedures, though defendants served many years before release. These legal reversals demonstrated the judicial system's capacity for self-correction, albeit often after devastating delays and damage to defendants' lives.

Scientific research simultaneously undermined core psychological assumptions behind ritual abuse allegations. Studies demonstrated that suggestive questioning techniques used with children could implant false memories that children would subsequently report as genuine experiences. Researcher Stephen Ceci showed that after multiple suggestive interviews, 58% of preschoolers would maintain false claims even when questioned by neutral interviewers. The American Psychological Association published guidelines in 1994 casting doubt on "recovered memory therapy" techniques that had generated many adult ritual abuse claims. The scientific consensus increasingly recognized that well-intentioned but flawed interviewing approaches had manufactured allegations rather than uncovering them, leading to reformed protocols that child protective services adopted nationwide.

On February 5, 1997, Michael Gottlieb, the UCLA doctor who first identified AIDS in 1981, stood on stage at the 4th Conference on Retroviruses and Opportunistic Infections in Washington, D.C. Sixteen years after his initial discovery of a mysterious immune deficiency affecting gay men, he delivered a presentation describing the remarkable success of newly developed antiretroviral therapy combinations. "For the first time," he told the assembled researchers, clinicians, and activists, "we are seeing a dramatic decline in AIDS deaths and a real possibility of long-term viral suppression." The annual AIDS death rate in the United States had fallen 23% between 1995 and 1996, the first significant decline since the epidemic began. A disease once considered an automatic death sentence had transformed into a manageable chronic condition for many patients who could access treatment.

This medical breakthrough represented one crucial element in the broader transformation of the AIDS crisis from peak hysteria to a more rational, science-based, and compassionate response. Unlike the Satanic Panic, which collapsed primarily through evidence dispelling unfounded claims, the AIDS crisis involved a genuine threat that required substantive solutions. Its resolution emerged through an interdependent process of scientific advancement, activist pressure, policy reform, cultural representation, and public education, demonstrating how combination approaches can effectively address complex societal challenges involving both medical and social dimensions.

Scientific and medical progress formed the foundation of this transformation. The identification of HIV as the causative agent in 1983-84 by French and American researchers established clarity about what was being confronted. The development of antibody testing in 1985 allowed for diagnosis, blood supply screening, and epidemiological tracking. AZT became the first approved treatment in 1987, though with limited effectiveness. But the true breakthrough came in 1996 with highly active antiretroviral therapy (HAART), drug combinations that dramatically reduced viral loads and restored immune function in many patients. These scientific advances transformed prognosis from near-certain death to potential long-term survival, fundamentally changing the nature of the crisis for those with treatment access.

Yet this scientific progress cannot be separated from the unprecedented activist movement that helped drive it. ACT UP and other AIDS organizations fundamentally changed how medical research was conducted, demanding and eventually achieving accelerated drug approval processes, expanded clinical trial access, and meaningful participation of affected communities in research decisions. By 1990, the FDA had implemented a "parallel track" system allowing patients to access experimental treatments outside formal trials. These institutional changes, achieved through disruptive protests, policy expertise, and strategic pressure, saved countless lives while establishing new models for patient advocacy that would influence healthcare more broadly.

Under the ancient stellar gaze, this extraordinary convergence of scientific discovery and human advocacy might appear as part of a larger pattern visible throughout history: how crisis can sometimes catalyze unprecedented collaboration across boundaries that seemed impermeable, how the urgency of suffering can accelerate innovation that might otherwise take decades, how those most directly affected by problems often develop the most creative solutions when given voice and agency. The stars have witnessed many such moments when human intelligence and compassion combine to overcome seemingly insurmountable challenges, creating not just technical solutions but new models for addressing future crises.

On the morning of September 16, 1987, representatives from 24 nations gathered in Montreal, Canada, to sign what would become one of the most successful international environmental agreements in history. The Montreal Protocol on Substances that Deplete the Ozone Layer committed signatories to reducing production of chlorofluorocarbons (CFCs) by 50% by 1999. As United Nations Environment Programme Executive Director Mostafa Tolba declared at the signing ceremony, "For the first time in the history of mankind, nations have agreed to regulations that control transboundary, global industrial products before extensive damage has been proven." This precautionary approach, acting decisively based on strong but incomplete evidence, represented a remarkable departure from traditional requirements for absolute certainty before intervention, establishing a model for environmental action that continues to influence international cooperation on planetary threats.

The Montreal Protocol's success only grew in subsequent years. Initially modest in scope, the agreement strengthened through five major amendments between 1990 and 1999, accelerating phase-out schedules and adding additional ozone-depleting substances to the controlled list. By 2010, the production and consumption of nearly 100 ozone-depleting chemicals had been phased out entirely in developed countries and significantly reduced in developing nations. As of 2023, the Protocol had achieved universal ratification by all 198 United Nations member states, the only UN treaty to reach this milestone. This remarkable international consensus demonstrated that effective global environmental governance is possible when certain enabling conditions align.

Scientific monitoring confirmed the agreement's effectiveness. By the late 1990s, atmospheric concentrations of major ozone-depleting substances had stabilized and begun declining. The Antarctic ozone hole stopped expanding, and while seasonal fluctuations continued, measurements showed the beginning of a long-term recovery trend. In 2018, NASA announced that the first direct observations of ozone increasing in the upper stratosphere had been recorded. Current projections suggest the ozone layer will return to 1980 levels in most of the world by mid-century. This measurable success validated the precautionary approach, showing that early intervention based on sound science could effectively address global environmental threats before their worst consequences manifested.

When January 1, 2000 arrived without major technological disruptions, the massive Y2K preparation effort immediately sparked contradictory interpretations. Senator Robert Bennett, who had chaired the Senate Special Committee on the Year 2000 Technology Problem, declared the smooth transition "a triumph of preparation over disaster." Technology consultant Mark Frautschi offered a contrasting assessment: "I think the whole thing was a self-fulfilling prophecy, the more we talked about it, the more we spent on it, and the more we convinced ourselves it would have been a disaster." This interpretive divide, seeing Y2K remediation as either essential prevention of catastrophe or wasteful response to exaggerated threat, revealed the fundamental challenge of evaluating preventive measures when their success means nothing dramatic happens.

The scale of Y2K preparation had been unprecedented. By conservative estimates, organizations worldwide spent between $300-500 billion on remediation efforts. Approximately 300,000 programmers dedicated years to reviewing and updating code. The United States federal government alone spent $8.4 billion preparing its systems. Major corporations established dedicated Y2K teams, sometimes comprising hundreds of employees. These massive investments reflected rational risk management given the potential consequences of system failures in critical infrastructure, even if the probability of worst-case scenarios remained uncertain.

The technical challenge had been genuine though often oversimplified in media accounts. Early computer programming had indeed used two-digit year representations to conserve then-precious memory resources. Without correction, these systems would incorrectly interpret "00" as 1900 rather than 2000, potentially causing calculation errors, data corruption, or system failures. Independent technical reviews consistently confirmed the validity of this concern. In sectors where remediation was less systematic, particularly in some developing countries, small businesses, and older embedded systems, minor problems did occur, though without cascading into broader disruptions. These limited failures validated the technical basis for concern while suggesting that the most catastrophic scenarios had overestimated technological brittleness and interdependence.

On June 27, 2011, the United States Supreme Court issued a landmark ruling in Brown v. Entertainment Merchants Association, striking down a California law restricting the sale of violent video games to minors. Writing for the 7-2 majority, Justice Antonin Scalia declared, "Video games qualify for First Amendment protection," adding that the government lacked sufficient evidence that violent games caused real-world aggression or harm to minors. This definitive legal affirmation of video games as protected expression marked the culmination of a gradual shift away from the moral panic about media violence that had intensified following the 1999 Columbine school shooting. The court's decision reflected broader evolutions in research evidence, industry practices, and cultural attitudes that had collectively transformed video games from perceived threat to mainstream entertainment medium.

Research developments played a crucial role in this transformation. Following Columbine, multiple government agencies commissioned studies examining potential links between violent media and aggressive behavior. The Federal Trade Commission, Surgeon General, National Institute of Mental Health, and Centers for Disease Control all conducted or sponsored research on the topic. These studies consistently found mixed or weak evidence for causal connections between media consumption and violent actions. A 2001 Surgeon General report concluded that media violence had "relatively small" effects compared to other risk factors for youth aggression. By 2004, the American Psychological Association's literature review found "some strong evidence" for short-term effects on aggression but noted "there's not a lot of research" showing a definitive link to violent crime. This accumulating research helped shift the discussion from moral certainty toward greater scientific nuance about complex influences on human behavior.

The stars, in their silent observation of our human dramas, might note how these various resolutions, from Satanic Panic to AIDS, from ozone depletion to Y2K, from video game fears to other moral concerns, reveal recurring patterns in how societies navigate from fear to understanding. They might observe how humans tend to oscillate between periods of heightened anxiety and calmer assessment, how evidence gradually accumulates to distinguish genuine threats from exaggerated fears, how institutions develop corrective mechanisms that build resilience against future panics. From their cosmic perspective, these patterns represent not aberrations but natural rhythms in how human communities process uncertainty and potential danger, cycles of concern, response, and adaptation that have characterized social evolution throughout recorded history.

Crowded into a hotel ballroom in Portland, Oregon on August 5, 2003, members of the American Psychological Association listened as psychologist Elizabeth Loftus presented "The Memory Wars: Past, Present and Future," a comprehensive assessment of how psychology had reckoned with its role in the Satanic Panic. Loftus, whose research on false memories had helped discredit the "recovered memory therapy" techniques that generated many ritual abuse allegations, reflected on the profession's ongoing process of accountability and reform. "We now know that suggestion can lead to rich false memories," she told colleagues. "We now know that therapists can unintentionally plant false memories. We now know that these false memories can be acted upon with devastating consequences." Her presentation embodied one of the most important aspects of societal recovery from moral panics, the capacity for professional and institutional self-correction following periods of excessive fear.

This process of institutional learning after panics demonstrated one of democracy's essential strengths, the ability to develop self-correcting mechanisms that gradually reduce vulnerability to future fear episodes. Child interview protocols for abuse investigations underwent comprehensive revision, incorporating empirical research on suggestion and memory while maintaining appropriate child protection measures. Health agencies developed principles for more effective risk communication during disease outbreaks, recognizing that transparent information typically reduces rather than amplifies public fear. Environmental communication increasingly balanced concerns about threats with practical steps for addressing them. Media organizations implemented more cautious approaches to reporting potential threats, introducing greater scientific context and multiple perspectives. These systematic adaptations, though imperfect and inconsistently applied, created institutional memory that made future panics less likely or less severe when similar issues emerged.

The recurrent pattern across different panic resolutions revealed several key success factors in navigating from fear to proportionate response. The methodical collection and application of empirical evidence provided essential foundation for countering exaggerated claims. Independent institutional voices offering factual perspective, such as FBI investigations of alleged ritual abuse, scientific consensus on ozone depletion mechanisms, or judicial review of video game restriction laws, proved particularly influential in challenging uncritical acceptance of fear narratives. Consumer adaptation through market choices, such as boycotting CFC-containing products or adopting age-appropriate content filtering, created change through distributed action rather than centralized control. Voluntary industry standards, such as video game ratings or pharmaceutical compassionate use programs, often addressed legitimate concerns while avoiding the rigidity or political polarization of government mandates. The most effective resolutions typically combined these elements rather than relying on any single mechanism.

If we could ask the stars for their ancient wisdom on these human struggles with fear and uncertainty, they might remind us that while the specific manifestations change, from witchcraft accusations to ritual abuse allegations, from miasma theories of disease to AIDS stigmatization, from comets as harbingers of doom to technological collapse anxieties, the underlying patterns of human response remain remarkably consistent. The stars have witnessed how societies throughout time have navigated the delicate balance between necessary vigilance against genuine threats and excessive fear of imagined ones. They have observed how each cycle of panic and resolution leaves behind both painful lessons and valuable adaptations that gradually increase collective wisdom. They might suggest that rather than seeing moral panics as evidence of particular modern weakness or irrationality, we might recognize them as recurring features of how human societies process uncertainty, challenges that each generation must navigate anew, hopefully with slightly more wisdom than the last.

Perhaps most significantly, ethical humility emerged as crucial for societies navigating the aftermath of moral panics. In each case examined, passionate advocates for specific perspectives, whether warning about dangers or questioning their severity, often expressed absolute certainty despite incomplete information. Both alarmists and skeptics frequently claimed unambiguous moral clarity while dismissing opposing viewpoints as either dangerously naive or irrationally fearful. Later evidence typically revealed greater complexity than either extreme position had acknowledged. This pattern suggests the value of maintaining provisional judgment and epistemic humility while taking reasonable precautions, recognizing that both unwarranted fear and complacent dismissal of genuine threats can produce harmful consequences. The most constructive post-panic reflections acknowledged the legitimacy of core concerns while critically examining their amplification into disproportionate fear.

The most valuable lasting lesson may be that societies require balanced approaches that neither automatically dismiss emerging concerns nor uncritically accept apocalyptic framings. The appropriate response to novel or evolving threats lies not in choosing between paranoid overreaction and complacent denial, but in developing systematic approaches for proportionate assessment and response. This balanced path acknowledges genuine concerns while subjecting them to evidence-based evaluation, considers worst-case scenarios without assuming their inevitability, takes precautionary measures proportionate to credible risks, maintains flexibility to adjust as new information emerges, and preserves essential freedoms while implementing necessary protections. Though challenging to maintain amid uncertainty and fear, this balanced approach represents democratic societies' most effective path through the recurring cycles of concern, alarm, and resolution that characterize our relationship with perceived threats.

NO MAN'S LAND: Crisis vs. Opportunity

Times of crisis primarily represent threats requiring protective measures to minimize harm and preserve existing systems against disruption or breakdown.

Pause. Notice what arises in you.

Times of crisis primarily create opportunities for beneficial innovation, institutional evolution, and positive transformation that might otherwise face resistance.

Pause. Notice what arises in you.

You do not have to agree with or justify either statement. Simply hold them both in your mind and observe what comes up.

This fundamental tension appeared throughout the moral panics and systemic anxieties we've examined. The AIDS crisis simultaneously threatened public health while creating transformative patient advocacy models that revolutionized medical research. The Satanic Panic damaged many lives through false accusations while ultimately generating significantly improved child interview techniques and greater awareness of suggestibility effects. The ozone hole represented genuine environmental danger while yielding unprecedented international cooperation frameworks. Y2K preparations consumed enormous resources addressing potential disruptions while producing valuable insights into technological interdependence and risk management. Video game controversies created chilling effects on creative expression while motivating industry self-regulation systems that balanced creator freedom with parental information needs.

In each case, the crisis contained elements of both threat and opportunity, neither perspective alone capturing the full reality. Viewing crises solely as threats often leads to defensive, preservationist responses focused on returning to previous conditions, which may address immediate dangers while missing transformative possibilities. Viewing crises solely as opportunities can minimize genuine suffering and risk while pursuing ideological agendas opportunistically, using human hardship instrumentally rather than addressing it directly. The most effective responses acknowledge both dimensions simultaneously, implementing protective measures to minimize harm while recognizing possibilities for constructive evolution that crisis conditions sometimes enable.

This dual perspective seems particularly valuable today as we face multiple overlapping crises involving climate, technology, public health, economic inequality, and democratic functioning. These complex challenges contain both genuine threats requiring protective response and significant opportunities for positive transformation. By holding both aspects in mind simultaneously, we can develop approaches that address immediate dangers while laying foundations for more resilient, just, and sustainable systems. Rather than choosing between naive optimism that minimizes genuine problems and paralytic pessimism that forsakes possibility, we can engage fully with both the protective imperatives and transformative opportunities that crisis moments present, maintaining hope without denying difficulty, and acknowledging challenges without surrendering to despair.

Conclusion

Pendulums & Progress

When I began this journey through history's spiral of fears and resolutions, I stood beneath a star-filled sky feeling overwhelmed by the urgencies of our time. As we conclude, I invite you to join me there again, looking upward at those ancient lights that have witnessed each turn of humanity's story.

The same stars that shone over Salem during the witch trials illuminated the streets of McCarthy's Washington. They watched over frightened communities during the AIDS crisis and glittered above Y2K preppers awaiting midnight on December 31, 1999. These celestial witnesses have observed each crisis arrive with its particular flavor of apocalyptic dread, each moral panic with its urgent calls for radical action, each societal division with its passionate certainty that this time is truly different.

And yet, we remain. Not unchanged, but persisting. Not perfect, but learning. Not moving in straight lines or perfect circles, but in that curious spiral pattern where we revisit similar fears while gradually ascending.

Across seven distinct historical cycles, we've witnessed remarkably similar patterns play out in different contexts:

During the Salem witch trials, a community under stress projected its deepest fears onto vulnerable members, creating an alternate reality where invisible forces threatened their way of life. Nearly three centuries later, communities in the 1980s convinced themselves that daycare workers were conducting satanic rituals, despite no physical evidence. In both cases, the accusations eventually collapsed under evidential scrutiny, but not before causing tremendous harm to the falsely accused.

The French Revolution's idealistic beginnings descended into the Terror as revolutionary purity became more important than human lives. During the Red Scare, similar patterns emerged as the protection of American ideals justified destroying the lives and reputations of suspected communists. In both cases, the pendulum eventually swung back toward due process and measured assessment as society recognized the dangers of unchecked fear.

Luddites smashed machines they believed would destroy their livelihoods and communities. Nuclear anxiety prompted Americans to build fallout shelters and practice duck-and-cover drills in schools. Y2K fears had reasonable technical foundations but expanded into apocalyptic scenarios. In each case, the feared collapse proved less catastrophic than anticipated, while legitimate concerns drove constructive adaptations.

These recurring patterns aren't evidence of human folly or weakness, but of our consistent psychological and social responses to perceived threats during periods of rapid change. History's repetitions are not failures but expressions of our persistent nature: our tribal instincts, our need for meaning and belonging, our tendency to find patterns even in randomness, and our capacity for both fear and hope.

Through each cycle, we've observed a fundamental tension between forces of change and those of preservation. This isn't a simple confrontation between "progress" and "backwardness," but a complex, necessary dialogue between innovation and stability.

The puritan communities of New England weren't simply close-minded zealots, but people trying to maintain cohesive societies in a threatening wilderness. The McCarthy era wasn't merely irrational paranoia, but also reflected genuine concerns about authoritarian ideologies during a period of international tension. Even the most misguided panics typically contain legitimate concerns at their core, however distorted they became through fear's magnifying lens.

Simultaneously, those pushing for change, whether technological innovators, social reformers, or cultural revolutionaries, weren't uniformly farsighted heroes, but complex actors with mixed motives and imperfect understanding of their innovations' full implications. The industrial revolution that Luddites resisted did indeed destroy traditional communities and ways of life even as it eventually created new opportunities. The counterculture movements of the 1960s produced both valuable social reforms and genuinely disruptive social dislocations.

This tension between change and stability, between reform and tradition, isn't a flaw in our social system but a feature. The pendulum swings between them not because we're trapped in endless conflict, but because we need both forces: the dynamic energy of innovation and the stabilizing wisdom of tradition. What appears as partisan battle often reflects this deeper dialogue about how societies should navigate change while preserving what's valuable from the past.

The stars, in their ancient patience, have witnessed this pendulum swing countless times across human civilizations. They have seen how societies that embrace change too rapidly without respect for stabilizing traditions often fracture and lose their way. They have equally observed how societies that resist all evolution eventually calcify and crumble when reality demands adaptation. From their cosmic perspective, the most resilient human communities have always been those that find balance: honoring their roots while reaching toward new possibilities, maintaining core values while adapting to changing circumstances. The stars recognize this not as contradiction but as the natural rhythm of healthy social evolution.

A striking pattern across our seven cycles has been how communication technologies consistently play dual roles in both spreading and eventually resolving fears. From the transatlantic pamphlets contributing to Salem's witch panic to television amplifying the Satanic ritual abuse claims, media has reliably served as both accelerant and eventual firefighter.

In each era, emerging media forms initially enable fears to spread more rapidly and widely than in previous cycles. Early printing presses distributed sensational accounts of witchcraft. Mass-circulation newspapers amplified fears about anarchists and communists. Television brought civil unrest and counterculture threats directly into American living rooms. Cable news channels created 24-hour cycles of fear during AIDS and Y2K. The internet enabled conspiracy theories to spread and communities of fear to form around vaccine hesitancy and digital threats.

Yet these same technologies subsequently became essential to resolving the very panics they helped create. Newspapers that initially published sensational accounts of satanic activity later published investigative pieces debunking them. Television that aired alarmist AIDS coverage eventually broadcast educational programs that reduced stigma. Online platforms that spread conspiracy theories also enabled expert voices to reach broader audiences with evidence-based corrections.

This pattern suggests that each new communication technology creates a period of vulnerability to fear contagion before society develops the literacy and institutional adaptations necessary to use these tools more wisely. The acceleration of this cycle with digital media presents both challenge and opportunity: faster spread of fears, but potentially faster corrections as well.

Perhaps the most valuable skill we can develop from studying these historical patterns is distinguishing between disproportionate fears and legitimate threats requiring response. The ozone hole represented a genuine environmental danger requiring coordinated action. The AIDS epidemic needed vigorous medical research and public health measures. Yet in both cases, legitimate concerns became entangled with exaggerated fears, moral judgments, and apocalyptic thinking that sometimes hindered effective response.

Several patterns can help us distinguish between warranted concern and moral panic:

Fears that target specific, often marginalized groups, whether witches in Salem, communists during McCarthyism, gay men during AIDS, or daycare workers during the Satanic Panic, deserve particular scrutiny. Throughout history, societies under stress have repeatedly projected anxieties onto convenient scapegoats, allowing complex problems to be simplified into battles against identifiable enemies.

Claims resistant to empirical investigation, where evidence of absence becomes reinterpreted as evidence of extraordinary concealment, often signal moral panic rather than legitimate threat assessment. When the lack of bodies at alleged satanic murder sites becomes evidence of particularly effective disposal methods, or when the absence of communist infiltration evidence becomes proof of especially clever subversion, we've entered circular reasoning that prevents reality-testing.

Apocalyptic framing that presents civilizational collapse as imminent without immediate, dramatic action serves psychological and social functions beyond rational risk assessment. Each generation faces genuine challenges, but the persistent human tendency to experience current problems as uniquely catastrophic reveals more about our psychology than about objective threat levels.

If we listen carefully, the stars might whisper to us about this curious human tendency to oscillate between catastrophic fear and dismissive complacency. From their vantage point across billions of years, they've observed how our species consistently struggles to calibrate its response to threats, how we amplify some dangers beyond reasonable proportion while overlooking others of genuine consequence. The stars do not judge this pattern but simply note it as a recurring feature of human perception, shaped by our evolutionary history, our social dynamics, and our need for meaning. They might suggest that wisdom lies in cultivating the calm awareness that allows us to see threats clearly: neither magnified by fear nor diminished by denial, but assessed with the measured perspective that comes from understanding our place in time's longer arc.

NO MAN'S LAND: WARNING VS. REASSURANCE

Those who warn about societal threats, looming crises, and systemic risks provide essential alerts that help prevent complacency, catalyze necessary precautions, and potentially avert worst-case outcomes.

Pause. Notice what arises in you.

Those who offer perspective, historical context, and reassurance about humanity's resilience provide essential balance that helps prevent paralyzing fear, enables thoughtful rather than reactive responses, and protects psychological wellbeing during periods of uncertainty.

Pause. Notice what arises in you.

You do not have to agree with or justify either statement. Simply hold them both in your mind and observe what comes up.

We need both these roles in a healthy society: the sentinel and the sage, the activist and the historian, the prophetic voice and the calming presence. Each provides balance to the other, preventing both dangerous complacency and debilitating fear. The most constructive approach acknowledges legitimate concerns while placing them in the longer arc of human experience, not to minimize current challenges, but to face them with both courage and context.

If history moved in perfect circles, these recurring patterns might justify despair: endless repetition of the same mistakes, the same fears, the same conflicts. But what we've observed across these seven cycles isn't a circle but a spiral, revisiting similar themes while gradually ascending.

Consider how the resolution of each cycle has typically established new foundations that subsequent societies built upon, even as similar fears reemerged:

The Salem witch trials eventually led to substantial legal reforms, with courts establishing higher evidential standards for testimony and greater skepticism toward spectral evidence. When the Satanic Panic emerged centuries later, these legal standards, though initially overwhelmed in some cases, ultimately provided the framework that helped courts correct course and overturn unjust convictions.

McCarthyism's eventual discrediting established stronger protections for civil liberties and due process, creating institutional knowledge that helped limit (though not eliminate) similar excesses during subsequent national security threats. The Church Committee reforms following Vietnam and Watergate further strengthened these protections, creating oversight mechanisms that have provided at least partial safeguards during the War on Terror and other security challenges.

The AIDS crisis, despite its devastating toll, transformed medical research processes, patient advocacy models, and eventually public health approaches in ways that created foundations for more effective and humane responses to subsequent health challenges, including COVID-19. While these later responses remained imperfect, they built upon lessons painfully learned in earlier crises.

Each cycle leaves behind both institutional knowledge and cultural memory that influence how subsequent societies respond to similar challenges. This doesn't prevent new fears or eliminate social conflict, but it creates the possibility of more sophisticated responses with each turn of the spiral, if we choose to access and apply these accumulated lessons.

This spiral pattern offers a realistic hope, neither the blind optimism that ignores genuine problems nor the fatalistic pessimism that sees only decline and repetition. It acknowledges that similar fears and conflicts will continue emerging with each generation while recognizing that we aren't simply running on a historical treadmill.

The witch hunts of Salem won't return in their original form. Modern surveillance technologies create new privacy challenges, but we face them with constitutional protections and civil liberties awareness that didn't exist in previous centuries. Climate change presents unprecedented global challenges, but we approach them with scientific understanding, international cooperation frameworks, and technological capacities unavailable to previous generations facing environmental threats.

This perspective doesn't promise that everything will work out on its own or that progress is automatic. The upward trajectory of the spiral depends on human choices: on our willingness to learn from past mistakes, to resist scapegoating when under pressure, to carefully distinguish between genuine threats and exaggerated fears, and to maintain both vigilance against real dangers and skepticism toward moral panics.

The comfort this history offers isn't passive reassurance that problems will solve themselves, but active hope grounded in humanity's demonstrated capacity to work through cycles of fear toward more nuanced understanding. It's not an invitation to disengage from today's legitimate challenges, but encouragement to approach them with the perspective that comes from recognizing our place in longer historical patterns.

The stars have traced humanity's spiral ascent throughout our existence. While each generation encounters challenges that seem unprecedented from their immediate vantage point, the cosmic perspective reveals how each turn of the spiral builds upon foundations laid during previous cycles. The stars have watched ethical principles evolve from tribal protections to universal human rights, scientific understanding grow from mystical speculation to empirical knowledge, and social organization develop from isolated bands to global cooperation frameworks. This ascent has never been steady or uninterrupted; there have been devastating setbacks, tragic regressions, and painful conflicts. Yet the overall trajectory, viewed across millennia rather than moments, reveals humanity's remarkable capacity to learn, adapt, and gradually create more sophisticated ways of understanding and addressing our recurring challenges.

Beyond its implications for understanding social patterns, this historical perspective offers something deeply personal: a different relationship with the anxieties that pervade modern life.

When the news cycle presents each current controversy as unprecedented, each political disagreement as existential, each technological change as either salvation or apocalypse, history offers a corrective lens. It reminds us that humans have repeatedly faced fundamental challenges to their ways of life, encountered seemingly irreconcilable value conflicts, and navigated disruptive technological transformations, and found paths forward.

This knowledge doesn't eliminate concern about genuine problems, but it can transform how we carry that concern: less desperately, less frantically, with greater capacity to distinguish between apocalyptic rhetoric and substantive issues requiring attention. It allows us to engage with today's challenges neither from the paralyzing despair that sees only crisis nor from the complacent denial that refuses to acknowledge problems, but from the grounded perspective that recognizes both real difficulties and human resilience.

In practical terms, this perspective creates space for thoughtful engagement rather than reactive alarm. It allows us to consider information more carefully, to resist both paranoid catastrophizing and dismissive minimizing, to engage with different viewpoints without immediately categorizing them as existential threats or comforting confirmations. It fosters what psychologists call "cognitive flexibility": the capacity to hold complexity without needing immediate resolution, to consider multiple perspectives without losing our own.

As we conclude this journey through history's cycling fears and resolutions, I return to where we began, looking upward at the stars on a clear night. That vast perspective doesn't eliminate my concerns about genuine challenges we face, doesn't make me dismiss climate threats or democratic fragility or technological risks or economic inequalities. But it does transform how I hold these concerns.

The same stars that watched over Salem's judges have seen societies navigate through panic after panic, crisis after crisis, sometimes with tremendous pain and injustice, sometimes with remarkable wisdom and adaptation, usually with some combination of both. They've witnessed the pendulum swing between stability and change, between tradition and innovation, between fear and hope, tracing that gradual upward spiral across generations.

They remind me that we aren't the first to feel we stand at history's precipice, that previously confident civilizations have felt the vertigo of fundamental change and somehow found new equilibrium. They offer not the false comfort that ignores problems, but the grounded perspective that helps us face them neither with paralyzing dread nor with complacent dismissal, but with the steady courage that comes from recognizing our place in time's longer arc.

I began this book offering permission to exhale, not to disengage, not to stop caring, but to step back from the frenetic urgency that treats each moment as unprecedented apocalypse or utopian opportunity. I end with an invitation to look upward occasionally, to remember those ancient witnesses to humanity's recurring fears and resilient adaptations, and to find in that vaster perspective not escape from today's challenges but a different way of engaging with them: with clarity rather than catastrophizing, with purpose rather than panic, with the steady determination that comes from knowing we're part of history's continuing story rather than its conclusion.

The stars remind us of a simple truth easy to forget amid breaking news alerts and viral outrage cycles: this moment, with all its noise and fury, is just one flickering point in humanity's long journey. The world is not ending. It never is. It's always transforming, challenging us to navigate change with wisdom, to distinguish between apocalyptic fears and genuine threats, to remember lessons from previous turns of the spiral as we face our own cycle's particular challenges.

The stars have seen it all before. And they'll be watching still as we write the next chapter of this never-ending story.

References

T he following sources represent the core materials consulted in the research and writing of this book. Readers seeking additional primary documents, scholarly articles, and supplementary sources can find a comprehensive bibliography at TheResilienceCompass.com.

CYCLE 1: RELIGIOUS FEAR & WITCH HUNTS (1600S-EARLY 1700S)

"A Brief History of Doubt — and the Emotion That Underpins It." *Church Times*, September 21, 2018. https://www.churchtimes.co.uk/articles/2018/21-september/features/features/a-brief-history-of-doubt-and-the-emotion-that-underpins-it.

"Copernicus, Galileo, and the Church: Science in a Religious World." *Inquiries Journal*. Accessed Feb 2025. https://www.inquiriesjournal.com/articles/1675/copernicus-galileo-and-the-church-science-in-a-religious-world.

"The Neuroscience of Witches." *Brain Facts*, October 30, 2019. https://www.brainfacts.org/neuroscience-in-society/law-economics-and-ethics/2019/the-neuroscience-of-witches-103019.

"René Descartes: A Yogi?" *Philosophy Now*, Issue 144. Accessed Feb 2025. https://philosophynow.org/issues/144/Rene_Descartes_A_Yogi.

Gilder Lehrman Institute of American History. "Cotton Mather's Account of the Salem Witch Trials, 1693." Accessed Feb

2025. https://www.gilderlehrman.org/history-resources/spotlight-primary-source/cotton-mathers-account-salem-witch-trials-1693.

Hogan Assessments. "Unraveling the Psychological Drivers of the Salem Witch Trials." 2021. https://www.hoganassessments.com/blog/unraveling-psychological-drivers-salem-witch-trials/.

Humanist Heritage. "Thomas Aikenhead (1676-1697)." Accessed Feb 2025. https://heritage.humanists.uk/thomas-aikenhead-1676-1697/.

Kramer, Heinrich, and Jacob Sprenger. *Malleus Maleficarum* [The Hammer of Witches]. 1487.

Locke, John. *A Letter Concerning Toleration*. London: Awnsham Churchill, 1689.

Mather, Cotton. *Remarkable Providences Illustrative of the Earlier Days of American Colonization*. London: John Russell Smith, 1684.

Mather, Cotton. *The Wonders of the Invisible World: Being an Account of the Tryals of Several Witches Lately Executed in New-England*. Boston: Benjamin Harris, 1692.

Mather, Increase. *Cases of Conscience Concerning Evil Spirits*. Boston: Benjamin Harris, 1692.

Parliament of England. *An Act Declaring the Rights and Liberties of the Subject and Settling the Succession of the Crown* [Bill of Rights]. 1689.

Parliament of England. *An Act for Exempting Their Majesties Protestant Subjects Dissenting from the Church of England from the Penalties of Certain Laws* [Toleration Act]. 1689.

Salem Witch Trials Documentary Archive. University of Virginia. Accessed Feb 2025. http://salem.lib.virginia.edu/.

Swift, Jonathan. *An Argument Against Abolishing Christianity*. London, 1708.

Thomas, Keith. *Religion and the Decline of Magic*. London: Weidenfeld & Nicolson, 1971.

William of Orange. *Declaration of His Highness William Henry, Prince of Orange, of the Reasons Inducing Him to Appear in Arms in the Kingdom of England*. 1688.

Cycle 2: Enlightenment Backlash & Revolution (1700s-Early 1800s)

Adams, John. Letter to Abigail Adams, July 3, 1776. Adams Family Papers: An Electronic Archive. Massachusetts Historical Society.

Amar, Akhil Reed. *America's Constitution: A Biography*. New York: Random House, 2005.

Anderson, Fred. *Crucible of War: The Seven Years' War and the Fate of Empire in British North America, 1754-1766*. New York: Alfred A. Knopf, 2000.

Andress, David. *The Terror: The Merciless War for Freedom in Revolutionary France*. New York: Farrar, Straus and Giroux, 2005.

Bailyn, Bernard. *The Ideological Origins of the American Revolution*. Cambridge: Harvard University Press, 1992.

Burke, Edmund. *Reflections on the Revolution in France*. London: J. Dodsley, 1790.

Continental Congress. *Journals of the Continental Congress, 1774-1789*. Washington: Government Printing Office, 1904-1937.

Declaration of the Rights of Man and Citizen. France, 1789.

Doyle, William. *The Oxford History of the French Revolution*. Oxford: Oxford University Press, 1990.

Hunt, Lynn. *Inventing Human Rights: A History*. New York: W.W. Norton, 2008.

Israel, Jonathan. *Democratic Enlightenment: Philosophy, Revolution, and Human Rights 1750-1790*. Oxford: Oxford University Press, 2011.

Jefferson, Thomas. Letter to William Stephens Smith, November 13, 1787. *The Papers of Thomas Jefferson*.

Law of Suspects. France, 1793.

Locke, John. *Two Treatises of Government*. London, 1689.

Madison, James. "The Federalist No. 51." *New York Packet*, February 6, 1788.

Marat, Jean-Paul. *L'Ami du peuple*, 1789-1793.

McPhee, Peter. *The French Revolution 1789-1799*. Oxford: Oxford University Press, 2002.

Paine, Thomas. *Common Sense*. Philadelphia: R. Bell, 1776.

Palmer, Robert R. *The Age of the Democratic Revolution: A Political History of Europe and America, 1760-1800*. 2 vols. Princeton: Princeton University Press, 1959-1964.

Popkin, Jeremy. *A New World Begins: The History of the French Revolution*. New York: Basic Books, 2019.

Schama, Simon. *Citizens: A Chronicle of the French Revolution*. New York: Alfred A. Knopf, 1989.

Tackett, Timothy. *The Coming of the Terror in the French Revolution*. Cambridge: Harvard University Press, 2015.

Washington, George. "Washington's Farewell Address." *American Daily Advertiser*, September 19, 1796.

Wood, Gordon S. *The Radicalism of the American Revolution*. New York: Alfred A. Knopf, 1991.

CYCLE 3: REACTION TO REVOLUTION & TECHNOLOGY (EARLY-MID 1800S)

Bailey, Brian. *The Luddite Rebellion*. New York: New York University Press, 1998.

Binfield, Kevin, ed. *The Writings of the Luddites*. Baltimore: Johns Hopkins University Press, 2004.

Burke, Edmund. *Reflections on the Revolution in France*. London: J. Dodsley, 1790.

Byron, George Gordon. Speech to the House of Lords on the Frame-Breaking Bill, February 27, 1812. *Hansard Parliamentary Debates*, Vol. XXI.

Carlsbad Decrees. 1819.

Deak, Istvan. *The Lawful Revolution: Louis Kossuth and the Hungarians, 1848-1849*. New York: Columbia University Press, 1979.

Eyck, Frank. *The Frankfurt Parliament 1848-1849*. New York: St. Martin's Press, 1968.

Final Act of the Congress of Vienna. 1815.

Gaskell, Peter. *The Manufacturing Population of England*. London: Baldwin and Cradock, 1833.

Great Britain. Parliament. *Parliamentary Papers*. Committee on Framework-Knitters' Petitions (1812), Vol. II.

Hammond, John Lawrence, and Barbara Hammond. *The Skilled Labourer 1760-1832*. London: Longmans, Green, and Co., 1919.

Hobsbawm, Eric. *Industry and Empire: From 1750 to the Present Day*. London: Weidenfeld & Nicolson, 1968.

Hungarian Declaration of Independence. April 14, 1849.

Jarrett, Mark. *The Congress of Vienna and its Legacy*. London: I.B. Tauris, 2013.

Kissinger, Henry. *A World Restored: Metternich, Castlereagh and the Problems of Peace, 1812-1822*. Boston: Houghton Mifflin, 1957.

Kossuth, Lajos. Speech to the Hungarian National Assembly, July 11, 1848.

Landes, David S. *The Unbound Prometheus: Technological Change and Industrial Development in Western Europe from 1750 to the Present*. Cambridge: Cambridge University Press, 1969.

Merchant, Brian. *Blood in the Machine: The Origins of the Rebellion Against Big Tech*. New York: Little, Brown and Company, 2023.

Metternich, Klemens. Various diplomatic correspondence and memoranda. In Siemann, Wolfram. *Metternich: Strategist and Visionary*. Cambridge: Harvard University Press, 2019.

Namier, Lewis. *1848: The Revolution of the Intellectuals*. Oxford: Oxford University Press, 1946.

Polanyi, Karl. *The Great Transformation*. New York: Farrar & Rinehart, 1944.

Rapport, Mike. *1848: Year of Revolution*. New York: Basic Books, 2008.

Sperber, Jonathan. *The European Revolutions, 1848-1851*. Cambridge: Cambridge University Press, 2005.

Thompson, Edward Palmer. *The Making of the English Working Class.* London: Victor Gollancz Ltd., 1963.

Thomis, Malcolm I. *The Luddites: Machine-Breaking in Regency England.* New York: Schocken Books, 1970.

Zamoyski, Adam. *Phantom Terror: Political Paranoia and the Creation of the Modern State, 1789-1848.* New York: Basic Books, 2014.

CYCLE 4: EUGENICS & SOCIAL PURITY PANICS (LATE 1800S-EARLY 1900S)

Addams, Jane. *Twenty Years at Hull-House.* New York: Macmillan, 1910.

Bederman, Gail. *Manliness and Civilization: A Cultural History of Gender and Race in the United States, 1880-1917.* Chicago: University of Chicago Press, 1995.

Begg, Paul. *Jack the Ripper: The Definitive History.* London: Pearson Longman, 2003.

Booth, Charles. *Life and Labour of the People in London.* 9 vols. London: Macmillan and Company, 1889-1891.

Brigham, Carl C. *A Study of American Intelligence.* Princeton: Princeton University Press, 1923.

Buck v. Bell, 274 U.S. 200 (1927).

Chinese Exclusion Act. United States Congress, May 6, 1882.

Clarke, William. "The Social Future of England." *Contemporary Review,* December 1893.

Comstock, Anthony. *Traps for the Young.* New York: Funk & Wagnalls, 1883.

Darwin, Charles. *On the Origin of Species by Means of Natural Selection, or the Preservation of Favoured Races in the Struggle for Life.* London: John Murray, 1859.

Galton, Francis. *Inquiries into Human Faculty and Its Development.* London: Macmillan, 1883.

George, Henry. *Progress and Poverty: An Inquiry into the Cause of Industrial Depressions and of Increase of Want with Increase of Wealth... The Remedy*. New York: D. Appleton and Company, 1879.

Grant, Madison. *The Passing of the Great Race*. New York: Charles Scribner's Sons, 1916.

Hofstadter, Richard. *The Paranoid Style in American Politics and Other Essays*. New York: Alfred A. Knopf, 1965.

Johnson-Reed Act (Immigration Act of 1924). 43 Stat. 153.

Kühl, Stefan. *The Nazi Connection: Eugenics, American Racism, and German National Socialism*. New York: Oxford University Press, 1994.

Laughlin, Harry H. *Eugenical Sterilization in the United States*. Chicago: Psychopathic Laboratory of the Municipal Court of Chicago, 1922.

Leo XIII. *Rerum Novarum: Encyclical Letter on Capital and Labor*. Vatican Press, 1891.

Lombroso, Cesare. *L'uomo delinquente* [*Criminal Man*]. Milan: Hoepli, 1876.

Marx, Karl. *Das Kapital* [*Capital*]. Vol. 1. Hamburg: Verlag von Otto Meissner, 1867.

Nordau, Max. *Entartung* [*Degeneration*]. Berlin: Carl Duncker, 1892.

Popenoe, Paul, and Roswell Hill Johnson. *Applied Eugenics*. New York: Macmillan, 1918.

Riis, Jacob. *How the Other Half Lives: Studies Among the Tenements of New York*. New York: Charles Scribner's Sons, 1890.

Skinner v. Oklahoma, 316 U.S. 535 (1942).

Stead, W. T. "The Maiden Tribute of Modern Babylon." *Pall Mall Gazette*, July 1885.

Stern, Alexandra Minna. *Eugenic Nation: Faults and Frontiers of Better Breeding in Modern America*. Berkeley: University of California Press, 2005.

UNESCO. *The Race Question*. Paris: UNESCO Publication 791, 1950.

Walkowitz, Judith R. *City of Dreadful Delight: Narratives of Sexual Danger in Late-Victorian London*. Chicago: University of Chicago Press, 1992.

CYCLE 5: IDEOLOGICAL PANICS & WAR (MID-1900S)

Adorno, Theodor W., et al. *The Authoritarian Personality*. New York: Harper & Brothers, 1950.

Anders, Günther. "Theses for the Atomic Age." *The Massachusetts Review* 3, no. 3 (1962): 493-505.

Arendt, Hannah. *The Origins of Totalitarianism*. New York: Harcourt, Brace, Jovanovich, 1951.

Bartley, Numan V. *The Rise of Massive Resistance: Race and Politics in the South During the 1950s*. Baton Rouge: Louisiana State University Press, 1969.

Boyer, Paul. *By the Bomb's Early Light: American Thought and Culture at the Dawn of the Atomic Age*. New York: Pantheon, 1985.

Brown v. Board of Education, 347 U.S. 483 (1954).

Caute, David. *The Great Fear: The Anti-Communist Purge Under Truman and Eisenhower*. New York: Simon & Schuster, 1978.

Ceplair, Larry, and Steven Englund. *The Inquisition in Hollywood: Politics in the Film Community, 1930-1960*. Berkeley: University of California Press, 1979.

Civil Rights Act of 1964. Pub. L. 88-352, 78 Stat. 241.

Congressional Record. Senate debates on McCarthy censure, 1954.

Eisenhower, Dwight D. Statement upon signing bill to include "under God" in the Pledge of Allegiance, June 14, 1954.

Flanders, Ralph. Senate speech introducing resolution against McCarthy, June 12, 1954.

Fried, Richard M. *Nightmare in Red: The McCarthy Era in Perspective*. New York: Oxford University Press, 1990.

Guralnick, Peter. *Last Train to Memphis: The Rise of Elvis Presley*. Boston: Little, Brown and Company, 1994.

Hofstadter, Richard. "The Paranoid Style in American Politics." *Harper's Magazine*, November 1964, 77-86.

Internal Security Act (McCarran Act). 64 Stat. 987 (1950).

Kennedy, John F. Inaugural Address, January 20, 1961.

Kershaw, Ian. *Hitler, 1936-1945: Nemesis*. New York: W. W. Norton & Company, 2000.

Lifton, Robert Jay. *Indefensible Weapons: The Political and Psychological Case Against Nuclearism*. New York: Basic Books, 1982.

Limited Test Ban Treaty. Signed August 5, 1963.

McCarthy, Joseph. Speech to Women's Republican Club, Wheeling, West Virginia, February 9, 1950.

Murrow, Edward R. "See It Now" broadcast on Senator McCarthy. CBS Television, March 9, 1954.

Navasky, Victor. *Naming Names*. New York: Viking Press, 1980.

Nixon, Richard. "Silent Majority" speech, November 3, 1969.

Oshinsky, David M. *A Conspiracy So Immense: The World of Joe McCarthy*. New York: The Free Press, 1983.

Red Channels: The Report of Communist Influence in Radio and Television. New York: American Business Consultants, 1950.

Schrecker, Ellen. *Many Are the Crimes: McCarthyism in America*. Princeton: Princeton University Press, 1998.

Truman, Harry S. Announcement of Soviet nuclear test, September 23, 1949.

Voting Rights Act of 1965. Pub. L. 89-110, 79 Stat. 437.

Welch, Joseph. Army-McCarthy hearings transcript, June 9, 1954.

Wertham, Fredric. *Seduction of the Innocent*. New York: Rinehart & Company, 1954.

Whitfield, Stephen J. *The Culture of the Cold War*. Baltimore: Johns Hopkins University Press, 1996.

CYCLE 6: CULTURAL REVOLUTION & SOCIAL ANXIETY (MID-LATE 1900S)

Agnew, Spiro T. Speech to Midwest Regional Republican Committee, Des Moines, Iowa, November 13, 1969.

Anderson, Terry H. *The Movement and the Sixties*. New York: Oxford University Press, 1995.

Carson, Rachel. *Silent Spring*. Boston: Houghton Mifflin, 1962.

Carter, Dan T. *The Politics of Rage: George Wallace, the Origins of the New Conservatism, and the Transformation of American Politics*. New York: Simon & Schuster, 1995.

Clean Air Act Amendments of 1970. Pub. L. 91-604, 84 Stat. 1676.

Cowie, Jefferson. *Stayin' Alive: The 1970s and the Last Days of the Working Class*. New York: The New Press, 2010.

Cronkite, Walter. CBS Evening News broadcast, February 27, 1968.

Endangered Species Act of 1973. Pub. L. 93-205, 87 Stat. 884.

Equal Pay Act of 1963. Pub. L. 88-38, 77 Stat. 56.

Farber, David. *The Age of Great Dreams: America in the 1960s*. New York: Hill and Wang, 1994.

Friedan, Betty. *The Feminine Mystique*. New York: W.W. Norton & Company, 1963.

Gitlin, Todd. *The Sixties: Years of Hope, Days of Rage*. New York: Bantam Books, 1987.

Haley, Alex. *Roots: The Saga of an American Family*. Garden City: Doubleday, 1976.

Herring, George C. *America's Longest War: The United States and Vietnam, 1950-1975*. 4th ed. Boston: McGraw-Hill, 2001.

Isserman, Maurice, and Michael Kazin. *America Divided: The Civil War of the 1960s*. New York: Oxford University Press, 2000.

Jacobs, Meg. *Panic at the Pump: The Energy Crisis and the Transformation of American Politics in the 1970s*. New York: Hill and Wang, 2016.

King, Martin Luther, Jr. "I Have a Dream." Speech delivered at the March on Washington for Jobs and Freedom, August 28, 1963.

King, Martin Luther, Jr. "Letter from Birmingham Jail," April 16, 1963.

Leary, Timothy. Speech at Human Be-In, Golden Gate Park, San Francisco, January 14, 1967.

National Advisory Commission on Civil Disorders (Kerner Commission). *Report of the National Advisory Commission on Civil Disorders.* Washington: Government Printing Office, 1968.

National Environmental Policy Act of 1969. Pub. L. 91-190, 83 Stat. 852.

Nixon, Richard. "Address to the Nation on the War in Vietnam," November 3, 1969.

Phillips, Kevin P. *The Emerging Republican Majority.* New Rochelle: Arlington House, 1969.

Proposed Equal Rights Amendment to the United States Constitution. Passed by Congress March 22, 1972.

Roe v. Wade, 410 U.S. 113 (1973).

Roszak, Theodore. *The Making of a Counter Culture: Reflections on the Technocratic Society and Its Youthful Opposition.* Garden City: Doubleday, 1969.

Savio, Mario. Speech at Berkeley Free Speech Movement rally, December 2, 1964.

Schell, Jonathan. *The Fate of the Earth.* New York: Knopf, 1982.

Schulman, Bruce J. *The Seventies: The Great Shift in American Culture, Society, and Politics.* New York: Free Press, 2001.

Title IX, Education Amendments of 1972. Pub. L. 92-318, 86 Stat. 235.

Wallace, George. Campaign speech in Madison Square Garden, October 24, 1968.

War Powers Resolution of 1973. Pub. L. 93-148, 87 Stat. 555.

Weart, Spencer R. *The Rise of Nuclear Fear.* Cambridge: Harvard University Press, 2012.

CYCLE 7: MODERN MORAL PANICS & INFORMATION AGE ANXIETY (LATE 1900S-1990S)

American Psychological Association. "Violence in Video Games: Myth vs. Reality." Literature review presented at APA Annual Convention, 2004.

Benedick, Richard Elliot. *Ozone Diplomacy: New Directions in Safeguarding the Planet.* Cambridge: Harvard University Press, 1998.

Best, Joel, and Gerald T. Horiuchi. "The Satanic cult scare." *The Sociological Quarterly* 26, no. 4 (1985): 473-485.

Buckley, William F., Jr. "Identify All the Carriers." *The New York Times*, March 18, 1986.

Byrd, Patrick. *The Y2K Survival Guide and Cookbook*. New York: Lyle Stuart, 2000.

Ceci, Stephen, and Maggie Bruck. *Jeopardy in the Courtroom: A Scientific Analysis of Children's Testimony*. Washington: American Psychological Association, 1995.

Centers for Disease Control. "Pneumocystis Pneumonia—Los Angeles." *Morbidity and Mortality Weekly Report* 30, no. 21 (June 5, 1981): 250-252.

Child Abuse Prevention and Treatment Act. Pub. L. 93-247, 88 Stat. 4, January 31, 1974.

Cohen, Stanley. *Folk Devils and Moral Panics: The Creation of the Mods and Rockers*. London: Routledge, 2002.

de Young, Mary. *The Day Care Ritual Abuse Moral Panic*. Jefferson, NC: McFarland & Company, 2004.

Epstein, Steven. *Impure Science: AIDS, Activism, and the Politics of Knowledge*. Berkeley: University of California Press, 1996.

Falwell, Jerry. "AIDS: The Judgment of God." Sermon delivered at Thomas Road Baptist Church, Lynchburg, Virginia, July 1983.

Farman, J. C., B. G. Gardiner, and J. D. Shanklin. "Large losses of total ozone in Antarctica reveal seasonal ClOx/NOx interaction." *Nature* 315, no. 6016 (March 1985): 207-210.

Hyatt, Michael S. *The Millennium Bug: How to Survive the Coming Chaos*. Nashville: Thomas Nelson, 1998.

Interactive Digital Software Association v. St. Louis County, 329 F.3d 954 (8th Cir. 2003).

Jenkins, Philip. *Moral Panic: Changing Concepts of the Child Molester in Modern America*. New Haven: Yale University Press, 2004.

Johnson, Judy. Police report filed with Manhattan Beach Police Department, October 1984, regarding Raymond Buckey and the McMartin Preschool.

Koop, C. Everett. "Understanding AIDS." U.S. Department of Health and Human Services, Public Health Service. HHS Publication No. (CDC) HHS-88-8404, 1988.

Kramer, Larry. *Reports from the Holocaust: The Story of an AIDS Activist.* New York: St. Martin's Press, 1989.

Lanning, Kenneth V. "Investigator's Guide to Allegations of 'Ritual' Child Abuse." FBI Behavioral Science Unit, Quantico, VA, 1992.

Los Angeles County Grand Jury. "Final Report on the McMartin Preschool Case." June 1990.

Montreal Protocol on Substances that Deplete the Ozone Layer. September 16, 1987.

Nathan, Debbie, and Michael Snedeker. *Satan's Silence: Ritual Abuse and the Making of a Modern American Witch Hunt.* New York: Basic Books, 1995.

Newsweek. "The Gay Plague: Why Is A Deadly New Disease Striking Only Homosexuals?" Cover story, August 9, 1982.

Pazder, Lawrence, and Michelle Smith. *Michelle Remembers.* New York: Congdon & Lattès, 1980.

People v. Buckey, Case No. A-750900. Los Angeles County Superior Court, 1990.

President's Council on Year 2000 Conversion. "First Quarterly Report." Washington: The White House, February 1999.

Rivera, Geraldo. "Devil Worship: Exposing Satan's Underground." NBC Television Special, October 25, 1983.

Ryan White Comprehensive AIDS Resources Emergency (CARE) Act of 1990. Pub. L. 101-381, 104 Stat. 576, August 18, 1990.

Shilts, Randy. *And the Band Played On: Politics, People, and the AIDS Epidemic.* New York: St. Martin's Press, 1987.

Time magazine. "The Y2K Bug: How to Protect Your Family, Your Money, and Your Life." Cover story, January 18, 1999.

Victor, Jeffrey S. *Satanic Panic: The Creation of a Contemporary Legend.* Chicago: Open Court Publishing, 1993.

Webster, Bruce F. Quoted in *The New York Times*, "After Y2K, Praise, Relief, and Doubt," February 22, 2000.

Year 2000 Information and Readiness Disclosure Act. Pub. L. 105-271, 112 Stat. 2386, October 19, 1998.

Yourdon, Edward, and Jennifer Yourdon. *Time Bomb 2000: What the Year 2000 Computer Crisis Means to You!* Upper Saddle River: Prentice Hall, 1998.